VMware Cloud on AWS Blueprint

Design, automate, and migrate VMware workloads on AWS global infrastructure

Oleg Ulyanov

Michael Schwartzman

Harsha Sanku

VMware Cloud on AWS Blueprint

Group Product Manager: Preet Ahuja

Publishing Product Manager: Surbhi Suman

Book Project Manager: Neil DMello

Senior Editor: Athikho Sapuni Rishana

Technical Editor: Rajat Sharma

Copy Editor: Safis Editing

Proofreader: Safis Editing

Indexer: Tejal Daruwale Soni

Production Designer: Gokul Raj S.T

Senior DevRel Marketing Coordinator: Linda Pearlson

DevRel Marketing Coordinator: Rohan Dobhal

First published: February 2024

Production reference: 1010224

Published by

Packt Publishing Ltd.

Grosvenor House

11 St Paul's Square

Birmingham

B3 1RB, UK

ISBN 978-1-80323-819-7

www.packtpub.com

To the VMware community,

It is with heartfelt gratitude and deep appreciation that we would like to extend our sincerest dedication to this vibrant and dynamic community, which includes VMware customers, partners, VMware Certified Professionals, VMware communities and User Groups, VMware Technology Alliance Partners, developers, consultants, solution architects, training and education providers, and VMware evangelists and enthusiasts.

Our collective commitment to pushing the boundaries of virtualization technology and fostering innovation has truly made a lasting impact over two decades. As we navigate the ever-evolving landscape of virtualization, your contributions continue to be the cornerstone of our success. The challenges we face and the solutions we forge together not only strengthen our individual expertise but also contribute to the growth of the entire VMware ecosystem.

Additionally, heartfelt appreciation extends to the visionary leadership at VMware and AWS for their unwavering commitment to excellence in bringing VMware Cloud on AWS to fruition. The collaboration between these two industry leaders has not only redefined the possibilities of cloud computing but also set a benchmark for seamless integration and innovation. The combined strategic vision and collaborative spirit have empowered customers to transcend traditional boundaries, unlocking a new era of flexibility, efficiency, and agility in the cloud.

Let us continue to inspire, support, and elevate each other as we embark on this journey of perpetual learning and innovation. The success of the VMware community is a testament to the power of collaboration, and we are honored to be part of this extraordinary journey.

With unwavering dedication,

The authors, Oleg Ulyanov, Michael Schwartzman, and Harsha Sanku

Contributors

About the authors

Oleg Ulyanov is a staff cloud architect with more than 15 years of experience. He is a subject matter expert in VMware hybrid cloud, cloud migration, networking, and storage. He has experience as a VMware professional services architect, helping customers achieve their technical and business goals through IT transformation and migrating to VMware hybrid clouds. He holds various industry certificates, including VMware VCP, VCAP6/7-DCV, SNIA, and Microsoft.

Michael Schwartzman, a senior Azure application innovation specialist at Microsoft, has over a decade of experience in cloud infrastructure, cloud security, and hybrid cloud solutions. Prior to his current role, Michael served as a lead cloud solution architect specializing in VMware Cloud on AWS. He has played a pivotal role in assisting global ISVs with the development and sale of SaaS solutions on Azure. Additionally, Michael's broad expertise encompasses support for both digital-native and traditional enterprises, including the optimization of their cloud systems. His dedication to remaining at the forefront of the rapidly evolving tech landscape has established him as a go-to expert for businesses seeking to leverage cutting-edge cloud technology.

Harsha Sanku is a senior solutions architect at AWS, specializing in AWS hybrid cloud and edge computing services. His proficiency extends to cloud infrastructure, encompassing networking and security. Over the past four years, he has excelled as a VMware Cloud on AWS specialist. Harsha has a strong background in designing and implementing data center infrastructure and private clouds, with a particular focus on VMware technologies. In his current role at AWS, he collaborates with customers to migrate and modernize their hybrid cloud infrastructure, ensuring they remain competitive in the ever-evolving business and IT landscape.

About the reviewers

Daniel Jonathan Valik is an industry expert and author in the cloud and software industry, living in the US. He has been in leadership positions for product management, engineering, and as a strategy adviser over the past 23 years. Currently leading Webex data analytics and AI at Cisco Systems, he has also worked in other global roles for Microsoft, Amazon, VMware, and Huawei in the infrastructure, platform, and communication services spaces.

He has a double master's degree in change and strategic management from the University of Westminster, UK, and the University of Austria and is the author of several technical and business-related books.

Dan Frith has 25 years of IT infrastructure experience across the government, managed services, and integrator sectors. For the last 20 years, he has been working with various data center technologies specifically focused on cloud, storage, data protection, and virtualization. He is a recipient of the vExpert awards from 2013 to 2023. His areas of expertise and key strengths are storage, data protection, virtualization, hyper-converged infrastructure, and hybrid cloud solutions.

In his spare time, he runs a blog on data center technologies and helps with the Brisbane VMware User Group. He currently works as a cloud infrastructure architect, helping customers effectively leverage VMware Cloud on AWS and other VMware Cloud solutions.

Table of Contents

2

Exploring Networking, Security, and AWS Integrations   37

3

Exploring VMware Cloud on AWS-Integrated Services   79

Part 2: Configuration, Maintenance, and Troubleshooting on VMware Cloud on AWS

4

Getting Started with VMware Cloud on AWS SDDC   105

5

Configuring vCenter, vSAN, and VMware Cloud Console   147

6

Understanding Networking and Security Configurations   183

7

Exploring Integrated Services Configuration   225

8

Building Applications and Managing Operations   261

9

10

Part 3: Leveraging Design Considerations and Best Practices

11

12

Preface

In the ever-evolving landscape of cloud computing, the journey from traditional on-premises environments to the agility of the cloud demands careful planning and strategic execution. Whether you are orchestrating a meticulous data center evacuation or navigating the intricacies of migrating vSphere workloads to VMware Cloud on AWS, this book serves as your comprehensive guide. Our aim is to equip you with the insights and knowledge needed to ensure a seamless onboarding process. We delve into every aspect, covering architecture, network intricacies, security measures, disaster recovery, AWS integrations, best practices, and preflight checklists. This book is designed to empower you with the understanding necessary to make informed decisions and execute successful transitions.

Offering an in-depth exploration of hybrid cloud challenges and presenting solutions specific to VMware Cloud on AWS, this book is an indispensable asset for individuals at all experience levels, from beginners to seasoned practitioners. It equips you with the tools to unleash the complete capabilities of VMware Cloud on AWS.

Who this book is for

The book is intended for cloud and solutions architects, DevOps engineers, **site reliability engineers (SREs)**, system and network admins, and cloud engineers with experience in on-premises VMware or AWS administration, facilitating the seamless integration of VMware Cloud technologies. A prior understanding of cloud computing, virtualization principles, VMware vSphere administration, vSAN, and NSX, along with AWS cloud basics will be helpful.

What this book covers

Chapter 1, *Foundation of VMware Cloud on AWS*, provides an introduction to VMware Cloud on AWS and addresses hybrid cloud challenges. In addition, you will identify various use cases, and understand the high-level architecture of VMware Cloud on AWS. You will learn how to navigate around the VMware vCenter, VMware **Cloud Services Platform** (**CSP**), and the VMware Cloud Console. Finally, you will understand VMware vSAN, which is the primary storage technology used for VMware Cloud on AWS.

Chapter 2, *Exploring Networking, Security, and AWS Integrations*, covers networking and security aspects of VMware NSX architecture in VMware Cloud on AWS, including the firewall architecture, **Compute Gateway** (**CGW**), **Management Gateway** (**MGW**), understanding the concept of micro-segmentation, IPS/IDS, Layer 7 firewall, and native AWS integrations architectures through **VMware Managed Transit Gateway** (**vTGW**).

Chapter 3, Understanding VMware Cloud on AWS Integrated Services, covers the large ecosystem of VMware Cloud on AWS integrated services that helps organizations migrate workloads using VMware **Hybrid Cloud Extension** (**HCX**), protect workloads for disaster recovery using **VMware Cloud Disaster Recovery** (**VCDR**) and **VMware Site Recovery** (**VSR**), and enable advanced logging with VMware Aria Operations for Logs to **Container-as-a-Service** (**CaaS**) services with Tanzu Services. You will understand the basic capabilities and design choices when planning, along with learning about implementing and operating all the integrated add-ons.

Chapter 4, Getting Started with Your First VMware Cloud on AWS SDDC, helps you navigate through the process of deploying a new VMware Cloud on AWS **Software-Defined Data Center** (**SDDC**) including creating a VMware Cloud organization, running the SDDC deployment wizard, and configuring **Role-Based Access Control** (**RBAC**) to access vCenter using identity management on the VMware CSP.

Chapter 5, Configuring vCenter, vSAN, and VMC Console, focuses on how to manage an SDDC, VM storage policies, compute policies, and the **Elastic Distributed Resource Scheduler** (**EDRS**) mechanism for automatically scaling the cluster based on resource usage through the VMware Cloud Console. You will learn how to manage VMware Cloud on AWS, vSAN storage policies, and compute policies, and how to engage with VMware for support and maintenance issues.

Chapter 6, Understanding Networking and Security Configurations, covers the basics of SDDC networking and security functionality, including NSX micro-segmentation, and networking and security configurations that are essential parts of day two operations. Configurations include SDDC networking, NSX micro-segmentation, connected VPC, AWS Direct Connect, VMware Transit Connect, IPFIX, and port mirroring.

Chapter 7, Exploring Integrated Services Configuration, focuses on the intricacies involved in configuring integrated services. These services encompass the NSX advanced security service, which offers layer 7 firewall and IPS/IDS security features. Additionally, you will explore VMware HCX, VMware Aria Operation for Logs, and Tanzu Kubernetes Grid Service. By delving into these topics, you will acquire the essential knowledge required for day-to-day operations.

Chapter 8, Building Applications and Managing Operations, covers how workloads that have been migrated can be modernized by leveraging native AWS services. Additionally, it covers operations and monitoring specifically for VMware Cloud on AWS, as well as details about maintenance and SDDC upgrades.

Chapter 9, Deploying Infrastructure as Code with VMware Cloud, explores using **Infrastructure as Code** (**IaC**) for provisioning and managing IT infrastructure and equips you with the knowledge and skills needed to facilitate seamless automation and management of your virtual infrastructure. Key topics covered in this chapter include an introduction to VMware Cloud APIs, insights into the CSP API, guidance on consuming the Console API through the developer center, and an exploration of the NSX-T Data Center REST API.

Chapter 10, Identifying Low-Latency Workloads to Run on VMware Cloud on AWS Outposts, discusses how to address low latency, local data processing, and data sovereignty requirements for workloads that need to stay on-premises or at the edge and run vSphere workloads locally while benefiting from the features of the VMware Cloud platform using VMware Cloud on AWS Outposts. The chapter covers architecture, physical connectivity, components, service link connectivity options, scalability, and available configurations, along with the support model.

Chapter 11, Knowing the Best Practices, FAQs, and Common Pitfalls, addresses the challenges of integrating a new service such as VMware Cloud on AWS. It emphasizes the importance of various factors to ensure the success of the project. The key focus is on facilitating a smooth adoption process including best practices, recognizing and avoiding common pitfalls, and providing valuable answers for **Frequently Asked Questions** (**FAQs**) that equip you with essential knowledge to enhance the efficiency and success of the adoption process for VMware Cloud on AWS within your enterprise infrastructure.

Chapter 12, Appendix – Preflight Checklist before Onboarding, focuses on critical configuration elements necessary for deploying the SDDC and configuring a hybrid cloud environment. It serves as a comprehensive guide to key setup considerations. The chapter anticipates and addresses the need for a thorough understanding of essential configurations before proceeding with the purchase and onboarding process. It acts as a valuable resource for those of you seeking a consolidated overview of the configuration prerequisites for a successful deployment and integration of the SDDC in a hybrid cloud environment.

To get the most out of this book

This book assumes that you possess strong foundational knowledge of VMware technologies, including vSphere, vSAN, NSX-T, and vCenter. It is designed for individuals who already have a comprehensive understanding of these core VMware components, enabling you to delve into more advanced concepts and practical implementations related to VMware Cloud on AWS. Familiarity with virtualization, software-defined networking, storage management, and centralized infrastructure administration will enhance your ability to grasp the nuanced discussions and effectively apply the knowledge shared throughout the book. While foundational VMware expertise is presumed, this book aims to further enrich your skills and knowledge, providing valuable insights into the integration and optimization of VMware technologies within the context of the AWS cloud environment.

Software/hardware covered in the book	Operating system requirements
VMware vSphere CLI VMware vCenter Server	Windows

Software/hardware covered in the book	Operating system requirements
VMware Cloud on AWS API SDDC API (vSphere API) NSX-T Data Center REST API VMware vSphere/ESXi VMware vSAN VMware NSX-T	Windows
Terraform for VMC on AWS PowerCLI for VMware Cloud on AWS vSphere Automation SDKs	Windows

Conventions used

There are a number of text conventions used throughout this book.

`Code in text`: Indicates code words in text, database table names, folder names, filenames, file extensions, pathnames, dummy URLs, user input, and Twitter handles. Here is an example: "Mount the downloaded `WebStorm-10*.dmg` disk image file as another disk in your system."

Bold: Indicates a new term, an important word, or words that you see onscreen. For instance, words in menus or dialog boxes appear in bold. Here is an example: "Select **System info** from the **Administration** panel."

> **Tips or important notes**
> Appear like this.

Get in touch

Feedback from our readers is always welcome.

General feedback: If you have questions about any aspect of this book, email us at `customercare@packtpub.com` and mention the book title in the subject of your message.

Errata: Although we have taken every care to ensure the accuracy of our content, mistakes do happen. If you have found a mistake in this book, we would be grateful if you would report this to us. Please visit `www.packtpub.com/support/errata` and fill in the form.

Piracy: If you come across any illegal copies of our works in any form on the internet, we would be grateful if you would provide us with the location address or website name. Please contact us at copyright@packt.com with a link to the material.

If you are interested in becoming an author: If there is a topic that you have expertise in and you are interested in either writing or contributing to a book, please visit authors.packtpub.com.

Share Your Thoughts

Once you've read *VMware Cloud on AWS Blueprint*, we'd love to hear your thoughts! Scan the QR code below to go straight to the Amazon review page for this book and share your feedback.

https://packt.link/r/1803238194

Your review is important to us and the tech community and will help us make sure we're delivering excellent quality content.

Download a free PDF copy of this book

Thanks for purchasing this book!

Do you like to read on the go but are unable to carry your print books everywhere?

Is your eBook purchase not compatible with the device of your choice?

Don't worry, now with every Packt book you get a DRM-free PDF version of that book at no cost.

Read anywhere, any place, on any device. Search, copy, and paste code from your favorite technical books directly into your application.

The perks don't stop there, you can get exclusive access to discounts, newsletters, and great free content in your inbox daily

Follow these simple steps to get the benefits:

1. Scan the QR code or visit the link below

https://packt.link/free-ebook/978-1-80323-819-7

2. Submit your proof of purchase

3. That's it! We'll send your free PDF and other benefits to your email directly

Part 1:
VMware Cloud on AWS Foundations and VMware HCX as a Migration Tool

Part 1 serves as an introductory guide to VMware Cloud on AWS, and highlights the challenges associated with hybrid cloud environments. It explores various use cases catered to by VMware Cloud on AWS and delves into its high-level architecture. Additionally, it covers hybrid and public cloud challenges, addressing components such as vCenter, VMware vSAN, and NSX-T networking, and security features such as micro-segmentation, IPS/IDS, a Layer 7 firewall, and **VMware-Managed Transit Gateway** (**vTGW**). Furthermore, it highlights integrated services that enable various use cases, such as HCX for migration, disaster recovery, advanced logging, and container services with Tanzu. It also covers the Cloud Service Platform and VMware Cloud Console.

This part consists of the following chapters:

- *Chapter 1, Foundation of VMware Cloud on AWS*
- *Chapter 2, Exploring Networking, Security, and AWS Integrations*
- *Chapter 3, Understanding VMware Cloud on AWS Integrated Services*

1

Foundation of VMware Cloud on AWS

This chapter provides an introduction to VMware Cloud on AWS, hybrid cloud challenges, and how VMware Cloud on AWS solves them. In addition, you will learn about the different use cases that VMware Cloud on AWS addresses and its architecture principles.

This chapter covers the following topics:

- Introduction to VMware Cloud on AWS
- Introducing hybrid and public cloud challenges
- Understanding VMware Cloud on AWS use cases
- Understanding the VMware Cloud on AWS high-level architecture
- Discovering vCenter, the Cloud Services Platform (CSP), and CSP console
- Demystifying VMware vSAN, the primary storage technology for VMware Cloud on AWS

Introduction to VMware Cloud on AWS

VMware Cloud on AWS is a product jointly engineered by VMware and AWS enabling customers to run proven, enterprise-grade VMware **software-defined data centers (SDDCs)** on top of bare metal AWS hardware. VMware Cloud on AWS enables enterprise IT and operations teams to continue to add value to their business in the AWS cloud while maximizing their VMware investments, without the need to buy new hardware. This offering enables customers to quickly and confidently scale capacity up or down, without change or friction, for any workload with access to native cloud services.

Understanding VMware Cloud on AWS is not possible without knowing the broad range of capabilities of the AWS cloud (https://aws.amazon.com/resources/analyst-reports/gartner-mq-cips-2021/). VMware Cloud on AWS helps customers design their environments using different cloud models, facilitating connections between on-premises deployments and public clouds

AWS was officially launched in 2006 and has grown rapidly to become one of the world's largest cloud providers. AWS operates in over 25 geographic regions worldwide, with plans to expand to more regions. This means that users can deploy their applications and services in locations closest to their customers, improving performance and reducing latency. AWS provides over 175 fully featured services for computing, storage, databases, analytics, machine learning, **Internet of Things (IoT)**, security, and more.

AWS is used by millions of customers worldwide, including start-ups, large enterprises, and government organizations

One of the key benefits of the AWS cloud is its flexibility and scalability. Users can quickly and easily provision the needed resources and only pay for what they use.

The AWS cloud also offers a range of deployment options, including private, public, and hybrid cloud models. This allows users to tailor their cloud environment to their specific needs, depending on security requirements, compliance regulations, and performance goals.

VMware Cloud on AWS is a jointly engineered and fully managed service that brings VMware's enterprise-grade SDDC software and Amazon **Elastic Compute Cloud (EC2)** bare-metal instances running on the AWS Global Infrastructure. This integration enables customers to seamlessly migrate their workloads to VMware Cloud on AWS without re-platforming their virtual machines (`https://aws.amazon.com/resources/analyst-reports/gartner-mq-cips-2021/`).

Introduction to cloud deployment models

Companies can choose from different models to deploy cloud services. The deployment model will be driven by the application requirements, business use cases, and existing IT investments. The following section describes the different approaches.

Public cloud

Cloud computing delivers IT services with flexible pay-as-you-go pricing and consumption models. Customers can access as many resources as they need, often immediately. Charges are only applicable to resources that have been used or reserved. Customers can consume fully managed services that encompass computing, storage, networks, databases, containers, application platforms, functions and much more.

An application can be created directly in the cloud, known as a **cloud-native application**, or migrated from an existing on-premises infrastructure to take advantage of the public cloud benefits through a modernization process. Customers break the application's monolith architecture into microservices, also known as **refactoring**.

Private cloud or on-premises

The private cloud approach is the deployment of resources on-premises, using physical facilities, hardware, virtualization infrastructure, and automation software dedicated to an organization in most cases.

Usually, customers will own the facilities and physical IT hardware in their on-premises environment. Private clouds are often used to meet compliance with data governance regulations or to leverage investment into existing IT infrastructure.

Customers who were not *born in the cloud* have a significant part of their workloads running in their on-premises infrastructure. VMware is a leader in the on-premises SDDC with its **VMware Cloud Foundation** (**VCF**) software stack and vSphere's virtualization solution.

Hybrid cloud

A hybrid cloud is an IT architecture and an operational deployment model that enables customers to leverage public and private clouds. A hybrid cloud enables delivering applications and connecting infrastructure with common orchestration and management tools between on-premises and public cloud providers.

Processes and workloads established for on-premises need to be integrated with the workloads and processes in the public cloud to ensure unified management of data, applications, and their associated governance, life cycle management, and security policies.

Hybrid cloud solution core principles

The following are the hybrid cloud solution core principles:

- Seamless workload mobility between private cloud and public cloud environments
- Provision and scale resources through an API or self-service portal in the public cloud provider
- Network connectivity between environments through a high-speed, reliable, and secure solution
- Automate processes across environments with a common automation process, toolset, and APIs
- Manage and monitor environments with unified tools between environments

Different approaches to the hybrid cloud

Public cloud providers have solutions bringing their *native* centralized data center services to run in their customer's on-premise environments – for example, Google with its Anthos solution for Kubernetes workloads, AWS with Outposts and Amazon EKS Anywhere for Kubernetes workloads, and Microsoft with Azure Stack and Azure Arc.

VMware's approach is to extend existing VMware on-premises infrastructure to the cloud rather than building new infrastructure in customer data centers that implement point solutions of the different hyperscales.

It can help organizations benefit from hybridity with public clouds without rethinking their application delivery and security model, governance, policies, or procedures.

Multi-cloud

Multi-cloud is an operational model that combines more than one public cloud and potentially a private cloud. Many customers rely on multiple public cloud providers. Often, this adoption of multi-cloud is developed bottom-up in organizations, where different business units and development teams procure their cloud services without IT knowledge or guidance, or through a merger and acquisition process where two organization operational teams need to converge after adopting different cloud strategies.

For instance, using the **Google App Engine** for **Platform as a Service (PaaS)** services and AWS for EC2 with Lambda for **Infrastructure as a Service (IaaS)** and **Function as a Service (FaaS)** services, while, at the same time, running a third private cloud with VMware on-premises.

> **Note**
> Workloads are not portable between public cloud providers by default, and vendor lock-in concerns customers.

The VMware hybrid cloud stack can run on major public cloud providers, not only AWS. It enables customers to migrate their IaaS workloads between different public clouds and their private cloud without public cloud vendor lock-in.

Hybrid cloud challenges

Customers trying to naively implement a hybrid cloud strategy encounter challenges in the five pillars of operational inconsistencies, different skill sets and tools, disparate management tools and security controls, inconsistent application **service-level agreements (SLAs)**, and incompatible machine formats. Without making proper adjustments to those pillars, customers may encounter decreased agility and an increase in cost and risk.

The following figure summarizes those pillars:

Challenges of Implementing a Hybrid Cloud Strategy

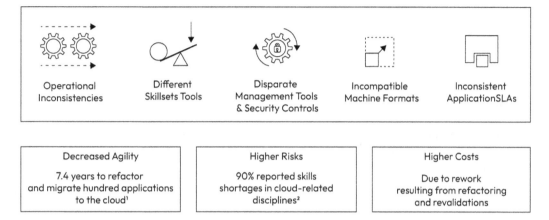

| Operational Inconsistencies | Different Skillsets Tools | Disparate Management Tools & Security Controls | Incompatible Machine Formats | Inconsistent ApplicationSLAs |

Decreased Agility	Higher Risks	Higher Costs
7.4 years to refactor and migrate hundred applications to the cloud[1]	90% reported skills shortages in cloud-related disciplines[2]	Due to rework resulting from refactoring and revalidations

A hybrid cloud with consistent infrastructure and operations overcomes these challenges

Figure 1.1 – Five challenges of implementing a hybrid cloud strategy

Now, let's explore those challenges in further detail in the following section.

Describing the challenges of the hybrid cloud

Cloud infrastructures have become more attractive to organizations driven by business transformation initiatives. The cloud improves agility with faster testing and development cycles and reduces costs and risks. Organizations are migrating to the cloud for those reasons.

While providing positive business values, many challenges arise when moving from on-premises to the public cloud. Many customers don't realize the changes they need to go through to properly take advantage of the public cloud's benefits. A cloud strategy that addresses the hybrid cloud challenges needs to consider people, processes, and technology.

Operational inconsistency

The tools and procedures that operation teams are leveraging to manage the life cycle of their applications and workloads on-premises are different from the public cloud.

For example, application and infrastructure monitoring and observability tools, automation, management, and CI/CD tools for deploying applications need to be repurposed from vSphere-based APIs/SDKs to AWS APIs and native monitoring services such as CloudTrail, CloudWatch, and adopting infrastructure as code with tools such as HashiCorp's Terraform.

Disparate security controls

Expanding on operational inconsistency, customers achieve security and compliance through existing security procedures and tools. Adaptation ranges from how users consume authentication, identity access management, network security controls – such as firewalls, **intrusion prevention systems** (**IPSs**), and **web application firewalls** (**WAFs**) – and application-level protection, monitoring, and logging for **Security Operation Center** (**SOC**) environments.

Skill sets and certifications

IT personnel managing VMware-based infrastructure require an investment in recertification and retraining to operate workloads in the public cloud. Skilled IT and DevOps personnel are in short supply in the market.

Inconsistent application SLAs

Migrating workloads in a high-availability architecture while providing production-grade SLAs requires application-level architecture adjustments to enjoy the resiliency of public cloud services. For instance, migrating a virtual machine to an EC2 service in the cloud doesn't make it highly available. On-premises resiliency mechanisms such as vSphere **High Availability** (**HA**) and **Distributed Resource Scheduler** (**DRS**) are unavailable on an EC2 service without making architecture adjustments.

Incompatible machine formats

Migration requires a manual conversion for each virtual machine, which includes the hypervisor format, operating system disks, and networking IP address configurations. This process takes into account unsupported configurations in the cloud, especially for legacy end-of-life and 32-bit operating systems. Additionally, the format conversion problem creates a vendor lock-in challenge.

Customers not considering those challenges in advance may experience a decrease in the developer's agility instead of an increase, an increase in the risk of the project instead of a decrease, and an increase in costs instead of a decrease.

VMware Cloud on AWS was designed to address all of those challenges of the hybrid cloud deployment model.

Understanding VMware Cloud on AWS use cases

This section will describe the most common use cases of hybrid cloud with VMware Cloud on AWS.

The use cases that we'll explore in this section are data center extension, next-generation application modernization, cloud migrations, and disaster recovery.

The following figure summarizes the four use cases:

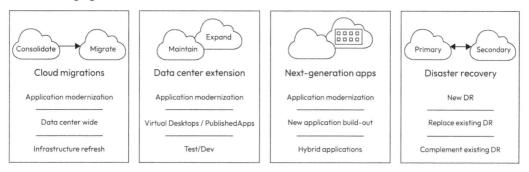

Figure 1.2 – The use cases of VMware Cloud on AWS

Let's describe each of the use cases in further detail in the following section.

Data center extension

Customers look to integrate their existing data center infrastructure into the public cloud. They want to enjoy the benefits offered by the public cloud without being affected by the hybrid cloud challenges described in earlier sections – for instance, when the on-premises environment fails to deliver IT capacity on time to meet business needs. Limited capacity can be because of a lack of physical space, supply chain issues, or a need for a temporary workload.

With VMware Cloud on AWS, a consistent infrastructure between vSphere environments in the data center and the vSphere SDDC that VMware manages in the AWS cloud enables customers to move applications to the AWS cloud or back seamlessly.

VMware Aria is a cloud management platform that allows customers to manage VMware Cloud on AWS as an extension to an existing customer data center. Workload types that are quick wins are testing/development and **virtual desktop infrastructure** (**VDI**) environments. Kubernetes workloads running on-premises can migrate into the VMware Cloud on AWS with the Tanzu portfolio integration.

Cloud migration

Cloud migration, also known as **re-platforming** or **lift-and-shift** in AWS terms or **relocating** in VMware Cloud on AWS terms, involves migrating existing brownfield applications to the public cloud from on-premises with minimal to no adjustments to the application code or VM format.

Business driver customers may have an expiring lease on a data center colocation facility, a management decision to evacuate an existing data center because of a cloud-first approach, or a hardware refresh because of end-of-life. An additional use case is mergers and acquisitions, where one company needs to absorb the IT infrastructure of the acquired company, as well as consolidate branch sites and data centers by migrating applications from the on-premises data center to the public cloud to reduce the total cost of ownership.

VMware Cloud on AWS is the fastest way for customers to migrate VMware vSphere-based workloads to the cloud because they can relocate their workloads in a way that is faster than a standard lift and shift. Consistent infrastructure is delivered using the same VMware on-premises stack leveraging vSphere as the hypervisor. Customers use this on-premises and the cloud enables the migration of workloads without lift-and-shift adjustments or refactoring their applications.

Next-generation apps

Customers looking to go through a development process of refactoring, such as breaking up a monolith application into a microservice architecture, can do this integrally on the platform leveraging the Tanzu portfolio, which is included in VMware Cloud on AWS.

VMware Cloud on AWS provides high bandwidth and low latency connectivity to native services that AWS offers. This integration provides a consistent and easy way for virtual machines and containers to access AWS services. These innovative AWS services can be seamlessly integrated with customers' applications to enable incremental refactoring and modernization enhancements.

Disaster recovery

The VMware **Disaster Recovery as a Service (DRaaS)** service is available with the VMware Cloud on AWS offering. It enables customers to recover and protect applications without needing to maintain an on-premises secondary or a third DR site. VMware delivers and manages it as a service. IT teams manage their cloud-based resources using familiar VMware tools without learning new skills or performing a lift-and-shift migration.

Customers using on-premises traditional DR build a secondary site with a replica of the production site. They need to prioritize which workloads will be protected because of costs. The operations of the secondary DR site are associated with complexity because of manual processes and siloed IT solutions.

DRaaS with VMware Cloud on AWS can reduce secondary site costs, simplify DR operations, and help customers meet or improve their **recovery time objective (RTO)** and **recovery point objective (RPO)**. **VMware Cloud Disaster Recovery (VCDR)** and **VMware Site Recovery Service (VSR)**, powered by **VMware Site Recovery Manager (SRM)**, are offered as part of the DRaaS service with VMware Cloud on AWS.

Understanding the VMware Cloud on AWS high-level architecture

This section will describe the high-level architecture of the main components that comprise VMware Cloud on AWS.

VMware Cloud on AWS is integrated into VMware's **Cloud Services Platform** (**CSP**). The VMware **Cloud Services Provider** (**CSP**) console allows customers to manage their organization's billing and identity, and grant access to VMware Cloud services. You can leverage the VMware Cloud Tech Zone *Getting Started* resource (`https://vmc.techzone.vmware.com/getting-started-vmware-cloud-aws`) to get familiar with the process of setting up an organization and configuring access in the CSP console.

The VMware CSP console allows you to manage VMware Cloud on AWS. You will use VMware CSP console to deploy VMware Cloud on AWS. Once the service is deployed, you leverage VMware CSP console to manage the SDDC.

The following figure shows the high-level design of the VMware Cloud on AWS architecture, showing both a VMware Cloud customer organization running the VMware Cloud services alongside an AWS-native organization running AWS services:

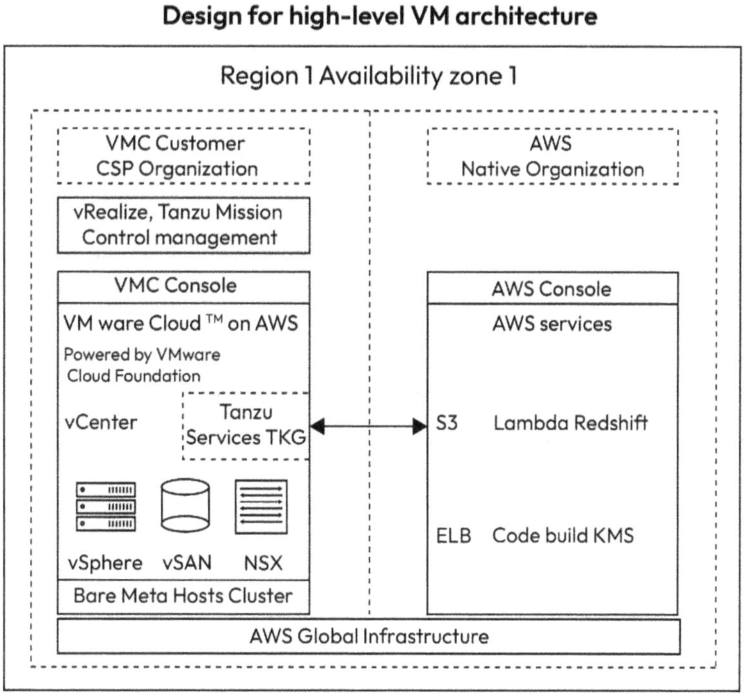

Design for high-level VM architecture

Figure 1.3 – High-level architecture of VMware Cloud on AWS

Now, let us switch to the Tanzu Kubernetes service available with VMware Cloud on AWS.

Tanzu Kubernetes with VMware Cloud on AWS

VMware Cloud on AWS includes VMware Tanzu Kubernetes Grid as a service. VMware currently offers several **Tanzu Kubernetes Grid** (**TKG**) flavors for running Kubernetes:

- **vSphere with Tanzu or the TKG service**: This solution has made vSphere a platform that can run Kubernetes workloads directly on the hypervisor layer. This can be enabled on a vSphere cluster and allows Kubernetes workloads to be run directly on ESXi hosts. Additionally, it can create upstream Kubernetes clusters in dedicated resource pools. This flavor is integrated into the VMware Cloud on AWS platform, providing a **Container as a Service** (**CaaS**) service, and is included in the basic pricing service.

- **Tanzu Kubernetes Grid Multi-Cloud** (**TKGm**) is an installer-driven wizard that sets up Kubernetes environments for use across public cloud environments and on-premises SDDCs. This flavor is supported but not included on VMware Cloud on AWS's basic pricing service, but it can be consumed with a separate license.

- **Tanzu Kubernetes Integrated Edition**: VMware Tanzu Kubernetes Integrated (previously known as **VMware Enterprise PKS**) is a Kubernetes-based container solution that includes advanced networking, a private registry, and life cycle management. It is beyond the scope of this book.

VMware **Tanzu Mission Control** (**TMC**) is a SaaS offering for multi-cloud Kubernetes cluster management and can be accessed through VMware CSP console. It provides the following:

- Kubernetes cluster deployment and management on a centralized platform across multiple clouds

- He ability to centralize operations and management

- A policy engine that automates access control policies across multiple clusters

- The ability to centralize authorization and authentication with federated identity

The following figure presents a high-level architecture of services available between the on-premises and the VMware Cloud solution in order to provide hybrid operations:

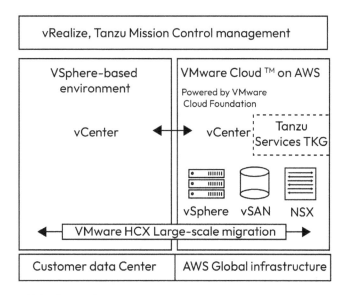

Figure 1.4 – Hybrid operation components connecting on-premises to VMware Cloud

SDDC cluster design

A VMware Cloud on AWS SDDC includes compute (vSphere), storage (vSAN), and networking (NSX) resources grouped together into one or more clusters managed by a single VMware vCenter Server instance.

Host types

VMware Cloud on AWS runs on dedicated bare-metal Amazon EC2 instances. When deploying an SDDC, VMware ESXi software is deployed directly to the physical host without nested virtualization. In contrast to the pricing structure for other Amazon EC2 instances running on AWS Nitro System (which generally follows a pay-per-usage model per running EC2 instance), the pricing model for VMware Cloud on AWS is priced for the entire bare-metal instance, regardless of the number of virtual machines running on it.

Multiple host types are available for you when designing an SDDC. Each host has different data storage or performance specifications. Depending on the workload and use case, customers can mix multiple host types within different clusters of an SDDC to provide better performance and economics, as depicted in the following figure:

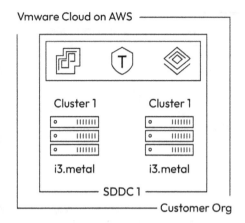

Figure 1.5 – VMware Cloud SDDC with two clusters, one each of i3.metal and i3en.metal host types

At the time of writing this book (2023), three different host types can be used to provision an SDDC.

i3.metal

The i3.metal type is VMware Cloud on AWS's first host type. I3 hosts are ideal for general-purpose workloads. This host instance type may be used in any cluster, including single-, two-, or three-node clusters and stretched cluster deployments. The i3.metal host specification can be found in the following table:

i3 .metal

Compute	
Type	Intel Xeon Broadwell
Number of Sockets	2
Number of Cores per Socket	18
Total Physical Cores	36 @ 2.3 GHz
Hyper-Threading	Disabled
Custom Core Counts	8, 16, 36
Memory	
RAM	512 GiB (~550 GB)
Storage	
Boot Volume	EBS
Disk Count	8
Disk Type	Self-Encrypting NVMe
Capacity per Disk	1.58 TiB (1.74 TB)
vSAN Disk Groups	2
Total Raw Cache Capacity	~3.16 TiB (~3.5 TB)
Total Raw Storage Capacity	~10.37 TiB (~11 TB)
VSAN Features	Compression, Deduplication
Network	
Physical NIC Speed	1x 25 Gb ENA

Figure 1.6 – i3.metal host specification

This instance type has a dual-socket Intel Broadwell CPU, with 36 cores per host.

As in all hosts in the VMware Cloud on AWS service, it boots from an attached 12 GB EBS volume.

The host vSAN configuration is comprised of eight 1.74 TB disks, and two disks per disk group are allocated for the caching tier and are not counted as part of the raw capacity pool.

It is important to note that *hyperthreading* is disabled on this instance type and that both *deduplication and compression* are enabled on the vSAN storage side. As VMware moves toward consuming new host types, it's anticipated that use cases for i3.metal will become rare.

i3en.metal

The i3en hosts are designed to support data-intensive workloads. They can be used for storage-heavy or general-purpose workload requirements that cannot be met by the standard i3.metal instance. It makes economic sense in storage-heavy clusters because of the significantly higher storage capacity as compared to the i3.metal host: it has four times as much raw storage space at a lower price per GB.

This host instance type may be used in stretched cluster deployments and regular cluster deployments (two-node and above).

The i3en.metal host specification can be found in the following table:

i3en.metal

Compute	
Type	Intel Xeon Broadwell
Number of Sockets	2
Number of Cores per Socket	24
Total Physical Cores	48 @ 2.5 GHz
Hyper-Threading	Enabled, 96 logical cores
Custom Core Counts	8, 16, 24,30, 36, 48
Memory	
RAM	768 GiB (~825 GB)
Storage	
Boot Volume	EBS
Disk Count	8
Disk Type	Self-Encrypting NVMe
Capacity per Disk	6.82 TiB (7.5 TB)
vSAN Disk Groups	4
Total Raw Cache Capacity	~6.36TiB (~7 TB)
Total Raw Storage Capacity	~45.84 TiB (~50 TB)
VSAN Features	Compression
Network	
Physical NIC Speed	1x 100 Gb ENA: 25Gb initial GA
NIC Hardware Encryption	East-West

Figure 1.7 – i3en.metal host specification

The i3en.metal type comes with hyperthreading enabled by default, to provide 96 cores and 768 GB of memory.

The host vSAN configuration is comprised of eight 7.5 TB physical disks, using NVMe namespaces. Each physical disk is broken up into 4 virtual disk namespaces, creating a total of 32 NVMe namespaces. Four namespaces per host are allocated for the caching tier and are not counted as raw capacity.

This host type offers a significantly larger disk, with more RAM and CPU cores. Additionally, there is *network traffic encryption* on the NIC level, and only *compression* is enabled on the vSAN storage side; *deduplication* is disabled.

> **Note**
>
> VMware on AWS customer-facing vSAN storage information is provided in TiB units and not in TB units. This may cause confusion when performing storage sizing.

i4i.metal

VMware and AWS announced the availability of a brand new instance type in September 2022 – i4i.metal. With this new hardware platform, customers can now benefit from the latest Intel CPU architecture (Ice Lake), increased memory size and speed, and twice as much storage capacity compared to i3. The host specification can be found in the following table:

Compute	
Type	Intel Xeon Broadwell
Number of Sockets	2
Number of Cores per Socket	32
Total Physical Cores	64 @ 2.9GHz / 3.5GHz Turbo
Hyper-Threading	Enabled, 128 logical cores
Custom Core Counts	8, 16, 24, 30, 36, 48, 64
Memory	
RAM	1024GiB (≈1TB)
Storage	
Boot Volume	Amazon Elastic Block Store (EBS)
Disk Count	8
Disk Type	Self-Encrypting NVMe
Capacity per Disk	3.75TiB (4.12TB)
vSAN Disk Groups	2
Total Raw Cache Capacity	~6.82TiB (~7.5 TB)
Total Raw Storage Capacity	~20.46TiB (~22.5TB)
VSAN Features	Compression
Network	
Type	Amazon Elastic Network Adapter (ENA)
Physical NIC Speed	1x 75 Gbps
NIC Hardware Encryption	East-West

Figure 1.8 – i4i.metal host specification

Based on a recent performance study (`https://blogs.vmware.com/performance/2022/11/sql-performance-vmware-cloud-on-aws-i3-i3en-i4i.html`) using a Microsoft SQL Server workload, i4i outperforms i3.metal on a magnitude of 3x.

In the next section, we will evaluate how the VMware Cloud on AWS SDDC is mapped to AWS Availability Zones.

AWS Availability Zones

The following figure describes the relationship between a Region and Availability Zones in AWS:

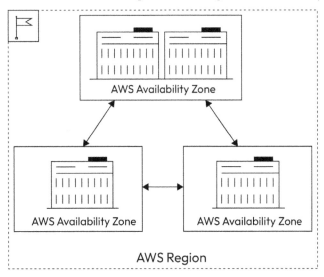

Figure 1.9 – Architecture of a Region and Availability Zones

Each AWS Region is made up of multiple Availability Zones. These are data centers that are physically isolated. High-speed and low-latency connections connect Availability Zones within the same Region. Availability Zones are placed differently in floodplains, equipped with uninterruptible power supplies and on-site backup generators.

If available, they can be connected to different power grids or utility companies. Each Availability Zone has redundant connections to multiple ISPs. By default, an SDDC is deployed on a single Availability Zone.

The following figure describes the essential building blocks of VMware Cloud on AWS SDDC clusters, which are, in turn, built from compute hosts:

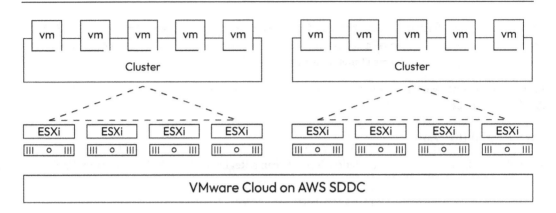

Figure 1.10 – Architecture of a VMware Cloud on AWS SDDC, with clusters and hosts

A cluster is built from a minimum of two hosts and can have a host added or removed at will from the VMware Cloud on AWS SDDC console.

Cluster types and sizes

VMware Cloud on AWS supports many different types of clusters. They can accommodate various use cases from **Proof of Concept** (**PoC**) to business-critical applications. There are three types of standard clusters (single availability zone) in an SDDC.

Single-host SDDC

A **cluster** refers to a compute pool of *multiple hosts*; a *single-host* SDDC is an exception to that rule, as it provides a fully functional SDDC with VMware vSAN, NSX, and vSphere on a single host instead of multiple hosts. This option allows customers to experiment with VMware Cloud on AWS for a low price.

> **Information**
>
> Customers need to know that single-host SDDC clusters can't be patched or software updated within their 60-day lifespan. These clusters cease automatically after 60 days. All virtual machines and data are deleted. VMware doesn't back up the data, and in the case of host failure, there will be data loss.

An SLA does not cover single-host SDDCs, and they should not be used for production purposes. Customers can choose to convert a single-host SDDC into a 2-host SDDC cluster at any time during their 60-day operational period. Once converted, the 2-host SDDC cluster will be ready for production workloads. All the data will be migrated to both hosts on the 2-host SDDC cluster.

VMware will manage the multi-host production cluster and keep it up to date with the latest software updates and security patches. This can be the path from PoC to production.

Two-host SDDC clusters

The 2-host SDDC cluster allows for a fully redundant data replica suitable for entry-level production use cases. This deployment is good for customers beginning their public cloud journey. It is also suitable for DR pilot light deployments that are part of VCDR services, which will be covered later in the book.

The 2-host SDDDC cluster has no time restrictions and is SLA-eligible. VMware will patch and upgrade all the hosts in the SDDC Clusters with zero downtime similar to how a multi-host SDDC cluster running production workloads is patched or updated.

The two-host cluster leverages a virtual EC2 m5.2xlarge instance as a vSAN *witness* to store and update the witness metadata; it allows for resiliency in case of a hardware failure in any one of the hosts. When scaling up to three hosts, the metadata witness is terminated. On the contrary, the metadata witness instance is recreated when scaled down from three hosts.

> **Note**
>
> At launch time, a three-host cluster couldn't be scaled down to two hosts; however, this limitation was addressed in early 2022. There are still limitations associated with the number of virtual machines that can be turned on concurrently (36) and support of large VM vMotion through HCX is limited with i3 host types.
>
> More information can be found at `https://vmc.techzone.vmware.com/resource/entry-level-clusters-vmware-cloud-aws`.

Three-host SDDC clusters

A three-host cluster can scale the number of hosts up and down in a cluster from 3 to 16, without the previously described limitations, and is recommended for larger production environments.

Multi-cluster SDDC

There can be up to 20 clusters in an SDDC. The management appliances will always be in cluster number 1. Each cluster needs to contain the same type of hosts, but different clusters can operate different host types.

The following figure describes at a high level how, in a single customer organization, there can be multiple SDDCs, and within the SDDC, multiple clusters, with each SDDC having its own management appliances residing in cluster 1:

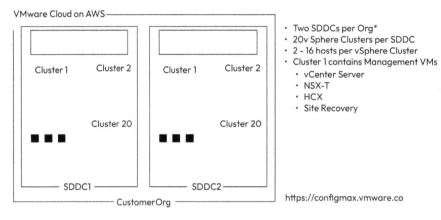

Figure 1.11 – Detailed view of multiple SDDCs and clusters in an organization

So far, we have gone through a single Availability Zone cluster type. Next, let's explore how customers can architect their SDDC resiliency to withstand a full **Availability Zone (AZ)** failure leveraging stretched clusters.

Stretched clusters

When designing application resiliency across AZs with native AWS services, resiliency must be achieved via application-level availability or services such as AWS RDS. Traditional vSphere-based applications need to be refactored to enjoy those resiliency capabilities.

In contrast, VMware Cloud on AWS offers AZ failure resilience via vSAN stretched clusters.

Cross-AZ availability is possible by extending the vSphere cluster across two AWS AZs. The stretched vSAN cluster makes use of vSANs synchronous writes across AZs. It has a zero RPO and a near-zero RTO, depending on the vSphere HA reboot time. This functionality is transparent for applications running inside of a VM.

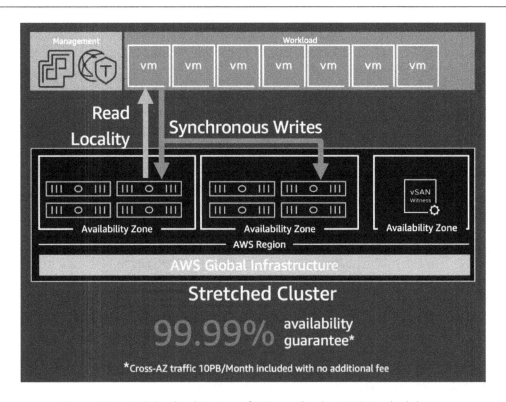

Figure 1.12 – High-level architecture of VMware Cloud on AWS standard cluster

Customers can select the two AZs that they wish their SDDC to be stretched across in the stretched cluster deployment. VMware automation will then pick the correct third AZ for your witness node to deploy in. The VMware Cloud on AWS service covers the cost of provisioning of the witness node, which operates on an Amazon EC2 instance created from an **Amazon Machine Images** (**AMI**) converted from a VMware OVA. The stretched cluster and witness deployments are fully automated once the initial parameters have been set, just like a single AZ SDDC installation.

Stretched clusters can span AZs within the same AWS Region and require a minimum number of four hosts. vSphere HA is turned on, and the host isolation response is set to shut down and start virtual machines. In an AZ failure, a vSphere HA event is triggered. vSAN fault domains are used to maintain vSAN data integrity.

The SLA definition of a standard cluster has an availability commitment of 99.9% uptime, and a stretched cluster will have availability commitment of 99.99% uptime. If it utilizes 3+3 hosts or more in each AZ, and a 2+2 cluster will have an availability commitment 99.9% uptime. This enables continuous operations if an AWS AZ fails.

The VMware SLA for VMware Cloud on AWS is available here: `https://www.vmware.com/content/dam/digitalmarketing/vmware/en/pdf/support/vmw-cloud-aws-service-level-agreement.pdf`.

Elastic Distributed Resource Scheduler

The **Elastic DRS** system employs an algorithm designed to uphold an optimal count of provisioned hosts, ensuring high cluster utilization while meeting specified CPU, memory, and storage performance criteria. Elastic DRS continually assesses the current demand within your SDDC and utilizes its algorithm to propose either scaling in or scaling out of the cluster. When a scale-out recommendation is received, a decision engine acts by provisioning a new host into the cluster. Conversely, when a scale-in recommendation is generated, the least-utilized host is removed from the cluster.

It's important to note that Elastic DRS is not compatible with single-host starter SDDCs. To implement Elastic DRS, a minimum of three hosts is required for a single-AZ SDDC and six hosts for a multi-AZ SDDC. Upon the initiation of a scale-out by the Elastic DRS algorithm, all users within the organization receive notifications both in the VMware Cloud Console and via email.

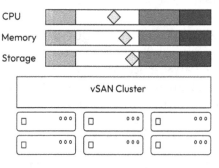

Figure 1.13 – Elastic DRS cluster threshold monitoring and adjustments

You can control the Elastic DRS configuration through Elastic DRS policies. The default Elastic DRS baseline policy is always active and is configured to monitor the utilization of the vSAN datastore exclusively. Once the utilization reaches 80%, Elastic DRS will initiate the host addition process. Customers can opt to use different Elastic DRS policies depending on the use cases and requirements. The following policies are available:

- **Optimize for best performance** (recommended when hosting mission-critical applications): When using this policy, Elastic DRS will monitor CPU, memory, and storage resources. When generating scale-in or scale-out recommendations, the policy uses aggressive high thresholds and moderate low thresholds for scale-in.

- **Optimize for the lowest cost** (recommended when running general-purpose workloads with costs factoring over performance): This policy, as opposed to the previous one, has more aggressive low thresholds and is configured to tolerate longer spikes of high utilization. Using this policy might lead to overcommitting compute resources and performance drops, but it helps to maintain the lowest number of hosts within a cluster.

- **Optimize for rapid scaling** (recommended for DR, VDI, or any workloads that have predictable spike characteristics): When opting for this policy, you can define how many hosts will be added to the cluster in parallel. While the default setting is 2 hosts, you can select up to 16 hosts in a batch. With this policy, you can address the demand of workloads with high spikes in resource utilization – for example, VDI desktops starting up on Monday morning. Also, use this policy with VCDR to achieve low cost and high readiness of the environment for a DR situation.

The resource (storage, CPU, and memory) thresholds will vary depending on the preceding policies.

Elastic DRS Policy	Storage Thresholds	CPU Thresholds	Memory Thresholds
Baseline Policy	Scale-Out Threshold: 80%	(Storage Only)	
Optimize for Best Performance	Scale-Out Threshold: 80%	Scale-Out Threshold: 90%	Scale-Out Threshold: 80%
Optimize for the Lowest Cost	Scale-Out Threshold: 80% Scale-In Threshold: 40%	Scale-Out Threshold: 90% Scale-In Threshold: 60%	Scale-Out Threshold: 80% Scale-In Threshold: 60%
Rapid Scaling	Scale-Out Threshold: 80% Scale-In Threshold: 40%	Scale-Out Threshold: 80% Scale-In Threshold: 50%	Scale-Out Threshold: 80% Scale-In Threshold: 50%

Table 1.1 – Elastic DRS policy default thresholds

> **Note**
> VMware will automatically add hosts to the cluster if storage utilization exceeds 80%. This is because the baseline Elastic DRS policy is, by default, enabled on all SDDC clusters; it cannot be disabled. This is a preventative measure to ensure that vSAN has enough "slack" storage to support applications and workloads.

Automatic cluster remediation

One of the ultimate benefits of running VMware SDDC on an AWS public cloud is access to elastic resource capacity. It tremendously helps to address not only resource demands (see the preceding *Elastic DRS* section) but also to quickly recover from a hardware failure.

The auto-remediation service monitors ESXi hosts for different types of hardware failures. Once a failure is detected, the auto-remediation service triggers the autoscaler mechanism to add a host to the cluster and place the failed host into maintenance mode if possible. vSphere DRS will automatically migrate resources or vSphere HA will restart the affected virtual machines, depending on the severity of the failure. vSAN will synchronize the **Virtual Machine Disk (VMDK)** files. Once this process is complete, the auto-remediation service will initiate the removal of the failed host.

The following diagram describes how the autoscaler service monitors for alerts in the SDDC and makes remediation actions accordingly:

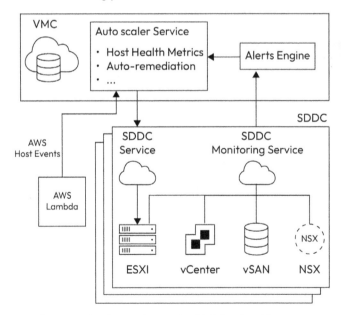

Figure 1.14 – Autoscaler service high-level architecture

All these operations are transparent to customers and also do not incur additional costs – a newly added host is non-billable for the whole time of the remediation.

Understanding Cloud Service Platform and VMware Cloud Console

In this section, we will depict how customers operate the VMware Cloud on AWS environment.

Cloud Service Platform and VMware Cloud Console

A VMware Cloud Services account gives customers access to the VMware Cloud Console and other VMware Cloud services, such as VMware vRealize Log Insight Cloud, HCX, and TMC. The VMware Cloud Services Console allows customers to manage their organization's billing, identity, access, and other aspects of VMware Cloud on AWS. VMware Cloud on AWS is based on an organization as a basic management object containing cloud services and users. Customers can subscribe to different Cloud services through service roles inside the organization.

The first user will need to have a valid MyVMware account to create a Cloud Service platform account and a VMware Cloud organization. There are three types of organization roles in an organization:

- **Fund Owner**: Prior to onboarding, your VMware representative will request that you identify a fund owner during the deal process. Once the deal is completed, a welcome email is sent to the fund owner. This email contains the link that you need to sign up for the Cloud Service platform. This link can only be used once. The link will redirect to the VMware Cloud Services Portal site, where you can log in to the VMware Cloud on AWS service with your MyVMware credentials. Your MyVMware account is used to create an organization and become an organization owner.

- **Organization Owner**: This user can add, remove, and modify users. This user can also access VMware Cloud services. Multiple owners are possible per organization.

- **Organization Members**: These users can access cloud services. However, they cannot add, remove, or modify users. The Cloud Services Console allows customers to assign service roles to specific organization members. The VMware Cloud on AWS service lets customers assign Administrator, Administrator (Delete Restricted), NSX Cloud Auditor, and NSX CloudAdmin roles.

As mentioned, the **Cloud Service Platform** (**CSP**) console handles the IAM with MyVMware accounts as the identity source. However, a federation with an external IDP source such as Okta or Azure AD is supported and configured from the CSP console. The CSP authentication and federation are unrelated to the VMware Cloud on AWS authentication path, which uses a different mechanism. Support tickets can be managed either from the CSP console or from the online chat inside the VMware Cloud service.

VMware Cloud console

The VMware Cloud console is a service within an organization accessed from the CSP described in the preceding section. The VMware Cloud console manages SDDCs, one or more clusters of bare-metal hosts installed with VMware ESXi, vSphere, vCenter Server (vCenter), VMware NSX, and VMware vSAN.

The VMware Cloud console facilitates access to the standalone NSX Manager UI through the reverse proxy. To access the vSphere Web Client, used to manage the VMware Cloud on AWS SDDC, you will use the default CloudAdmin user. The initial provision of the CloudAdmin user includes a randomly generated password that can be accessed via the SDDC view on the VMware Cloud console.

> **Note**
> VMware Cloud Console does not reflect the current password of Cloud Admin if the password has been changed using the Web Client or API. The VMware Cloud console can manage multiple SDDCs. Each SDDC can reside in a different Region. An SDDC is created within one AWS Region. An organization can create up to 2 SDDCs by default, but this is a soft limit that can be extended to 20.

The SDDC console offers quick summary information about each SDDC and its clusters. It includes the Region, AZ, host count, and cluster resources available (CPU, RAM, and storage). Once an SDDC has been created, the customer can control the SDDC's capacity by adding/removing hosts and clusters and modifying the Elastic DRS policy. The VMware Cloud console also provides access to the SDDC groups.

SDDC groups are where the VMware Transit Connect service is managed, which is based on the AWS **transit gateway** (TGW) service. VMware Transit Connect is a **VMware-managed TGW** (vTGW) that can be used to connect multiple SDDCs and VPCs over a high bandwidth router utilizing a VPC attachment and TGW attachment. The vTGW can be used to connect to native AWS TGW and VPC to form hybrid architectures – more on this later in the NSX section.

The SDDC Console provides additional operational functionality:

- Activation of complementary services such as HCX, NSX advanced firewall, **VMware site recovery** (VSR), and Aria Automation
- Activation of Microsoft **Services Provider License Agreement** (SPLA) licenses
- Open support tickets and live chat with technical support
- Support-related environment information such as SDDC and organization ID
- Network connectivity troubleshooting
- VMware maintenance notifications

- Subscription management for hosts, site recovery, and NSX advanced firewall

- Activity logs for SDDC-related activities, alerts, audit trails, and notifications

- API explorer for the different services and access SDKs

VMware vCenter Server

vCenter Server facilitates the management of the VMware Cloud on AWS SDDC. vCenter running in VMware Cloud on AWS is the same product that customers use in their on-premises environment to manage VMware vSphere. The **Cloud gateway appliance** (**CGA**) enables the linking of vCenters through a hybrid-linked mode to the on-premises environment, enabling hybrid operations with a single pane of glass.

The following screenshot shows how two vCenter Servers are managed with a single pane of glass through the cloud gateway from the vSphere Web Client:

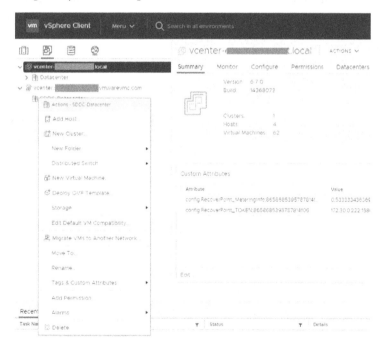

Figure 1.15 – Cloud gateway managing two vCenters in a single management pane of glass

You use vSphere Web Client to access VMware Cloud on AWS vCenter Server and operate the VMware Cloud on AWS SDDC. It's vital to understand the access model used within the VMware Cloud on AWS SDDC.

Restrictive access model

The VMware Cloud on AWS SDDC permissions model allows VMware's **Site Reliability Engineering** (**SRE**) and customers to manage the vCenter deployment mutually according to the *shared responsibility model*. The permissions model has the following high-level goals:

- Enable access to VMware operators and VMware Cloud on AWS customers

- Permit customers to manage their workloads and users/groups using **Active Directory** (**AD**) / **Lightweight Directory Access Protocol** (**LDAP**), tags, permissions (on their inventory items), roles (from subsets of their permissions), and so on

- Protect administrator-managed objects (management appliances, users/groups, global policies, roles, permissions, hosts, storage, and so on)

- Enable SRE teams to manage vSphere and underlying AWS infrastructure life cycle management, including deployment, configuration, upgrade, patching, monitoring, remediating, and applying emergency updates for security vulnerabilities

Because of this access model, certain third-party vendors that require root ESXi access and **vSphere Installation Bundle** (**VIB**) installation are not compatible with VMware Cloud on AWS.

> **Note**
>
> To see which third-party solutions are certified with VMware Cloud on AWS, please refer to the VMware compatibility guide at `https://www.vmware.com/resources/compatibility/search.php?deviceCategory=vsanps` or the third-party vendor's certification website.

If a host goes down or is found to be inoperable, a new host is added to the cluster. All data from the affected host is then rebuilt on the new host. After being fully replaced by the new host, the faulty host will be removed from the cluster using the DRS capability and EC2 API automation.

VMware Cloud automation automatically configures all VM kernels and logical networks when a new host is connected to the cluster; the customer doesn't have access to the host or cluster configuration. After the host is connected, the vSAN database is automatically expanded. This allows the cluster to take advantage of the newly added storage capacity. This happens completely automatically without any intervention from the customer or VMware SRE.

CloudAdmins can't modify the default level 3 DRS migration threshold. This is to avoid unnecessary vMotion operation.

> **Note**
>
> A new mechanism known as **compute policies** is used in VMware Cloud on AWS to create affinity or anti-affinity rules.

The following figure graphically summarizes the restricted access and shared responsibility model between customers and VMware:

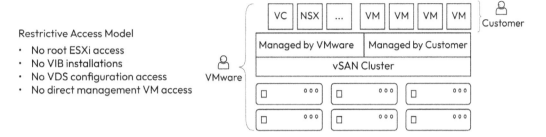

Restrictive Access Model

- No root ESXi access
- No VIB installations
- No VDS configuration access
- No direct management VM access

Figure 1.16 – Restricted access and shared responsibility model

> **Information**
>
> More information can be found at https://docs.vmware.com/en/VMware-Cloud-on-AWS/solutions/VMware-Cloud-on-AWS.39646badb412ba21bd6770ef62ae00a2/GUID-31CC90E5EB22075B2313FA674D567F2A.html.

Let's look further into the default user role and group in VMware Cloud on AWS.

CloudAdmin user

Customers will be able to access vCenter via the `cloudadmin@vmc.local` username account.

CloudAdmin role and group

The SDDC CloudAdmin role determines the highest level of permissions of the customer.

The CloudAdmin group was granted a CloudAdmin role with Global permissions and the data center object in vCenter. It has been granted read-only permission set to vCenter's management resources (storage, networks, resource pools, virtual machines, and the `Discovered Virtual Machines` folder). Customer users within AD/LDAP are assigned to the CloudAdmin group (or AD/LDAP groups with a custom role and a subset of permissions) within vCenter.

vSphere architecture

Now, let's describe in detail the vSphere configuration and vCenter inventory.

Data center

An SDDC has a single virtual data center named `SDDC-Datacenter`. This data center contains the compute resources organized in vSphere clusters.

vSphere HA is enabled on VMware Cloud On AWS by default. DRS is a feature that balances computing workloads on available resources. These features can only be configured by VMware. In the event of a host failure, application workloads are restarted on all healthy hosts within the cluster using vSphere HA.

The following figure describes at a high level the vSphere configuration inside a vCenter virtual data center managed by VMware and customer administrators:

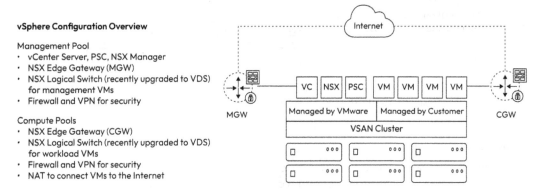

Figure 1.17 – Overview of vSphere configuration inside an SDDC data center

All hosts in the SDDC will be present within a cluster. An SDDC will have a single cluster called **Cluster-1**, which will serve both management appliances and end user workloads. The SDDC can have additional clusters as required. Clusters are named with the naming convention `Cluster-x`, where `x` is the cluster's number. Clusters, by default, are limited to a single AWS AZ. Stretched clustering allows hosts in a cluster to be distributed across two AZs in an AWS Region.

> **Note**
>
> Customers cannot add a stretched cluster to an SDDC that is deployed in a single AZ. This needs to be a decision that is made at deployment time – that is, stretched or standard cluster.

Resource pools

An SDDC's resource pools primarily protect management appliances. They are a way to preserve compute resources for management appliances and they serve as the target object when permissions are granted to management appliances.

The SDDC creates two resource pools from the base cluster:

- `Mgmt-ResourcePool` is a resource pool that contains management appliances
- `Compute-ResourcePool` is a resource pool that accommodates end user workloads

Datastores

The SDDC-based cluster contains two datastores:

- `vsanDatastore` is only used to store SDDC management appliances
- `WorkloadDatastore` can be used to store workloads for end users

These datastores represent the same underlying vSAN pool but are presented as separate entities to enforce permissions within SDDC. Specifically, `vsanDatastore` can't be modified. Management appliances can only be found in the first cluster.

Additional clusters to the SDDC will appear as an additional datastore for end user workloads. The datastores will be named `WorkloadDatastore x`, where x refers to the cluster number.

Demystifying vSAN and host storage architecture

Let us explore the architecture of the storage subsystem within the VMware Cloud on AWS SDDC.

VMware vSAN overview

vSAN stands for **virtual storage area network**, an object-based storage solution leveraging locally attached physical drives. VMware has offered vSAN technology to the market for some time. Now, it's a mature storage solution, well represented in Gartner's magical quadrant and powering millions of customer workloads.

vSAN combines locally attached hard disks into a single, cluster-wide datastore, supporting simultaneous access from multiple ESXi hosts. All vSAN traffic traverses over a physical network using a dedicated vSAN VM kernel interface. A shared datastore across all hosts in a vSphere cluster enables usage of distinguished vSphere features, including live vMotion between hosts, vSphere HA to restart virtual machines from a failed host on the surviving host in the cluster, and DRS.

The vSAN distributed architecture with local storage fits perfectly into the cloud world, eliminating dependencies on external storage. Easily scalable with the addition of a new host, providing enterprise-level storage functionality (deduplication, compression, data-in-rest encryption, etc.), vSAN builds the foundation of VMware Cloud on AWS.

vSAN on VMware Cloud on AWS high-level architecture

While VMware Cloud on AWS leverages VMware vSAN in a way very similar to on-premises, there are still a number of distinguished architecture differences.

NVMe HDDs with a 4096 native physical sector size are used by all instance types in VMware Cloud on AWS.

At the moment, VMware Cloud on AWS features vSAN v1 (OSA) with a distinction between the caching and capacity tiers. Each host type features its own configuration of disk groups. With the release of vSphere 8, VMware brings a new vSAN architecture model, the so-called vSAN ESA. With the recent 1.24 SDDC release, vSAN ESA has been made available to selected customers under preview (`https://vmc.techzone.vmware.com/resource/vsan-esa-vmware-cloud-aws-technical-deep-dive`).

To facilitate logical separation between customer-managed and VMware-managed virtual machines, a single vSAN datastore is represented as two logical datastores. Only workload datastores are available for customer workloads. Both logical datastores share the same physical capacity and throughput.

Storage encryption

In VMware Cloud on AWS, vSAN encrypts all user data-a-rest. Encryption is automatically activated by default on every cluster deployed in your SDDC, and cannot be disabled. Additionally, with newer host types (i3en and i4i) vSAN traffic between hosts is encrypted as well (so-called data-in-transit encryption).

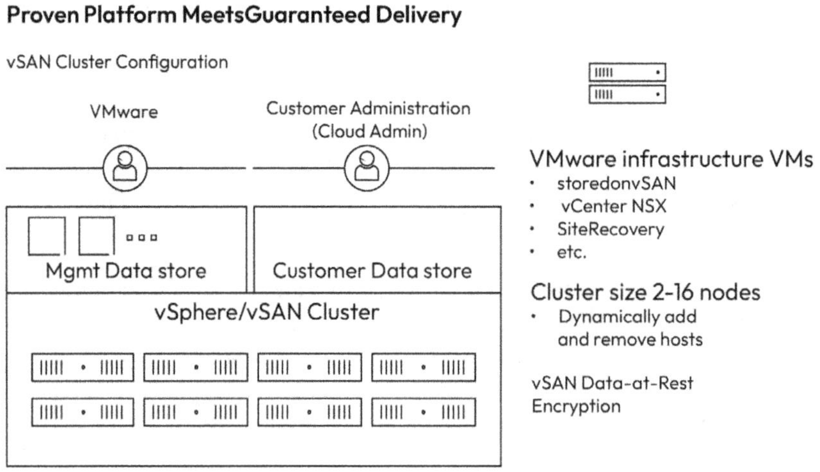

Figure 1.18 – vSAN cluster configuration and shared responsibility model

Storage policies

vSAN has been designed from the beginning to support major enterprise storage features. However, there is an important architectural difference between external storage and vSAN. When using an external storage, you will enable storage features on a physical **Logical Unit Number** (**LUN**) level and each LUN will be connected as a separate datastore, featuring different performance and availability patterns. With vSAN, all of these features are activated on a virtual machine or even on an individual VMDK level. To control performance and data availability for your workload, you assign different storage policies. vSAN storage policy management and policy monitoring are done from the vCenter using the vCenter Web Client. Customers control their configurations through virtual machine (VM) storage policies, also known as **storage policy-based management** (**SPBM**).

Each virtual machine or disk has a policy assigned to it, and the policy includes, among others, disk RAID and fault tolerance parameters and additional configurations such as disk stripers, I/O SLA, and encryption.

In the following diagram, you can see a graphical summary of the SPBM values:

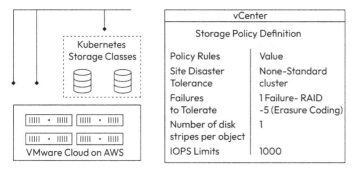

Figure 1.19 – SBPM configuration graphical summary

Let's go deeper and review the configuration available with vSAN storage policies.

Failures to Tolerate

Failures to Tolerate (**FTT**) defines the number of disk device or host failures a virtual machine can tolerate within a cluster. You can choose between 0 (no protection) and 3 (a cluster can tolerate a simultaneous failure of up to three hosts without affecting virtual machine workloads).

> **Note**
>
> VMware Cloud on AWS SLAs dictate a minimum FTT configuration to be eligible for SLA credit.

FTT is configured together with the appropriate **Redundant Array of Independent Disks** (**RAID**) policy according to the number of hosts in the cluster. Customers can choose a RAID policy optimized for either performance (mirroring) or capacity (erasure coding).

The FTT policy overhead per storage object depends on the selected FTT and RAID policy. For example, an FTT1 and RAID-1 policy creates two copies of a storage object. FTT2 and RAID-1 creates three copies of the storage object, and FTT3 and RAID-1 creates four copies of the storage object.

The following list describes the trade-offs between different RAID options:

- RAID-1 uses **Mirroring** and requires more disk space overhead, but gives better write I/O performance, can survive a single host failure with FTT1, and is available from two hosts and above. RAID-1 is also used in conjunction with FTT2 for clusters larger than six hosts as an alternative to RAID-6 for improved write I/O performances, or FTT3 for clusters larger than seven hosts.

- RAID-5 uses **Erasure Coding** and has less disk space overhead, which results in lower performance, but it can survive a single host failure and is available from four hosts and above.

- RAID-6 is similar to RAID-5; however, it can survive two host failures (FTT2). This RAID type is available starting with six hosts.

- RAID-0 (**No Data Redundancy**) uses no extra disk overhead and provides potentially the best performance (eliminating overhead to create redundant copies of the data), but cannot survive any failure.

> **Note**
> The RAID-0 policy is configurable but not eligible for SLA. If the host or disk fails, this can result in data loss.

The following table summarizes the RAID configuration, FTT policy options, and the minimal host count:

RAID Configuration	FTT Policy	Hosts Required
RAID-0 (No Data Redundancy)	0	1+
RAID-1 (Mirroring)	1	2+
RAID-5 (Erasure Coding)	1	4+
RAID-1 (Mirroring)	2	5+
RAID-6 (Erasure Coding)	2	6+
RAID-1 (Mirroring)	3	7+

Table 1.2 – Table summary of the RAID, FTT, and minimal host count options

Managed Storage Policy

VMware Cloud on AWS is provided as a service to customers. As a part of the service agreement, VMware commits to SLAs for customers using the service, including a VM uptime guarantee. Depending on the SDDC configuration, the SDDC is eligible for either a 99.9% (standard cluster) or 99.99% (stretched cluster with 6+ hosts) uptime availability commitment. To facilitate this strength of SLAs, VMware dictates a certain level of FTT configuration for customer workloads.

The following figure describes VM storage policies required for SLA-eligible workloads:

Table 1: Standard Clusters (Single-AZ)

Number of Hosts	Policy Configuration
5 or less	1 Failure - Raid-1 (mirroring)
6 or more	2 Failure - Raid-6 (Erasure Coding)

Table 2: Stretched Clusters (Multi-AZ)

Number of Hosts	Policy Configuration
Any	Dual Site Mirroring 1 Failure - Raid-1 (mirroring)

Figure 1.20 – Table of storage policy configuration for SLA eligibility

---

Information

A single-host SDDC is not covered by an SLA and should not be used for production workloads.

VMware Cloud on AWS introduced a new concept called **Managed Storage Policy Profiles** to help customers adhere to SLAs. Each vSphere cluster has a default storage policy managed by VMware and configured to adhere to SLAs requirements (e.g., FTT1, RAID-1 in a cluster with 3 ESXi hosts). As the cluster size changes, the Managed Storage Policy Profile is updated with the appropriate RAID and FTT configuration.

Customers can create their own policies, based on their needs, which may differ from the managed policies, and in that case, it will be the customer's responsibility to adjust the policy parameters to meet the SLA compliance requirements. Customers can configure values not aligned with the SLA parameters – for instance, use RAID-1 FTT1 in a six-host cluster. In that case, customers will receive notifications that they have non-SLA-compliant storage objects in a cluster in their SDDC. Such a cluster is not entitled to receive any SLA credits. As in the following example, customers using non-compliant policies will receive periodic email notifications about it:

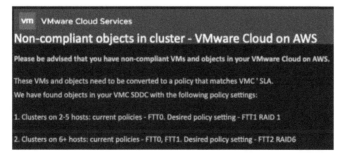

Figure 1.21 – Screenshot of a non-SLA-compliant storage object email notification

The Managed Storage Policy Profile offers customers an easy way to deploy workloads with SLA-compliant storage policies without overthinking the current cluster configuration.

> **Note**
> Do not modify the default storage policy in your SDDC. Your changes will be rewritten by the next invocation of SDDC monitoring. These changes might cause performance penalties for your workload causing vSAN to reapply changes within a short period of time. Instead, create a custom policy and assign it only to a subset of your virtual machines.

Summary

In this chapter, we have learned about AWS Cloud, hybrid cloud challenges, and how VMware Cloud on AWS solves these challenges. We have described the different use cases that VMware Cloud on AWS addresses and described the architecture of VMware Cloud's main components, including CSP, VMware Cloud console, vCenter, vSAN, and NSX. We also looked at the different cluster types, underlying hosts, and high-level networking architecture.

NSX and networking are essential and extensive topics; therefore, we have decided to dedicate the following chapter to describe the unique NSX architecture in VMware Cloud on AWS, including the security and firewall architecture, security capabilities such as micro-segmentation, IPS/IDS, networking capabilities such as routing, VPN, and native AWS integrations in detail.

In the next chapter, you will discover the best practices on how to implement networking and security in VMware Cloud on AWS.

2

Exploring Networking, Security, and AWS Integrations

This chapter is dedicated to the networking and security aspects of VMware NSX architecture in VMware Cloud on AWS, including the firewall architecture, a **Compute Gateway** (**CGW**), a **Management Gateway** (**MGW**), understanding the concept of micro-segmentation, IPS/IDS, a Layer 7 firewall, and native AWS integration architectures through **VMware Managed Transit Gateway** (**vTGW**).

The chapter will cover the following topics:

- Exploring VMware NSX

- VMware Cloud on AWS networking architectures

- VMware Cloud on AWS SDDC connectivity to the AWS cloud

- VMware NSX and AWS security architecture and capabilities

- VMware NSX micro-segmentation

- Discovering the NSX advanced security add-on

Exploring VMware NSX

Careful networking design and planning are essential for a successful cloud project, and this section will examine the basics of NSX and AWS networking.

A VMware NSX overview

VMware NSX network virtualization offers a complete logical overlay network and security abstraction service, independent from the underlying physical infrastructure.

Distributed functions such as routing, switching, and firewalls are available as kernel-level modules to the hypervisor hosts. Edge components provide external connectivity and stateful services such as

VPN, NAT, and a firewall. VMware Cloud on AWS relies on the proven capabilities of VMware NSX, extended with configuration constructs specific to the AWS cloud.

VMware NSX architecture

The networking architecture of an SDDC comprises a multi-tier topology of tier-0/1 gateways, distributed routers, and service routers.

A tier-0 gateway

A **tier-0** (**T0**) gateway serves as the border point of connectivity for all north-south traffic that traverses through networking constructs, such as AWS **Internet Gateway** (**IGW**), **Direct Connect** (**DX**), IPsec VPNs, a connected VPC **Elastic Network Interface** (**ENI**), and vTGW. All external traffic in the SDDC is terminated at the T0 gateway. T0 external connectivity services run inside an NSX Edge virtual appliance, by default deployed in HA (active/passive) configuration, distributed across different ESXi hosts.

All ESXi hosts share the **Distributed Router** (**DR**) component of the T0 and **Tier-1** (**T1**) routers. The CGWs, MGWs, and T0 Edge distributed router components are responsible for routing their workloads' traffic locally on the ESXi hosts to their destination segment.

The centralized services component, also known as a **Service Router** (**SR**), runs services that the DR cannot distribute, such as **Network Address Translation** (**NAT**), **Dynamic Host Configuration Protocol** (**DHCP**), and Edge Firewall. The SR runs inside the virtual edge appliance.

The following figure illustrates the traffic flow of a VM reaching the internet through a T0 SR component, running on a virtual edge appliance and using a segment connected to the T1 compute gateway, with the corresponding SR and DR components.

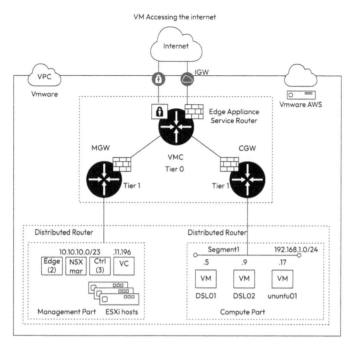

Figure 2.1 – Traffic from a VM to the internet over T1 and T0 routers

During an SDDC deployment, you have an option to choose the SDDC appliance size – medium or large:

Appliance size	Medium	Large
Recommended for	Up to 30 hosts or 3,000 VMs	Greater than 30 hosts or 3,000 VMs
Resources required	34 vCPU and 116 GB	68 vCPU and 240 GB memory

Table 2.1 – SDDC appliance sizes

By default, the SDDC is deployed with a medium appliance that includes a single NSX Edge (implemented as a pair of VMs running active/passive configuration). The T0 services run on this default single NSX Edge.

SDDCs that run network-intensive heavy workloads have the potential to overload the resources on the single NSX Edge. If you anticipate a high volume of network traffic traversing the NSX Edge, you can opt to use the multi-edge feature, as shown in *Figure 2.2*.

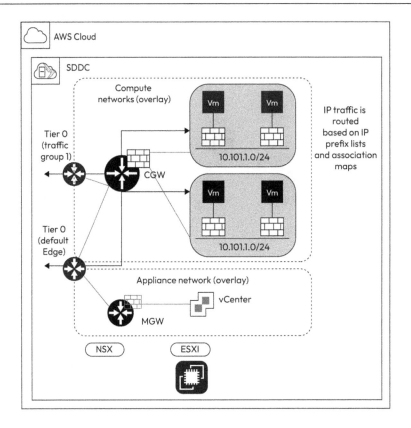

Figure 2.2 – A multi-edge SDDC with traffic groups

The prerequisites to configuring a multi-edge SDDC include the following:

- SDDC requires a minimum of more than four hosts
- The SDDC appliance size has to be upgraded to large (from medium)
- SDDC must use a VMware Transit Connect (vTGW)

Once the prerequisites are met, you can create an IP prefix list with one or more IP prefixes and map it to a traffic group. Each traffic group will create an additional pair of NSX Edge appliances that will route the traffic flows corresponding to the traffic group.

A tier-1 gateway

Tier-1 gateways handle all east-west traffic between the network segments inside the SDDC. There are two types of tier-1 gateways:

- **Management Gateway (MGW)**
- **Compute Gateway (CGW)**

They act as a router for the networks they serve and provide them with networking and security services. Workloads use the compute segments managed by the CGW, while the MGW hosts segments for management appliances and ESXi hosts.

> **Note**
>
> Each SDDC is deployed with a single CGW. You can create an additional CGW (a custom CGW) as required by your design. This feature helps you to design for advanced networking requirements.

MGWs

All infrastructure management components, such as vCenter Server, NSX manager controllers, and ESXi hosts receive networking and security services from the MGW. VMware manages these components, and customers can't deploy workloads under the MGW-attached segments. MGW is primarily used to enable user access to management components using predefined ports.

> **Note**
>
> At deployment time, the default deny rule is configured on an MGW. You need to create new firewall rules to enable connectivity to management components, including vCenter Server.

CGWs

CGWs provide network connectivity and gateway firewall service for workload VMs. There can be more than one compute segment behind a CGW. The CGW firewall rules and NAT rules for the east-west traffic between the compute segments run on the CGW routers. There are several types of compute segments:

- **Routed segments**. Routed segments are default network segments connected to a CGW and are added to the T0 route table to establish communication with networks outside of the SDDC. During the creation of a routed segment, you must specify the default gateway for the segment. The specified default gateway IP address and subnet mask will define the **Classless Inter-Domain Routing (CIDR)** range of the segment and will be used to assign IP addresses to the VM workloads attached to the segment.

> **Note**
>
> At deployment time, a default network segment is created if you deploy an SDDC with three hosts or less. This segment has the default gateway configured to 192.168.0.1/24. Larger SDDCs do not have a default segment. You need to create a segment before creating a VM.

- **Disconnected segments** have no uplinks to a CGW and are not routed. Disconnected segments are used, for example, by HCX network extensions and are useful for security appliances and disaster recovery bubble network testing.

- **Extended segments**. Extended (Layer 2) segments are automatically created when you configure L2VPN or HCX-based Layer 2 stretched networking.

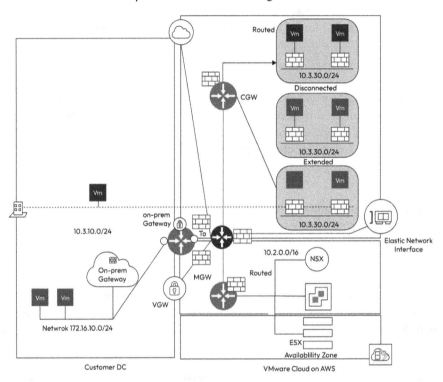

Figure 2.3 – Routed, disconnected, and extended segments in an SDDC

Customers create one or more logical segments that connect to a CGW. VM workloads attached to these logical segments communicate to each other using the CGW. Certain customers have advanced networking requirements such as multi-tenancy, an overlapping IP address space, and route aggregation, which require the use of more than one CGW. The multi-CGW capability allows you to create more than one. Depending on the type of CGW, the workloads can exhibit capabilities such as network isolation, NAT, and disaster recovery. Let's take a look at the types of CGWs:

CGW	Type of CGW
Default CGW	Routed
Custom CGW	Routed
	Isolated
	NATed

Table 2.2 – The CGW types

Let's look at these types of CGWs in more detail:

- **Routed CGW**: A non-default CGW configured as a routed CGW is capable of establishing communication with other routed CGWs (including the default CGW), and also the NSX Edge and beyond, to communicate with on-premises workloads and also the internet. Unlike in the case of the default CGW, you can choose to explicitly configure addresses in route aggregation prefix lists that should be advertised externally. This gives you more control over the routing.

- **NATed CGWs**: The segments on a NATed CGW are not advertised by default to the NSX Edge. A NAT rule needs to be configured to ensure connectivity between the NATed CGW and the NSX Edge. Once a NAT rule is configured for the T1 CGW, then the routes are advertised to the NSX Edge. This enables the segments behind the NATed CGW to have overlapping CIDRs in the SDDC, which is a good use case for customers supporting multi-tenancy or legacy applications that cannot be reconfigured with new IP addresses.

- **Isolated CGWs** are disconnected from the NSX Edge. The isolated CGW serves as a local router without connectivity to the rest of the routed and NATed CGW or MGW segments, or to the external environment. However, all the workload VMs on the segments connected to isolated CGWs can communicate among themselves.

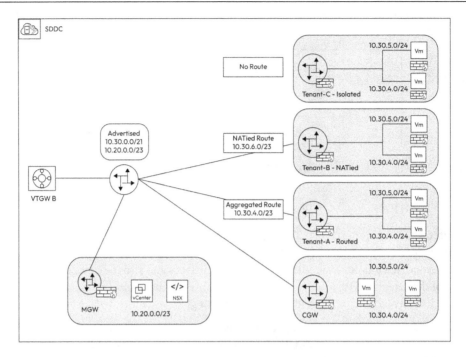

Figure 2.4 – Routed, NATed, and isolated segments behind custom CGWs in an SDDC

Now that we have gained understanding of different configuration options, let us explore the ways to configure networking for your SDDC.

Accessing and managing networking configuration in the VMware Cloud on AWS SDDC

It is recommended to manage VMware Cloud on AWS networking using the VMware NSX Web UI.

The VMware NSX Web UI provides access to all VMware NSX features and supersedes the functionality of the **Networking & Security** tab. We advise you to use the NSX Web UI to access, configure, and monitor network operations in your SDDC.

You can access the VMware NSX Web UI by either using a public IP, by leveraging the **Open NSX Manager** button on the SDDC **Summary** page, or opting to use a private IP for enhanced security. To access the NSX Manager UI over a private IP, you need to configure a VPN or AWS DX first and, after that, change the mapping of the NSX **Fully Qualified Domain Name** (**FQDN**) to a private IP on the **Setting** tab in your SDDC console.

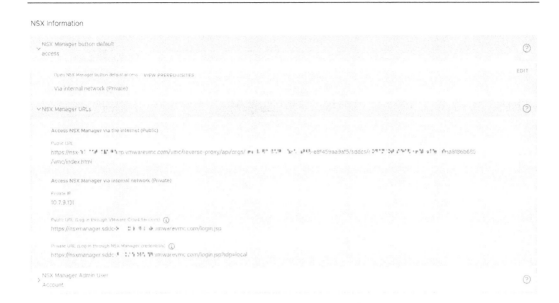

Figure 2.5 – NSX Manager URLs

The next section will dive deeper into how NSX overlay networking and NSX architecture works.

Understanding the network architecture of the VMware Cloud on AWS SDDC

In this section, we will cover network design principles and architecture considerations for different network services in the VMware Cloud on AWS SDDC.

AWS networking

This section provides background on the AWS networking constructs in the VMware Cloud on AWS SDDC.

Amazon **Virtual Private Cloud** (**VPC**) is a logically isolated virtual network that spans across an AWS Region. You can create a VPC using you own IP CIDR range. Additionally, you then create subnets that are mapped to **Availability Zones** (**AZs**). Once subnets are created, you can create resources that are part of them. The resources in the VPC subnet can establish communication with other VPCs and network constructs using route tables.

A VMware-owned and managed AWS account is dedicated to each VMC on AWS customer. A VPC and several subnets are created in this account where all the Amazon EC2 bare-metal hosts reside.

This VPC also acts as a network underlay, on which VMware deploys an NSX overlay, on which the VMC on AWS compute segments are created, which are then used to connect to the VMs.

The underlying AWS account and VMware-owned and managed VPCs are abstracted by VMware. Customers will not have access to this AWS account and instead use the VMware **Cloud Services Portal (CSP)** to access the VMware CSP Console to manage their SDDC environments.

Additionally, an AWS account that is customer-owned and managed runs an Amazon VPC, also referred to as the connected VPC. During the SDDC deployment, VMware runs an orchestration workflow that links the VMware-owned and customer-owned accounts using a set of cross-account **Elastic Network Interfaces (ENIs)** that establish a high-bandwidth low-latency connectivity between the VMC on AWS workloads and the native AWS services.

External connectivity options

NSX has a robust set of capabilities for workload connectivity from the SDDC to the outside world, such as on-premises or AWS native environments. NSX provides networking services over AWS constructs such as AWS DX, **Internet Gateway (IGW)**, **Virtual Private Gateway (VGW)**, **Transit Gateway (TGW)**, an NAT gateway, and VPC services such as **Elastic IP (EIP)**.

All external connectivity components are configured on the T0 router, hosted on the redundant pair of NSX Edges appliances in active/passive configuration. NSX Edge has three main interfaces, plus a fourth VPN interface.

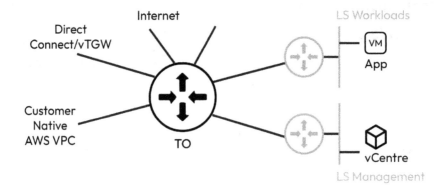

Figure 2.6 – NSX T0 uplink interfaces

Internet uplink

NSX provides public internet connectivity via the AWS IGW, deployed in the VMware-owned VPC associated with this SDDC. The SDDC Edge uses a default route of 0.0.0.0/0 with the IGW as its next hop. It is represented as an internet uplink on the T0 router when reviewing firewall rules in the CGW. Networking egress costs over this link are billable through VMware from the customer's fund.

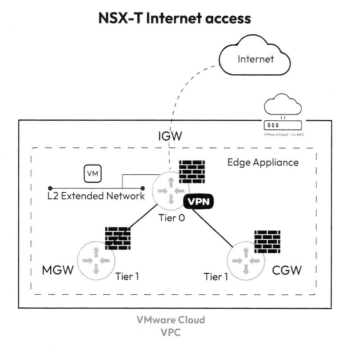

Figure 2.7 – NSX-T internet uplink architecture

AWS DX uplink

Connecting to an on-premises environment via an AWS DX connection can be achieved through two methods. The first involves using a Private VIF to establish a direct connection to the SDDC. The second approach entails connecting via a Transit VIF, which is linked to an AWS **Direct Connect Gateway (DXGW)**, which then connects to a **VMware Transit Connect Gateway (vTGW)**.

The NSX Edge has a DX uplink interface is used when connecting to an on-premises using an AWS DX private VIF. The NSX edge will advertise and receive network prefixes over the uplink.

There are AWS DX-related limitations while integrating a VMC on AWS SDDC using private VIFs:

- A SDDC can advertise only 20 route prefixes over an AWS DX private VIF
- The SDDC can learn 100 route prefixes over the same AWS DX private VIF

> **Note**
> It's important to keep in mind that advertising over 100 routes through the **Border Gateway Protocol (BGP)** session can result in it going into an idle state, causing the session to go *down*.

AWS Direct Connect is a network service that provides a dedicated and private high-bandwidth network connections from an on-premises data center or colocation facility to AWS. Organizations can use an AWS Account (also referred to as customer-owned AWS account) to request an AWS **Direct Connect (DX)** connection to connect to both native AWS workloads along with VMware Cloud on AWS SDDCs. A single DX connection can support up to 50 private VIFs that can be used for both native Amazon VPC and VMware Cloud on AWS SDDCs. However, since the DX connection is hosted in the Organization's AWS Account all the port charges and data transfer costs incurred will be accrued on the Organization's AWS account (also referred to as the customer-owned AWS account).

More information about AWS DX, including advanced architectures using transit VIFs and SDDC groups, and vTGW is available in the later sections of this chapter.

Connected VPC

Each host of SDDC is connected through cross-account ENI connections with a customer-owned VPC, provisioned using a customer-owned AWS account, also known as a **connected VPC**. This connection enables low latency and high-speed access to AWS services deployed to the connected VPC.

It's important to note the following design constraints:

- The connected VPC traffic passes through T0 externally to the SDDC. If you have a plan to deploy a resource-intensive service (for example, Amazon FSx) in your connected VPC, make sure that your T0 infrastructure is capable of handling the traffic flow.

- The active T0 edge appliance is running on a particular ESXi host, and the AWS VPC routing table will reflect that, showing the SDDCs routed segments with the active edge appliance ENI as a next hop. If there is a failover of the active edge VM to another host, the customer VPC main routing table will be updated with the new host ENI. It might cause traffic disruption between VMs in the SDDCs and AWS services in the connected VPC.

> **Note**
> Note that all additional routes tables created in the connected VPC are not updated automatically. As a best practice, it's not recommended to use additional routing tables in the connected VPC.

The connected VPC routing table has the CGW, MGW subnets, and the ENI as a next hop, pointing toward the host running the active NSX T0 edge virtual appliance.

The following figure shows the ENI connectivity to the connected VPC over the T0 Edge:

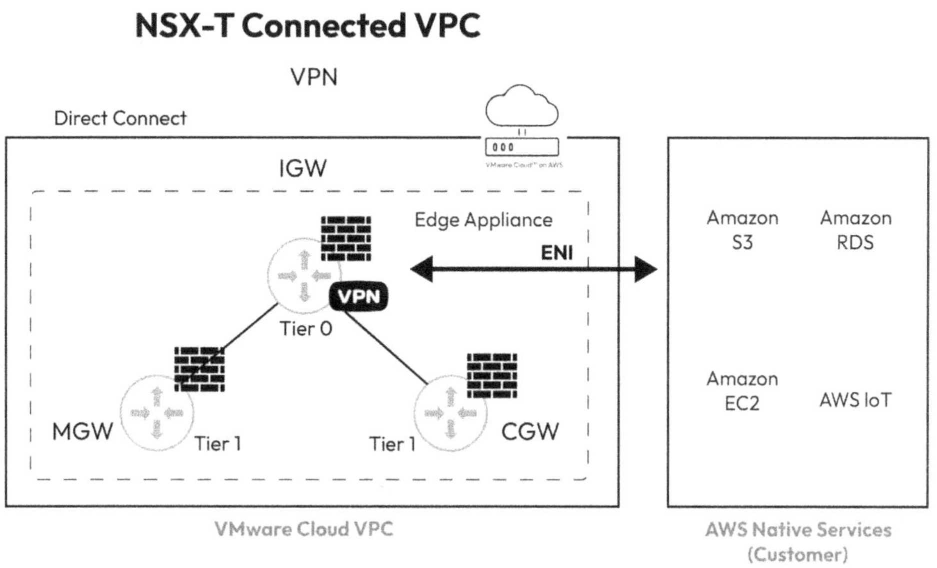

NSX-T Connected VPC

Figure 2.8 – Connected VPC NSX architecture

> **Information**
>
> SDDC hosts are deployed within the same AZ as their cross-link subnet, allowing customers to avoid cross-AZ charges between their SDDC and AWS resources located within the same AZ and/or connected VPC.

Understanding hybrid connectivity options

Once a VMware Cloud on AWS SDDC has been deployed, you will have a functional vSphere environment within the AWS cloud. You have the option to utilize the SDDC resources as a standalone vSphere environment or establish a network connection between your on-premises data center and the VMware Cloud on AWS SDDC. This connection can facilitate the migration of VM workloads and/or facilitate management and control plane traffic.

AWS DX

AWS DX is a dedicated network service that allows customers to establish a connection between AWS's and on-premises locations. DX provides a private, high-speed backbone connection to a VMware Cloud SDDC.

> **Note**
>
> Customers can leverage an existing AWS DX connection (subject to DX limits and bandwidth) to create additional private VIFs or use an existing transit VIF associated with a DXGW to establish on-premises connectivity, without having to procure an additional dedicated DX for VMC on AWS deployment.

Customers often implement DX solutions when they need a high-bandwidth, low-latency, and private connectivity between an on-premises location and a VMware Cloud on AWS SDDC. Security and compliance might be another reason to implement an AWS DX.

> **Note**
>
> By default, all traffic within AWS DX is not encrypted. With the introduction of the MACsec security capability, the AWS DX service now offers you the ability to provide data encryption in transit, without the need to use a VPN over AWS DX. Not all AWS DX connection supports MACsec now.

AWS DX offers customers multiple configuration options, depending on how they plan to use the service. Customers can create public, private, and transit AWS DX **Virtual Interfaces** (**VIFs**).

Public VIFs

A public VIF allows customers to access AWS's public network segments. AWS will advertise all public IP spaces via BGP over the DX connection. A public VIF terminates at AZ's public-facing AWS address space. SDDC public-facing components such as the T0 public IPs, NSX VPN public endpoints, and the public IP of the vCenter can be reachable over a public VIF.

While the use cases to use public VIFs are limited, it is still one of the methods used to establish reliable connectivity to the public internet.

Private VIFs

You attach a private VIF to the VMware-managed VPC and configure using the VMware NSX UI. VMware NSX offers a simplified way to assist in private VIF configuration, by providing a separate UI section to attach or detach a VIF. A BGP is the only supported routing protocol to exchange routing information between a VMware Cloud on AWS SDDC and on-premises. Private VIFs provide direct access to all SDDC networking.

Private VIF is a good design choice for customers, having a simple AWS networking design and an easy way to access all resources in their SDDC, including the ability to access vCenter Server, live-migrate the workload using vMotion, and provide connectivity for HCX appliances with a service mesh. When using a private VIF, it's recommended to leverage at least two AWS DX lines and provision a VIF from each line for redundancy.

> **Note**
>
> VMware Cloud on AWS offers the unique capability to provide additional redundancy for the AWS DX uplink, by leveraging a route-based VPN over the internet as a backup for AWS DX. This option is simple to configure, with just a single checkbox in the VMware NSX UI. A number of prerequisites applies (e.g., exactly the same BGP route distribution must be used for the VPN and DX, and the possibility of asymmetric routing).

Each SDDC requires a dedicated private VIF, and customers are required to manage route distribution independently. Also, the lack of an SDDC group and VMware Transit Connect prevents VPC-VPC or VPC-SDDC connections.

The following diagram illustrates a DX architecture leveraging a private VIF:

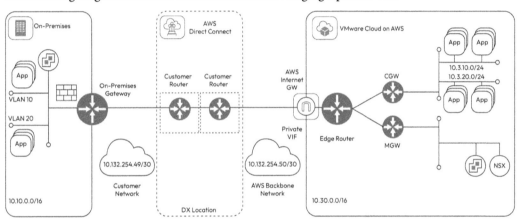

Figure 2.9 – AWS DX architecture connecting to SDDC

Transit VIFs

If your design requires a complex network architecture involving multiple VMware Cloud on AWS SDDCs and/or AWS VPCs, you can use AWS DX Gateway and attach your AWS DX to it. After that, you can either leverage vTGW or establish a VPN session from T0 in your SDDC to the DXGW.

This topology might help to overcome difficulties associated with managing separate private VIFs per each SDDC, enabling intra-Region and inter-Region peering using a single AWS DX connection. However, there are a number of limitations and constraints associated with using a transit VIF, which are outside of the scope of this book.

IPsec VPNs

An IPsec VPN is another option to connect your environments together. IPsec tunnels connect two private environments over the WAN or DX and encrypt the network traffic. All VPN tunnels to

VMware Cloud on AWS SDDC are terminated on the NSX Edge. VMware Cloud on AWS supports **Policy-Based VPNs (PBVPNs)** and **Route-Based VPNs (RBVPNs)**.

RBVPNs

As the name suggests, an RBVPN is a VPN flavor where a routing table entry is determined by BGP, a dynamic routing protocol. Traffic that hits the **VPN Tunnel Interface (VTI)** is encrypted and decrypted according to the IPSec settings. BPG peering is established over VTI.

The following figure shows the topology of a redundant RBVPN connection:

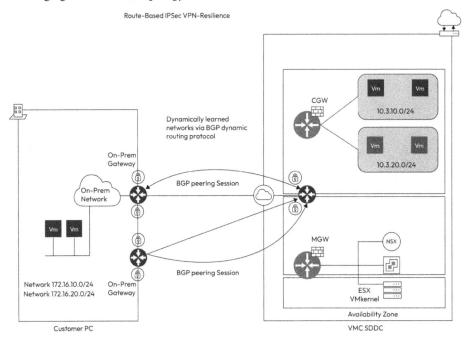

Figure 2.10 – A resilient RBVPN connection topology from VMC to on-premises

---

Note

BGP must be used with RPVPNs. Static routes are not supported.

RBVPNs allow redundant tunnels for high availability and load balancing purposes using **Equal-Cost Multi-Path (ECMP)** routing, improving bandwidth by aggregating multiple tunnels.

> **Information**
>
> A single tunnel can provide up to 1.25 Gbps of throughput.

RBVPNs can be used in connectivity architectures beyond on-premises networks, such as AWS TGWs and VGWs.

RBVPN is recommended for large-scale deployments because networks are learned and advertised automatically with BGP and do not require manual policy adjustments after a connection is established.

PBVPNs

A PBVPN does not use a dynamic routing protocol but is configured manually instead. The policy parameters need to match on both sides of the VPN, including all the connected networks. Otherwise, the VPN will fail to be established. This is not recommended for large-scale environments, as every segment change on either side will require manual policy adjustments.

Additionally, features such as ECMP and tunnel redundancy are not supported with a PBVPN. Also, the default route cannot be advertised using a PBVPN. Customers concerned about running BGP over their on-premises firewall may use it.

> **Tip**
>
> It is a *best practice* to avoid PBVPNs and use RBVPNs instead.

The following figure illustrates the topology of PBVPN with on-premises:

Policy–Based IPSec VPN

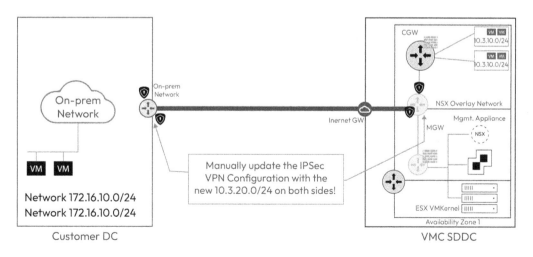

Figure 2.11 – A PBVPN from SDDC to on-premises

> **Information**
>
> RBVPN routes take precedence over PBVPN ones, and they also take precedence if there are overlapping subnets or a default route.

Layer 2 VPNs

A Layer 2 **Virtual LAN (VLAN)** is a single subnet and a single broadcast domain, and Layer 2 VPNs allow you to extend a VLAN over a disjoint broadcast domain using L3 connectivity to forward the broadcast traffic. A L2 VPN allows customers to migrate workloads to an SDDC without altering the workloads' IP addresses.

There are two supported ways to establish a L2 VPN – leveraging the standalone NSX Edge on-premises or the VMware HCX network extension service.

NSX L2VPN

VMware NSX provides support for one L2 VPN tunnel terminated on the NSX Edge over DX or an internet uplink. A single L2 VPN tunnel can encapsulate multiple VLANs. NSX VPNs require an NSX Edge deployed on-premises. You can either leverage the existing NSX infrastructure or deploy a standalone NSX Edge appliance.

> **Information**
>
> There are certain licensing and export control limitations regarding which version can be used, whether it's an NSX-T or an NSX-V standalone Edge. Consult VMware support for more details.

Extended networks are only available for customer workloads. Extending management subnets, including a vMotion network, is not supported. *Figure 2.12* provides more details on L2 networking.

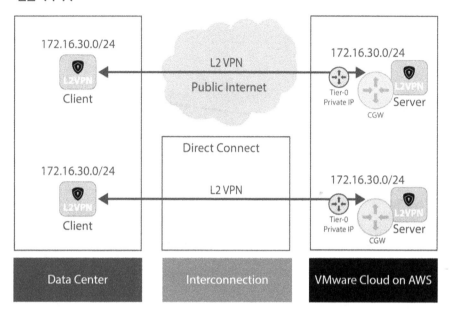

Figure 2.12 – L2VPN using NSX over the internet or DX

The extended network will appear inside the SDDC as an *extended* segment, and the default gateway will remain on-premises. This means the network traffic will always need to hairpin on-premises to route between segments, access the internet, or even access destinations within the AWS cloud, including a connected VPC. The following figure represents the routing between two layer 3 segments while leveraging an L2 VPN:

L2 VPN Hairpinning

Figure 2.13 – L2VPN hairpinning traffic on-premises between segments

> **Information**
>
> L2 VPN is not a replacement for an L3 VPN (policy or route-based) and cannot be established over a Layer 3 VPN.

HCX L2VPN

VMware HCX is a migration tool that, among other services, provides network extension services over the internet or AWS DX. It is an alternative to the NSX option and has more advanced features, but it requires the design and deployment of a VMware HCX infrastructure. It can be used in topologies connecting on-premises to VMware Cloud or cloud to cloud.

The topology of HCX is different from the other NSX-based VPNs previously described, as the tunnel is terminated on an HCX virtual **Network Extension** (**NE**) appliance. The extended networks appear as disconnected or routed segments when **Mobility Optimized Routing** (**MON**) is enabled. MON addresses the design limitation of hairpinning traffic over the on-premises Gateway (or Router) when routing between segments within the same VMware Cloud on AWS SDDC. Traffic to other destinations (e.g., the internet, AWS services, a connected VPC, or other VMware Cloud on AWS SDDCs) will use the on-premises gateway as the next hop.

The following diagram illustrates how HCX is included in the VMware NSX architecture:

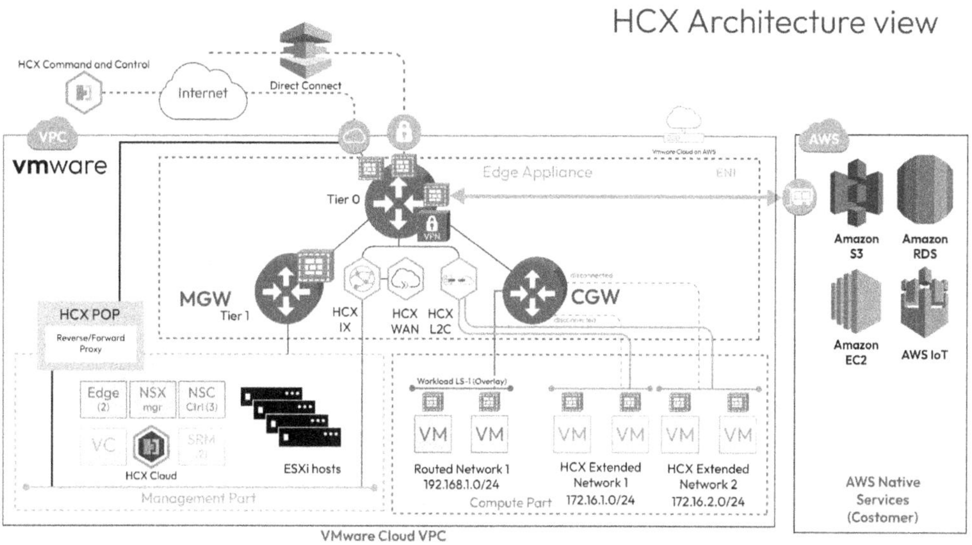

Figure 2.14 – HCX architecture within NSX-T

Complimentary networking services

NSX also manages complimentary networking services beyond VPN, routing, and switching.

DNS

An effective **Domain Naming System** (**DNS**) design is critical for the proper functioning of management and compute workloads in VMware Cloud on AWS. DNS configuration of a VMware Cloud on an AWS SDDC is managed through DNS zones. By default, an SDDC has two default DNS zones – a **Management Gateway DNS zone** and a **Compute Gateway DNS zone**.

The Management Gateway DNS zone and the Compute Gateway DNS zone are mapped to the **Compute Gateway DNS forwarder** and the **Management Gateway DNS forwarder**, respectively. Both the DNS forwarders relay queries from VMs to the specified DNS servers, which leads to improved DNS performance through the caching capabilities of the CGW and MGT.

By default, all DNS requests are automatically directed to public DNS servers, as both DNS forwarders are set up to use Google's DNS Servers, 8.8.8.8 and 8.8.4.4. However, in hybrid environments, the Management Gateway DNS forwarder must have the capability to resolve on-premises FQDNs. Consequently, using public DNS servers will not suffice, and private DNS servers managed by an organization must be used as DNS forwarders.

DHCP

Using DHCP, customers can simplify IP address management and avoid the complexity of allocating IP addresses to workloads. DHCP services can be provided to all workload segments in an SDDC. A DHCP allocation includes an IP address, subnet mask, default gateway, and DNS servers, and some advanced options are supported. On VMware Cloud on AWS SDDC, you can configure workloads to use DHCP in one of three ways:

- A segment DHCP server
- A relay DHCP server (e.g., a customer-managed DHCP Server/**IP Address Management** (**IPAM**)
- A gateway DHCP server

A segment **DHCP server** creates a DHCP service that caters to IP assignment requests originating only from the segment on which the DHCP service is configured. This segment DHCP server will not cater to DHCP requests originating from other segments on the SDDC.

The **DHCP relay** option enables workloads on the VMC on AWS segments to receive IP addresses from a remote customer-managed DHCP server that resides outside of a VMC on AWS SDDC. This option can be leveraged by customers who have large environments that are catered by a centralized DHCP service, or an IPAM tool for both on-premises and cloud environments.

The **gateway DHCP** server creates a DHCP service that provides IP addresses to VMs on all segments connected to the CGW.

NATs

NAT services divide into **Source NATs** (**SNATs**) for outbound internet access of workloads and **Destination NAT** (**DNAT**) for inbound traffic toward services in an SDDC. NSX uses an AWS **Elastic IP** (**EIP**). Customers can request and allocate EIPs for a NAT in the NSX console. The default SNAT EIP associated with internet access in the 0.0.0.0/0 route is predefined and can be seen on the **Networking** tab of the VMware NSX UI.

The following diagram shows a VM accessing the internet using the default SNAT predefined rule:

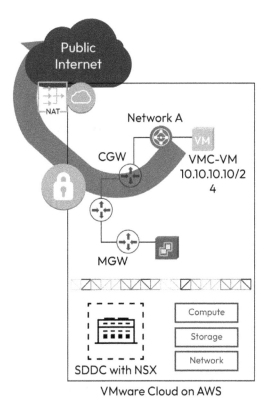

Figure 2.15 – VM internet access through a SNAT default route

If customers wants to define a specific VM to use a different SNAT EIP, a static DNAT rule with all-traffic parameter needs to be applied to an internal VM IP address, and in that case, both SNAT and DNAT will be used by that VM. The NAT rules table works similarly to a routing table, using the most specific match.

The following diagram shows the flow of a DNAT to a specific VM in an SDDC:

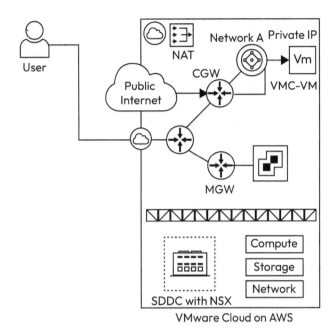

Figure 2.16 – A DNAT static rule for a workload VM behind the CGW

EIP usage such as egress traffic has additional costs associated with it. Customers will be billed for EIPs through VMware as per the AWS list price.

> **Information**
>
> EIPs are associated with an SDDC and are not transferable between SDDCs, organizations, or AWS accounts.

In the following section, we'll dive even deeper into AWS networking integrations, such as vTGW.

Understanding connectivity to the AWS cloud

VMware Cloud on AWS supports multiple options to establish connectivity to workloads running in an AWS VPC. We will take a closer look at various options, including vTWG and a connected VPC.

VMware Transit Connect

The AWS TGW service can be described as a managed router within an AWS Region. It connects using high-speed VPC attachments without the complexities of traditional routing protocols.

The AWS TGW simplifies the networking operations and supports the attachment types illustrated in the following diagram:

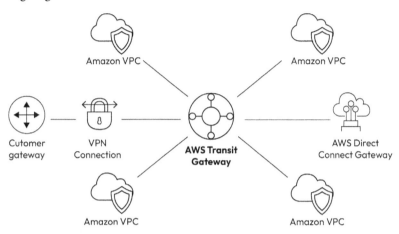

Figure 2.17 – AWS TGW attachment options

The primary function of an AWS Transit Gateway is to establish connectivity between Amazon VPCs, site-to-site VPNs, and AWS DX connections. The AWS TGW is capable of performing transitive routing between the various networks connected to it. To be able to route between the various networks, the TGW uses one or more TGW route tables that are populated by dynamic route propagation, based on the routes learned from the various VPC attachments, VPN attachments, and DXGW associations.

When a route propagation is established for VPC connections, the CIDR of the VPC is added to the routing entries of the TGW route table. Each VPC connection is capable of providing burstable transmission speeds of up to 50 Gbps.

For VPN connections, a BGP session is established between the customer router and the AWS Transit Gateway that is used to exchange routes. All routes learnt by the TGW will be added to the routing table when a route propagation is created. Each VPN connection is capable of providing speeds up to 1.25 Gbps. Higher VPN throughputs can be achieved by aggregated multiple VPN connections, using ECMP.

In the case of AWS DX connections, the customer's router and an AWS DXGW establish a BGP session, and then the DXGW is associated with the AWS Transit Gateway. When route propagation is created, the route table of the AWS Transit Gateway is updated with the routes learned from the DXGW.

VMware Transit Connect is a VMware-managed TGW known as vTGW. VMware Cloud on AWS customers can connect multiple SDDCs and also connect to external AWS networking constructs, such as VPCs, TGWs, and **Direct Connect gateways (DXGWs)**. Connections are managed using an *SDDC group* from the SDDC console.

> **Note**
>
> To connect multiple SDDCs with vTGW, they must have a non-overlapping management network range and should not have overlapping workload segments.

The following figure illustrates the connectivity options available with vTGW:

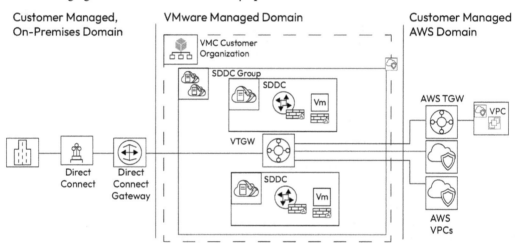

Figure 2.18 – The vTGW attachment options

> **Note**
>
> Please note that a VPN is not available today as a vTGW service.

When connected to an AWS-native VPC or TGW, vTGW is represented in the customer AWS console under **Resource Access Manager** as a shared resource. The customer must accept this shared resource before creating VPC attachments for customer-owned native VPCs. As mentioned previously, AWS DX is the only method for on-premises connectivity with VMware Transit Connect. However, a transit VPC security architecture that terminates the VPNs on an AWS transit VPC or a TGW can be implemented to overcome this architecture limitation.

VMware Transit Connect removes the difficulties of deploying, operating, and scaling complex networking configurations required to establish a connectivity network across VMware Cloud on AWS SDDCs and Amazon-native environments. This solution provides high-bandwidth and low-latency connectivity, and it is easy to set up and manage. It also includes automated provisioning and control, meaning it automatically scales according to the workloads that are added or removed from the SDDC group.

vTGW routing tables

VMware Cloud implements two route tables (per Region):

- **Members Route table**: This route table aggregates all routes learned from SDDCs as well as external attachments including **Direct Connect Gateways** (**DXGs**), Virtual Private Cloud (VPC, and AWS TGW. This ensures that all SDDCs can connect to external attachments (DXG, VPC, and TGW) and vice-versa, however all external attachments cannot connect to each other.

- **External Route table**: This route table aggregates all routes learned from SDDCs, but it does not include routes from external attachments. This ensures that SDDCs are able to communicate with all other SDDCs in the SDDC Group, and are restricted from communicating with external attachments.

Both these route tables are managed by VMware, and are separate from the NSX Edge's routing table. The NSX Edge is propagated with static routes targeted to vTGW as a next-hop over the DX interface shared with vTGW. Static routes are supported, including a default route on the external route table, thus enabling security VPC topologies.

In terms of billing, attachment hourly rates and cost per GB are billed through VMware.

vTGW firewalling

Routing allows connectivity, but it does not alter the firewall policy on the NSX CGW or MGW.

Customers need to add a rule in the CGW firewall and apply it to the DX interface to allow traffic through vTGW.

Connectivity best practices

In a vTGW traffic flow, an SDDC must either be the origin or the destination of the network path, which means that vTGW cannot be transient. Here are some examples of supported traffic flows:

- SDDC to SDDC
- SDDC to VPC
- SDDC to an AWS-native TGW
- SDDC to DXGW

The following figure shows an SDDC-to-SDDC design, where two SDDCs are part of the SDDC group, while the third SDDC is not part of the group, and traffic is not allowed:

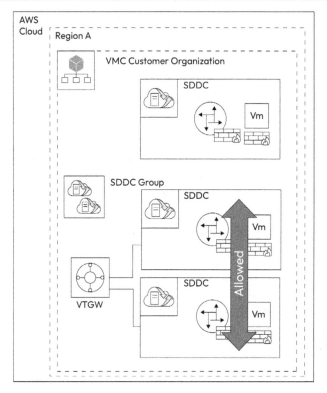

Figure 2.19 – Allowed traffic between two SDDCs in the same group

Another example in the following figure is SDDC to VPC. In this specific design, this is a *transit VPC*, which means that it is used to connect to external environments, such as on-premises or other cloud environments. Security network appliances of third-party security vendors, such as Check Point or Palo Alto Networks, can be placed in that transit VPC. A static default route toward the transit VPC is supported in the SDDC group to achieve this traffic flow.

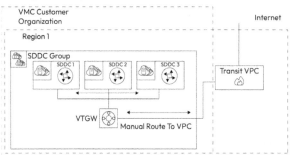

Figure 2.20 – vTGW to AWS transit VPC architecture

> **Information**
>
> Third-party security appliances are not officially supported to run inside the VMware SDDC, and it also makes the SDDC ineligible for SLA credits. Placing security appliances inside a transit VPC is a way to overcome this design constraint.

The following example (*Figure 2.21*) illustrates vTGW connectivity to a native AWS **TGW**. The concept of connecting to a security VPC can be achieved with this option and the transit VPC connectivity described in *Figure 2.19*.

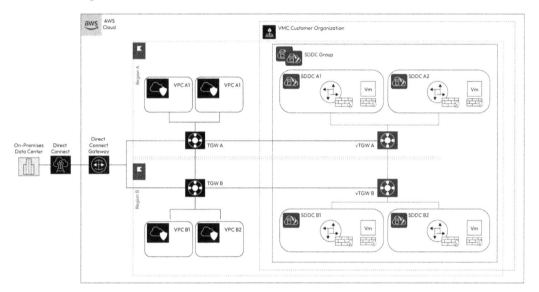

Figure 2.21 – vTGW to AWS TGW architecture

The next figure illustrates the connectivity between a DXGW connecting an on-premises data center and an SDDC over vTGW:

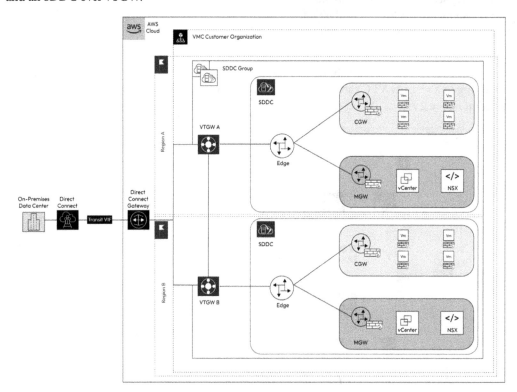

Figure 2.22 – DXGW to vTGW architecture

vTGW allows you to connect VMware Cloud on AWS SDDCs to on-premises environments using AWS DX private VIFs.

This is useful for high-speed connectivity on-premises using DX. Customers with existing DXGW connections to an SDDC directly can migrate their DXGW attachment from the NSX-T Edge toward vTGW.

Unsupported flow

The general design principle is that vTGW cannot be a transient router between external environments – for example, the VPC-to-on-premises and VPC-to-VPC traffic flows are not supported via vTGW, as illustrated in the following figure:

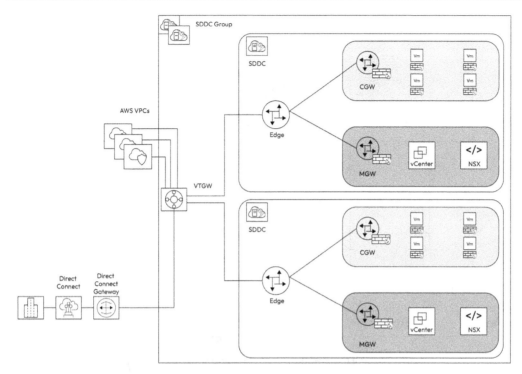

Figure 2.23 – vTGW's unsupported traffic flows

In the following section, we'll describe transit VPC architecture.

Transit VPCs/security VPCs

A common AWS architecture best practice is to leverage multiple accounts and VPCs to meet customers' business and technical needs. Customers may need to connect multiple VMware SDDCs to a single AWS VPC, or multiple AWS VPCs to a single VMware SDDC. AWS offers two alternatives to this requirement. These are the transit VPC and transit GW.

AWS customers use the transit VPC to interconnect multiple VPCs, on-premises locations, or SDDCs based on IPSec VPNs to allow hub and spoke communication. The following figure illustrates an example:

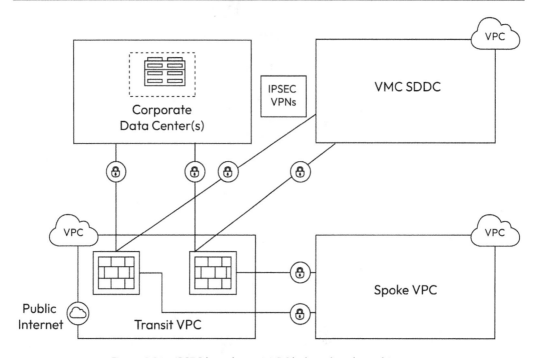

Figure 2.24 – IPSEC-based transit VPC hub and spoke architecture

TGW connectivity over VPN

Connectivity to an AWS transit GW can be achieved through a VPN tunnel from the NSX-T T0 Edge and the TGW over the internet, as illustrated in the following figure:

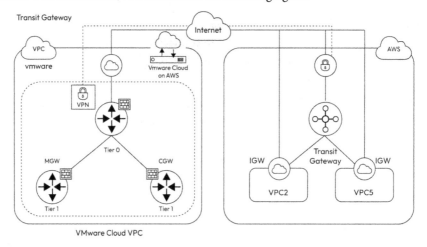

Figure 2.25 – An IPSEC connection between an SDDC and TGW

This topology has the obvious drawbacks of not leveraging the vTGW constructs, eliminating the solution's high throughput, scale, and simplicity. However, this still is a supported topology that can be used to reduce costs associated with vTGW.

Exploring NSX and AWS security architecture and capabilities

In the following section, we'll describe the firewalling and security capabilities of a VMware Cloud on AWS SDDC and AWS.

AWS security groups

An AWS security group regulates all the incoming and outgoing traffic of the resources. These resources can include Amazon EC2, elastic network interfaces, Amazon **Elastic File System** (**EFS**), and Amazon FSx filesystems. A security group is associated with resources within the VPC it was created for. Unlike **Network Access Control Lists** (**NACLs**), which are applied to VPC subnets, a security group is tied to individual resources. Additionally, security groups are stateful, which means they are bidirectional. In other words, if inbound traffic is permitted, the corresponding response packets in the opposite direction are always allowed by default.

The AWS security groups control the traffic flow from and to the connected VPC. The security groups control traffic on the AWS side and the security controls in the SDDC CGW firewall.

The following diagram show traffic flowing to an AWS service deployed to the connected VPC:

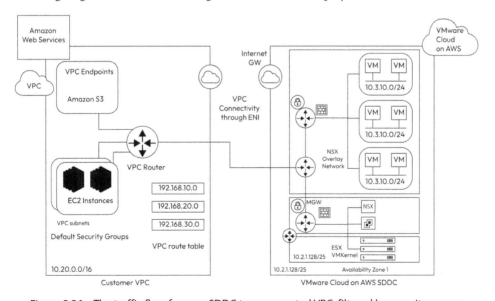

Figure 2.26 – The traffic flow from an SDDC to a connected VPC, filtered by security groups

Security

VMware NSX includes feature-rich security capabilities, including out-of-the-box capabilities such as stateful firewalling and **distributed firewalling** (**DFW**), also known as *micro-segmentation*. Advanced network security features such as IPS/IDS, layer 7 firewalling, and identity-based firewalls are available as a paid add-on service.

The firewalls' security policies are enforced by using two different technologies. DFW enforces an SDDC's compute network policy for east-west traffic between VMs, while GW firewalls enforce policies at network borders for north-south traffic.

GW firewalls

GW firewalls can be compared with centralized firewalls, and they are logically a subset of the NSX T0/T1 routers. They are responsible for enforcing network security policies at the borders of their respective networks, with a slight nuance of enforcement points compared to on-premises deployment. There are two points of enforcement for the GW firewalls security policies in VMC:

- A T0 edge router for the CGW GW firewall
- A T1 MGW firewall

The CGW has a *default deny* policy that requires security administrators to define what traffic is allowed through firewalls. Firewall rules need to be applied to both ingress and egress.

The MGW has a default rule for the outbound vCenter Server and ESXi traffic and a *Deny any rule* at the bottom of the Gateway Firewall rules list.

> **Note**
> Firewalls are stateful, so responses for allowed traffic will always be permitted.

The T0 router is the entry point for all SDDC networks. This router acts as the GW firewall's enforcement point for the CGW workloads.

The MGW router that borders the management networks has a separate firewall positioned on the T1 router. While the MGW protects the management network, firewall rules do not need to be opened again in the T0 firewall. For each of the management appliances, only a predefined set of ports are allowed for inbound connectivity to further reduce the attack surface. In addition, each rule requires an explicit definition of the source IPs – setting the source to *Any* is not allowed. Security administrators can use the MGW to protect their management network from external and internal networks.

The NSX Manager UI displays two rulesets, one for the MGW and one for the CGW

The following figure reiterates the T0 and CGW/MGW topology and where CGW and MGW firewall rules are applied:

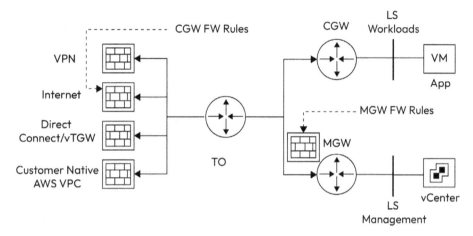

Figure 2.27 – CGW and MGW firewall rules

> **Note**
>
> The CGW firewall rules are applied on the T0 interfaces in the preceding figure, meaning that traffic is allowed between workload VMs without CGW enforcement. DFW needs to be used to enforce security within the CGW workloads.

The CGW rules are applied over the uplink interfaces through the logic described in the routing section.

> **Note**
>
> Note that VPN interfaces relate *only* to RB-VPN. PB-VPN firewall rules are applied over the internet uplink interface. The vTGW connectivity is represented by the DX interface.

Learning NSX micro-segmentation

NSX supports advanced ways of defining firewall rules beyond traditional sources – destination IPs. When leveraging micro-segmentation powered by **Distributed Firewall (DFW)**, customers can use native vSphere objects to control the traffic flow.

The benefits of micro-segmentation architecture

Micro-segmentation allows customers to logically separate an SDDC into security zones and provide security control for services that run across each zone, as described in the example of securing a multi-tiered application. DFW is unique, as it is applied to all network parts and dissociates network security policies from network architecture. It allows for the maintenance of security policies while the network infrastructure is modified. Workloads can be migrated, and IP addresses can change while applying the same security policies. Security administrators can leverage traditional non-contextual parameters, such as IP addresses and ports for policies, and include application context, such as OS names, VM names, services, application types, and tags, simplifying the implementation of granular security controls. This allows customers to build security rules that are based on business logic. Customers can use tags or naming conventions to specify a physical address, business application, and whether a workload will be a test, development, or production without considering its IP address scheme.

Micro-segmentation restricts attackers' ability to move laterally between different segments of a given SDDC once a workload is compromised. If business logic does not require it, lateral movement can be mitigated by stopping two workloads from speaking on the same subnet. This helps reduce the attack surface of the SDDC.

DFW is a virtual stateful Layer 4 firewall capable of inspecting traffic up to Layer 4. Layer 7 application-level inspection capabilities are introduced with the advanced security-add-on described in the following section.

Understanding NSX Distributed Firewall

NSX **Distributed Firewall** is a stateful firewall distributed to all ESXi hosts in an SDDC. It protects the SDDC's east/west traffic with micro-segmentation. It offers advanced protection for workloads within the same L2 domain. The rules do not have to be based on the traditional infrastructure parameters such as subnets but, rather, can leverage NSX tags or VM naming conventions to build a security policy. The following figure shows a traditional segmentation approach for a three-tier application:

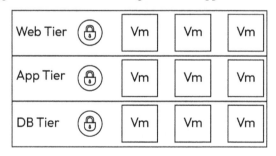

Figure 2.28 – Traditional segmentation

DFW removes the need for centralized GW firewalls. It's not enforced at a single location, as is the case with gateway firewalls, instead it is enforced on the **virtual machine network interfaces (vNICs)** of each VM in the network. This allows for new flexible ways to manage network security, which are impossible to implement in a traditional data center network.

For example, NSX enables the creation of grouping objects for DFW and Edge firewalls. NSX will automatically identify and place workloads in the group-based criteria, such as IP address and VM instance naming conventions.

NSX firewall policies follow a top-to-bottom evaluation process. The first rule that matches a connection is applied. For all new network connections, the rulesets for both SDDC ingress and SDDC egress are assessed and firewall policies are applied bidirectionally.

> **Note**
>
> The default explicit security policy for DFW is *Allow any*. This means all traffic is allowed unless specified otherwise by the administrator.

The following figure shows a micro-segmentation approach for a three-tier web application placed on the same subnet, in contrast to the traditional approach:

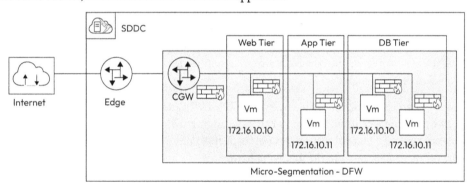

Figure 2.29 – Micro-segmentation

Only the compute network is eligible for DFW, not the management networks. DFW's purpose is to allow the security administrator to create a security policy applied within a compute network.

Discovering the NSX Advanced Firewall Add-On

The NSX Advanced Firewall Add-On is available to customers as a purchase option on top of the SDDC costs, and it has to be activated for all hosts in the SDDC cluster. NSX Advanced Firewall helps customers enhance the NSX security capabilities beyond distributed Layer 4 firewall security to advanced application security capabilities, such as distributed IPS/IDS, Layer 7 Context Profiles (app IDs), FQDN filtering, and Identity-Based Firewall.

IPS/IDS

NSX Distributed IPS/IDS inspects all traffic inside an SDDC without any dependency on its architecture, which contrasts with traditional IPS/IDS solutions where networking architecture needs to be taken into significant consideration when deploying an IPS/IDS solution.

Security administrators can create a virtual zone in a SDDC using the DFW and IDS/IPS features. IPS/IDS can detect and prevent the lateral movement of attackers who infiltrate data centers, leveraging attack signatures on top of the prevention mechanism of micro-segmentation and implementing a multi-tiered security approach.

Customers with regulatory requirements may also need to implement IPS/IDS to protect data from being stolen or leaked. It is relevant to achieve regulatory compliance with **Health Insurance Portability and Accountability Act (HIPAA)** and **Payment Card Industry Security Standards Council (PCI)** or **Sarbanes-Oxley Act (SOX)** standards.

The IPS/IDS feature leverages signature detection engines to detect and block malicious traffic patterns. Malicious traffic patterns are matched against signatures, and other techniques such as protocol compliance and anomaly detections are leveraged. As attacks and vulnerability exploitations constantly evolve, IDS/IPS stays updated with the latest threat signatures and anomaly detection algorithms to identify malicious activity inside an SDDC.

As with the DFW architecture, the uniqueness of the IPS/IDS capability is its distributed nature. This eliminates the traditional centralized monitoring and enforcement that all traffic must pass through, known as a hairpin, and instead distributes the inspection task to all the vNICs inside an SDDC. Traffic hairpinning is illustrated in the following figure:

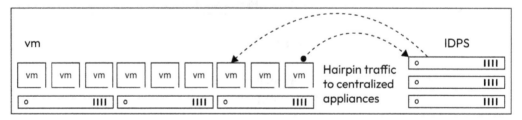

Figure 2.30 – The traffic hairpinning problem with centralized IPS/IDS

Distributed IPS/IDS throughput capacity scales linearly as new hosts add additional workloads to the cluster. It enables the complete coverage of all traffic that enters, and hosts don't need to choose which traffic can be inspected due to architecture or throughput constraints, eliminating blind spots in the data center.

The following figure shows traffic passing between two VMs in an SDDC being inspected through IPS/IDS, without hairpinning:

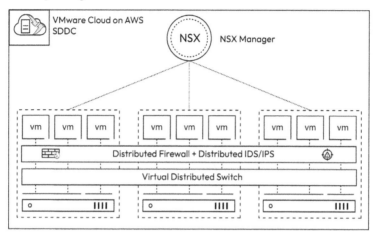

Figure 2.31 – DFW distributed across all hosts in an SDDC

The IDS/IPS engine has rich context for each guest VM. It can match signatures to account for both the application context and the sensitivity of the protected workload – for instance, prioritizing the domain controller alerts over other workloads and filtering for only attacks relevant to domain controllers. This helps the cloud admin quickly respond to threats and enable policies based on workload sensitivity and context.

Layer 7 (app ID) capabilities enable deep packet inspection across all vNICs within an SDDC, on top of the IPS/IDS capabilities described in the following section.

Layer 7 app IDs

App IDs enables application-level rules to match an application or protocol across any port.

App IDs are preconfigured for common enterprise applications such as Microsoft Active Directory, WINS, Kerberos, GitHub, and MySQL, ss well as protocol-level rules – for instance, versions and cipher suites of **Secure Sockets Layer/Transport Layer Security (SSL/TLS)** and **Common Internet File System/Server Message Block (CIFS/SMB)**.

The following figure shows a three-tier application micro-segmentation policy, independent of IP addresses and ports. The TLS version 1.2 protocol is enforced on the ingress web tier. HTTP traffic is allowed between the web tier and the application tier, and SQL traffic is allowed between the application tier and the DB tier. This policy is achieved independently of IP addresses and TCP ports, using an app ID.

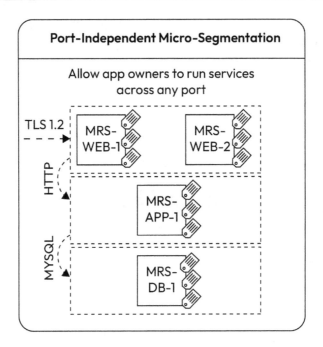

Figure 2.32 – Port-independent application DFW rule enforcement

Application-based security rules increase policy simplicity and enhance security, as applications can be detected dynamically even when a non-standard application port is used.

FQDN filtering

Domain filtering can lower the attack surface by blocking applications from accessing problematic domains or unrequired domains.

> **Tip**
> You must set up a DFW DNS rule before creating an FQDN rule. VMware NSX uses DNS snooping to map the IP address and the FQDN.

As described in the following figure, customers can apply an FQDN rule as part of their DFW policies – for example, blocking Linux servers and certain legacy Windows OSs from accessing https://update.microsoft.com.

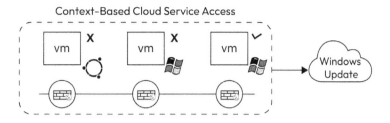

Figure 2.33 – FQDN filtering for Windows updates

FQDN filtering is useful for reducing the SDDC attack surface and blacklisting a known malicious domain.

Identity Firewall

Customers can use NSX Distributed Firewall with a user ID known as Identity Firewall to create Active Directory user-based **Distributed Firewall** (**DFW**) rules.

Integration between DFW and Active Directory allows the control of which user can access which app. DFW enforces rules based on the user ID at the source.

For instance, protecting **Virtual Desktop Infrastructure** (**VDI**) workloads allows only different users on shared infrastructure access to enterprise applications, based on their identity, as illustrated in the following figure:

Figure 2.34 – Identity Firewall access for a VDI user to a finance app, based on user identity

Additional advanced security capabilities are constantly added to the advanced security add-on.

Summary

In this chapter, we learned about the unique NSX architecture running over VMware Cloud on AWS, including security and firewall architecture, the roles of the CGW and MGW, and advanced security features such as micro-segmentation and IPS/IDS. We also looked at advanced networking architectures such as native AWS TGW integrations. With those lessons in hand, we can now move on to designing and implementing a scalable and secure deployment of applications in VMware Cloud.

In the next chapter, we will further explore add-on services, such as migrations with HCX, monitoring with vRLI, and Kubernetes with Tanzu services.

3

Exploring VMware Cloud on AWS-Integrated Services

VMware Cloud on AWS is part of a larger ecosystem of services and add-ons that enable organizations a wide variety of use cases, including migration with VMware **Hybrid Cloud Extension (HCX)**, disaster recovery with **VMware Cloud Disaster Recovery (VCDR)** and **VMware Site Recovery (VSR)**, advanced logging with **Aria Operations for Logs**, and **Containers as a Service (CaaS)** services with Tanzu services.

In this chapter, you will learn the basic capabilities and architecture of these services and understand the design choices when planning, implementing, and operating the HCX, VCDR, VSR, and Tanzu services.

The following are the topics that will be covered in this chapter:

- VMware HCX
- VSR
- VCDR
- The VMware Aria Operations for Logs service
- VMware Cloud with Tanzu services

VMware HCX

One of the main advantages of VMware Cloud on AWS is its operational consistency and ability to move applications to public clouds, without taking on significant risks and without the need to refactor an application when it doesn't bring value to a business. VMware HCX provides hybrid cloud capabilities to connect between an existing on-premises site and the VMware Cloud SDDC, as well as multi-cloud connectivity capabilities.

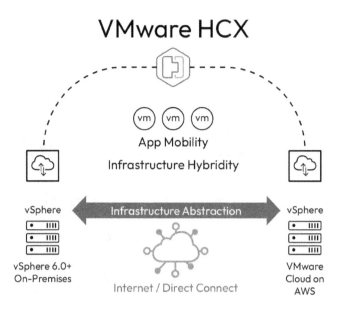

Figure 3.1 – The HCX VM migration capabilities for VMware Cloud on AWS

VMware HCX Enterprise is included with VMware Cloud on an AWS subscription with no additional charges, and it can be activated directly from the SDDC Console.

HCX offers the following technical capabilities:

- **Workload migration using dedicated network tunnels between HCX appliances**: You can choose between various migration methods depending on the design requirements. We'll discuss this in more detail later on in this section.

- **A layer 2 extension**: HCX provides a simple and powerful mechanism to extend existing VLANs to the cloud, enabling fully live migration capabilities. If you need to use extended VLANs after the migration is completed, HCX offers numerous additional capabilities, including high availability of the L2 extension service and **mobility-optimized networking** (**MON**) to improve traffic flow for stretched VLANs.

- WAN optimization to reduce network traffic and speed up migration.

HCX can not only be used for on-premises to cloud migration but also for cloud to cloud (between two HCX endpoints – endpoints can reside in any other cloud) and reverse migration (from the cloud to on-premises).

It has several technical prerequisites that your on-premises environment must adhere to. These depend on the HCX version used; please check the VMware documentation for more details (`https://docs.vmware.com/en/VMware-HCX/4.7/hcx-user-guide/GUID-BFD7E194-CFE5-4259-B74B-991B26A51758.html`).

An HCX component overview

HCX architecture is composed of several components or virtual appliances. These virtual appliances are deployed symmetrically at both the source and destination sites. HCX appliances provide a range of management and network services, such as migration and network extension.

The first component we'll review is the HCX Manager.

VMware HCX is first deployed via the HCX Manager virtual appliance and a vCenter plugin that enables the HCX UI to be integrated into the vSphere Client. Once the HCX Manager virtual appliance is deployed, it's responsible for orchestrating the deployment of all other appliances through a *service mesh*. The following figure illustrates the site pairing between the source HCX Connector and the HCX Cloud Manager:

Figure 3.2 – HCX Cloud Manager pairing between on-premises and the cloud

The service mesh defines what HCX services are enabled between the paired sites and includes the following components:

- An HCX Interconnect appliance
- An HCX Network Extension appliance
- An HCX WAN optimization appliance

You also define the resource containers to be used on-premises to deploy appliances and the network path for communication between them. On VMware Cloud on AWS, all HCX appliances are deployed into the management resource pool and attached to the **Management Gateway** (**MGW**). Required firewall rules are created automatically during the service mesh deployment. Depending on the available network connectivity between on-premises and the VMware Cloud on AWS SDDC, you can choose between connecting appliances using the following methods:

- Internet
- AWS Direct Connect

You can deploy multiple service meshes between the same site pairs to improve the migration performance and fully utilize the available cross-site link.

Let us review the functions of different appliances.

HCX Interconnect

The **HCX Interconnect** (**HCI-IX**) appliance offers **virtual machine** (**VM**) mobility services using the VMware vSphere Replication, vMotion, and **Network File Copy** (**NFC**) protocols over the internet and private lines. The following figure illustrates the different services and functions the HCX-IX appliance can deliver.

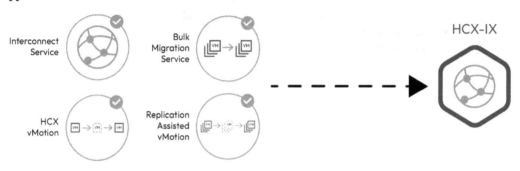

Figure 3.3 – HCX IX appliance services

HCX WAN optimization

You can opt to deploy an optional **WAN Optimizer** (**WO**) appliance to reduce the data transfer over the WAN link. The WO appliance offers data deduplication and compression, but it also might affect the bandwidth and cause high CPU usage with a high amount of traffic. It's recommended when migrating over the internet with a slow connection line from your on-premises data center.

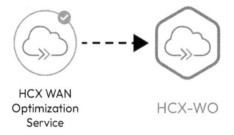

Figure 3.4 – The HCX WO appliance service symbol

HCX Network Extension (NE)

An HCX NE appliance facilitates the layer 2 extension of VLANs between two sites by seamlessly distributing the layer 2 broadcast traffic between two broadcast domains. HCX NE builds a VPN tunnel to encapsulate the extension traffic and supports the extension of multiple VLANs (eight per NE appliance).

For all extended VLANs, the default gateway still resides on-premises (or, in the case of a cloud-to-cloud extension, where the segment was originally created). All the network communication that requires routing, including traffic to AWS services, will first be routed back to the original gateway location. You can leverage the **mobility optimized network (MON)** feature to provide local routing within the SDDC.

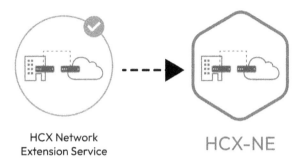

Figure 3.5 – The HCX NE Service symbol

OS Assisted Migrations (OSAM) is used for non-vSphere to vSphere virtual machine migrations. Guest virtual machines establish a connection and register with a **Sentinel Gateway (SGW)** appliance at the source site. Subsequently, the SGW initiates a forwarding connection with a **Sentinel Data Receiver (SDR)** appliance at the destination vSphere site. The HCX Sentinel software is installed on each guest virtual machine slated for migration to initiate the discovery and data replication process. Once the software is installed, a secure connection is formed between the guest virtual machine and the HCX SGW. As the Sentinel software is deployed on the guest virtual machines, HCX builds an inventory of candidates eligible for migration. The following figure shows the OSAM service mapping to the HCX-SGW appliance:

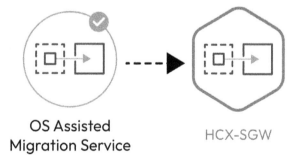

Figure 3.6 – HCX OSAM

Migration types

HCX offers multiple migration options, depending on your design requirements, acceptable downtime, bandwidth availability, latency, and other factors.

The following figure shows a summary of the different migration types, as well as their associated VM state and data transfer protocols:

Migration Using HCX	VM State	Data Transfer	VM Migration
Cold Migration	Off	NFC	Cold
HCX vMotion	On	vMotion	Live
HCX Bulk	On	HBR	Warm
Replication Assisted vMotion	On	HBR+ vMotion	Live

Figure 3.7 – A summary of the migration options in HCX

HCX-assisted vMotion

HCX uses vSphere vMotion capabilities to migrate VMs within a configured pair of sites. The main advantage of this migration type is that your workload stays online for the whole migration process and is instantly available on VMware Cloud on AWS SDDC, if combined with a layer 2 extension of the VLAN.

However, vMotion is a very resource-intensive process and has an extensive set of pre-requisites (https://docs.vmware.com/en/VMware-Cloud-on-AWS/services/com.vmware. vmc-aws-operations/GUID-DAE9B318-294A-4422-BBF4-82AE9DDFF043.html), updated with the latest version of HCX. Another important consideration is that HCX only supports vMotion of a single virtual machine at a time. You can schedule a group of virtual machines to be migrated, but the process is serial and might take considerable time to complete.

Bulk migration

Bulk migration provides efficient low downtime migration. Unlike migration with vMotion migration, bulk migration requires a restart at the destination, the workload remains available during the replication process, and the switchover can be scheduled on a maintenance window. This allows large-scale migrations of hundreds (up to 250 in a single group) of workloads to VMware Cloud on AWS SDDC.

The bulk migration option is designed for moving large amounts of VMs in parallel. It does this by using host-based replicating, which allows workloads to stay online during the seeding/delta replication stages. After data replication has been completed, we have two options – either schedule the switchover for a specific maintenance window or switch over immediately to the target location. This happens over the HCX WAN optimized mesh and is backwardly compliant as far as vSphere 6.0. HCX also offers the option to upgrade VMTools and hardware compatibility in bulk migrations. This allows organizations with older versions of vSphere the opportunity to make these upgrades simultaneously.

Replication Assisted vMotion

Replication Assisted vMotion (**RAV**) combines the best of the vMotion and bulk migration capabilities to make migrating large numbers of live workloads easier. RAV uses bulk migration for the initial replication process and allows parallel operations and cutover scheduling. vMotion is used to finalize the migration of the delta data and VM memory and networking state for the zero-downtime migrations.

You will naturally choose RAV over bulk migration if your design includes an extension of VLANs and requires a workload to be accessible over a network for the whole duration of the migration process. Bear in mind that all the prerequisites for vMotion are still applicable.

The following figure illustrates the RAV migration process:

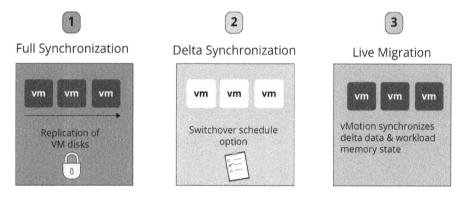

Figure 3.8 – A RAV migration process summary

Cloud to cloud

You can leverage HCX to not only migrate workloads from on-premises to VMware Cloud on AWS but also within a cloud, or between different clouds.

Within VMware Cloud on AWS, you can leverage HCX to migrate workloads between SDDCs deployed in the same region or different regions. For example, you can leverage HCX to move to the i4i host type from an i3-based SDDC. You would need to pay attention to the traffic flow and avoid ingress costs if possible.

Additionally, this feature can enable a multi-cloud migration from VMware Cloud on AWS to another hyperscaler's VMware cloud infrastructure offering, such as Azure, GCP, or Oracle. The following figure shows a conceptual cloud-to-cloud migration between VMware on AWS and **Azure VMware Solution** (**AVS**), using HCX:

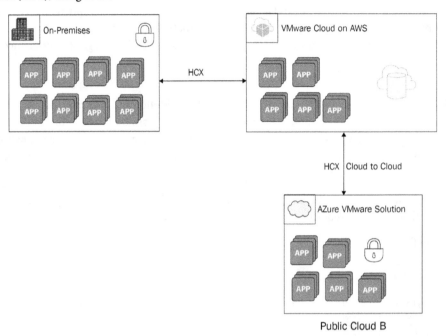

Figure 3.9 – The HCX multi-cloud migration option

HCX cloud-to-cloud migration is a great way to provide flexibility, choice, and control over multiple service offerings.

HCX for hybrid network extension

One of the many unique functionalities of VMware HCX is its Layer 2 extension. We have already provided a quick summary of its features. In this section, we will cover architecture and design decisions that will help cloud architects to create a network design for hybrid deployments.

From a high-level network perspective, a Layer 2 extension allows us to extend the level 2 broadcast domain (ARP and reverse ARP flows) between two disjointed network infrastructures, while retaining the same IP addresses for the application workload. In the absence of this feature, communication could only be established with IP routing and requires the reassigning of IP addresses.

Retaining IP addresses during migration shortens drastically the downtime, preparation window, and overall risks; however, it also poses a couple of challenges:

- **Traffic flow**: To facilitate proper ARP communication, all broadcast network traffic must be captured and retransmitted between two segments. This retransmission happens over the WAN connection (either over the internet or AWS **Direct Connect** (**DX**) and might pose security challenges for the network security team.

- **Bandwidth**: Traffic flow needs to be intercepted and retransmitted. This is accomplished by NE appliances, deployed in pairs. Each pair establishes its own tunnel to broadcast traffic with 1.5 GB/s maximum throughput per extended VLAN.

- **Availability**: By default, the extension is handled by a single appliance pair. If one of the appliances fails, VMs residing on the extended segment are not able to communicate with the rest of the network.

- **Routing**: Each VLAN has only a single default gateway. This gateway normally resides on the source side of the network extension. For the target (extended) environment, all network traffic sent to a destination outside of the segment must traverse back to the source side through the HCX NE tunnel.

However, the version of HCX available with VMware Cloud on AWS mitigates some of the aforementioned challenges:

- **Traffic flow**: HCX supports encryption of the Layer 2 extension traffic via an IPSec VPN. The VPN tunnel is established between HCX appliances and is independent of the underlying connectivity between the on-premises site and the VMware Cloud on AWS SDDC.

- **Bandwidth**. Even if each tunnel has fully supported throughput, you can increase performance by adding multiple NE pairs and distributing VLANs between them.

- **Availability**: With the recent addition of the NE high availability feature, the HCX version deployed with VMware Cloud on AWS now supports the creation of an NE group, consisting of four appliances. Inside each group, two pairs are established – one is active and transmits the traffic, and the other is a stand-by.

- **Routing**: With the recently introduced MON feature, HCX now supports optimized traffic flow in the target SDDC. VMs residing on the extended segment can communicate with other segments within the same SDDC or reach the AWS S3 endpoint.

We are used to the HCX network extension being actively used during migration, with switchover to a routed segment once the migration completes. However, with this new capability, you can opt to continue to run your workloads on an extended segment forever.

It is important to emphasize that HCX does not include a Layer 2 loop validation protocol, such as the spanning tree protocol. Therefore, best practice architecture is critical. The following unsupported topologies can create a Layer 2 broadcast storm.

HCX for disaster recovery

HCX provides limited **disaster recovery** (**DR**) functionality alongside its workload migration features, providing a basic low-cost DR solution. HCX uses the same migration replication engine for DR by protecting workloads. VSR features, such as support for protection groups, recovery plans, and advanced automated recovery workflow capabilities, are unavailable through VMware HCX.

HCX offers limited **disaster recovery (DR)** functionality alongside its workload migration features, providing a basic DR solution. Utilizing the same migration replication engine, HCX transmits data efficiently over an optimized WAN. While it can be employed for DR to safeguard development platforms against low-cost threats or ensure temporary environment protection, advanced VSR features like support for protection groups, recovery plans, and sophisticated automated recovery workflow capabilities are not available through VMware HCX.

> **Information**
>
> One point to emphasize is that even though HCX DR replication and orchestration is not recommended for production DR use cases, HCX layer 2 extension capability can be leveraged in combination with VSR and VCDR. Make sure that possible dependencies on the source network (i.e., the location of the default gateway) are taken into consideration while preparing the DR plan.

VMware Site Recovery service

VMware Site Recovery VSR uses the time-tested VMware SRM product to deliver VSR as a VMware Cloud on AWS integrated add-on service. This service simplifies traditional DR operations. The service is designed to provide a disaster recovery solution that can mitigate the need for a physical secondary site and quickly scale to a full production environment, simplifying DR operations. The following figure illustrates protecting a organization data center with VMware Cloud on AWS using VSR.

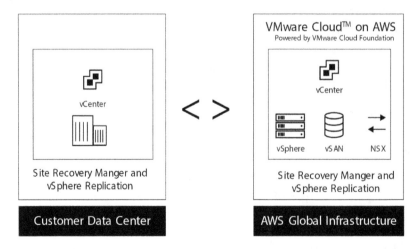

Figure 3.10 – VSR architecture

VSR leverages **vSphere Replication** (**vR**) to provide native hypervisor-based replication. All infrastructure services are delivered through software, and the orchestration is done through the VSR add-on. Organizations can replicate VM images and create automated recovery plans. These plans include the startup order, recovery steps, and recovery plan. The following figure shows the different components included in the replication process on the on-premises and VMware Cloud on AWS sides:

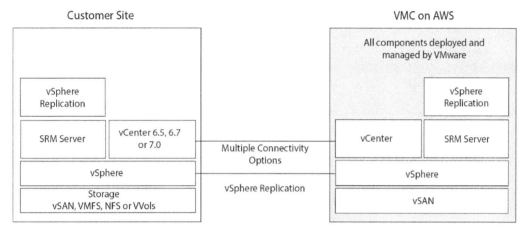

Figure 3.11 – vR architecture

Admins can then run tests to validate your environment within a bubble network. This allows you to prepare for a disaster fully.

VSR can protect multiple on-premises sites or another VMware Cloud on AWS SDDC, as shown in the following diagram:

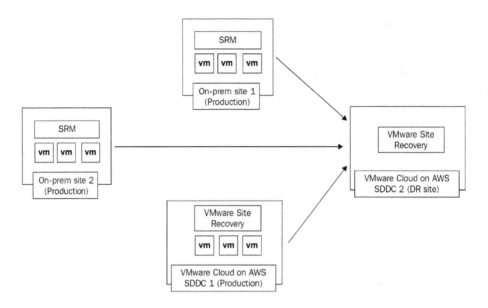

Figure 3.12 – VSR protecting multiple sources

VSR uses automated recovery programs that can be quickly set up and are easy to maintain through automation. Many of the steps in the recovery process are automated.

Auditors can also see the benefits of non-disruptive tests. They can verify a company's resilience to disasters and ability to meet **recovery time objectives (RTOs)**. They regularly test recovery plans and check for configuration drift. Organizations can run their recovery plans anytime they like, without worrying about impacting users or applications. Admins can address configuration drift or fix problems with recovery plans that environmental changes may have caused:

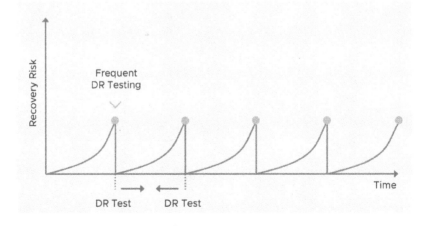

Figure 3.13 – Configuration drift and recovery risk

This non-disruptive testing can reduce the recovery risk and discover configuration drifts earlier. The Site Recovery service can then begin to execute its recovery process once a disaster has been declared through a series of automated workflows.

Failback can be enabled with bidirectional workflows. Workloads can be automatically migrated to their original site using manual user intervention.

The downside of using **VMware Site Recovery** (**VSR**) service is the fact that it relies on the VMware Cloud on AWS SDDC running vSAN-based storage as the target replication target. While vSphere-based replication on the target vSAN-based storage is robust and resilient, organizations will need a 2-Host SDDC Cluster Pilot light environments that have costs associated with compute and storage capacity. The following section will explore this challenge and provide a cost-effective **Disaster Recovery as a Service** (**DRaaS**) solution, where cloud storage compute resources are disaggregated and paying in advance for compute resources is not required.

VMware Cloud Disaster Recovery (VCDR) service

VCDR is a DRaaS provided by VMware. VCDR enables protection of on-premises vSphere environments and VMware Cloud on AWS SDDC by using an innovative concept of zero-compute DRaaS solutions. The main component of VCDR is the **Scale-Out Cloud File System** (**SCFS**) deployed in AWS Cloud. SCFS provides the ability to store large amounts of data efficiently and effectively, with hundreds of recovery points. You can replicate entire VMs with a **recovery point objective** (**RPO**) as low as 30 minutes. The SCFC facilitates storage of data during normal operations of your production sites. If the infrastructure needs to be restored, VCDR uses VMware Cloud on AWS SDDC to register VMs and start the environment.

The following figure depicts the high-level architecture of VCDR:

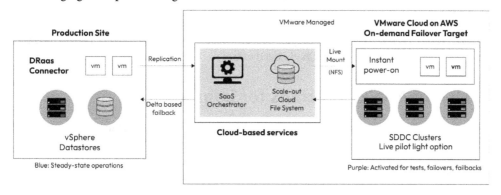

Figure 3.14 – VCDR replication architecture

The main goal of VCDR is to simplify DR protection, reduce costs, and orchestrate the recovery. However, the main advantage of this service is flexibility – with different deployment options, organizations can choose between the speed of recovery and costs of the solution. VCDR supports the following deployment options:

- **Just-in-time deployment**: When opting for this option, no VMware Cloud on AWS SDDC exists during normal operations. When the infrastructure needs to be restored, VCDR first will initiate the creation of the SDDC using the predefined configuration. Once the deployment completes, VCDR will mount the SCFC datastore and bring the VMs online. This option is the most cost-effective but increases the RTO, and it requires the IT team to perform certain tasks to finalize the SDDC configuration, before the environment is ready to be used.

- **Pilot-light deployment**: To shorten the RTO, organizations can opt to pre-deploy an SDDC in the minimal configuration – with just two hosts. The ability to pre-deploy the SDDC helps you to fulfil most of the configuration tasks beforehand – establish connectivity to the vCenter Server, add connectivity to on-premises, and pre-deploy a vital infrastructure service (Active Directory, DNS, DHCP, etc). You can also use the SDDC to run other workloads if needed. If the failover is required, VCDR will inflate the pilot light SDDC by adding hosts using rapid-scale in policy, with up to 12 hosts in parallel. This option helps to shorten the RTO and minimize the configuration work required to bring the VMware Cloud on AWS SDDC to production. Conversely, you will need to pay for the pilot light deployment under normal operations.

- **Ahead-of-time deployment**: You can opt to pre-deploy a full environment beforehand. All the compute capacity is instantly available in case of failover. You still can use the capacity of the SDDC to run other workloads if required. This option has the best RTO but comes with the highest costs.

Which option you choose depends on organization requirements, the desired RTO/RPO, and the available budget. Pilot-light deployment is recommended for all organizations protecting an on-premises workload – with this option, you can make sure that your recovery platform is fully ready to accommodate production workload ahead of time.

The VMware Aria Operations for Logs service

The **VMware Aria Operations for Logs** service is the logging platform included in the VMware Cloud on AWS service.

VMware Cloud SDDC's restricted access model does not allow cloud admins to directly access ESXi hosts and operational management logs. Logs can only be accessed through two tools – vCenter and the VMware Aria Operations for Logs service.

Each new organization has access to a full trial version of VMware Aria Operations for Logs service for the period of 30 days. After the trial ends, you can either subscribe to the full service or continue using the service with a limited subset of features.

The VMware Aria Operations for Logs service offers unified visibility to VMware Cloud on AWS network packet logs. This capability allows organizations to analyze and troubleshoot their application flows, using visibility of packets corresponding to specific NSX firewall rules. Organizations can turn on logging on firewall policy usage and analyze the traffic patterns of applications.

Organizations can access the VMware Aria Operations for Logs Service from the VMware Cloud portal, parallel to VMware Cloud, and they can ingest logs from various sources, including cloud-native AWS, VMware Cloud on AWS, on-premises vSphere, and applications directly, as shown in the following figure:

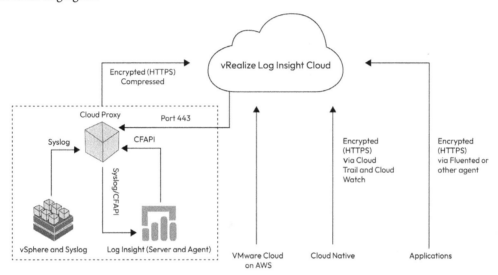

Figure 3.15 – The VMware Aria Operations for Logs service data sources

In summary, the VMware Aria Operations for Logs service allows organizations to do the following:

- Perform troubleshooting of basic administration tasks, including network firewall rules

- Demonstrate compliance by complying with auditing regulation requirements

- Gain visibility into activities in the VMware Cloud on AWS deployment, including which users performed what actions and when

VMware Cloud with Tanzu services

VMware Cloud with Tanzu services is included along with the VMware Cloud on AWS subscription.

Tanzu services portfolio includes a fully managed Kubernetes services that offers an easy path to enterprise-grade Kubernetes deployments and management, accelerating application modernization initiatives.

Crafted specifically for Tanzu services on VMware Cloud offerings such as VMware Cloud on AWS, Tanzu Mission Control Essentials provides a set of essential capabilities to organize your Kubernetes clusters and namespaces for scalable operations, and secure them with access control policies.

The enterprise-grade Kubernetes includes a multi-cloud management solution and a Kubernetes-based CaaS platform, running on a VMware Cloud on AWS **Infrastructure as a Service (IaaS)**.

Tanzu CaaS offerings are based on the on-premises vSphere with Tanzu, also known as **Tanzu Kubernetes Grid (TKG)**, provided as a managed service. **Tanzu Mission Control (TMC) Essentials** provides a multi-cloud Kubernetes management plane. The following figure shows the Tanzu services included with the VMware Cloud on AWS services – Tanzu Kubernetes Grid and TMC Essentials:

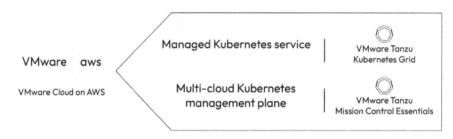

Figure 3.16 – VMware Cloud with Tanzu services

Organizations can leverage the platform to train and enable IT admins to Kubernetes operators, while using the same operational model with the familiar vCenter interface for all workloads VMs and containers alike. Organizations can consume enterprise-grade Kubernetes clusters that are secure, upstream-compliant, and isolated from one another within a few minutes.

vSphere administrators can create namespaces to separate resources and grant owners access. Before granting permissions, the vSphere administrators will assign resources, such as disk, memory, CPU, and storage, to the namespace. Any user assigned to this namespace will be able to create Kubernetes-based clusters up until they exceed their vSphere Admins' quotas.

Organizations can manage multiple TKG clusters with observability and troubleshooting in vCenter Server. The following figure shows how IT admins can now manage both their vCenter VM and Kubernetes workloads using Tanzu services over a VMware managed public cloud infrastructure:

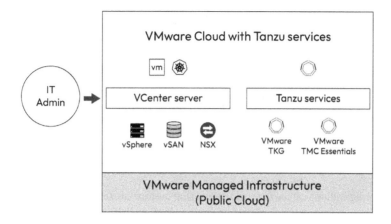

Figure 3.17 – IT administrators can upskill their Kubernetes skills

TKG was built upon the ClusterAPI open source project, and this API provides Kubernetes-like APIs to facilitate platform operators' life cycle management. The deployments work off a desired state configuration. Platform operators specify a cluster configuration and submit it to the Supervisor cluster for provisioning. The Supervisor Kubernetes cluster is specialized and contains all the ClusterAPI components. It can be used to provision Tanzu Kubernetes clusters where organizations' workloads can run, and it is used to scale **Tanzu Kubernetes Clusters** (**TKCs**), resize nodes, upgrade clusters, and delete clusters. The TKCs are fully conformant with upstream Kubernetes, which means they will run any Kubernetes app. The following figure shows conceptually how the **Tanzu Kubernetes Grid Supervisor Cluster**, integrated into vSphere, provisions and manages Tanzu Kubernetes workload clusters:

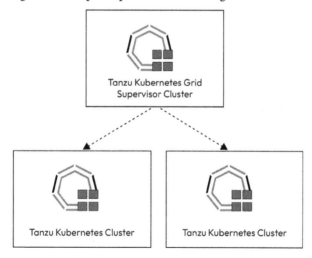

Figure 3.18 – The Tanzu Kubernetes Grid Supervisor and workload clusters

While the source of the Kubernetes distribution is identical for both Supervisor and **Tanzu Kubernetes Clusters (TKCs)**, it is crucial to acknowledge the following distinctions:

- Kubernetes distributions provisioned on Supervisor and Tanzu Kubernetes Cluster are separate and independent of each other
- The Kubernetes packaged in Supervisor represents an opinionated installation of Kubernetes
- On the other hand, the Kubernetes packaged in Tanzu Kubernetes Clusters is an upstream-aligned, fully conformant distribution of Kubernetes delivered through **Tanzu Kubernetes releases (TKrs)**

Tanz Kubernetes configurations can be overridden by using custom cluster configurations at deployment time. Tanzu Kubernetes clusters are deployed in two types of availability options:

- **Single node**: One control plane node for the cluster
- **High availability**: Three control plane nodes for the cluster

Organizations can enable the Tanzu Kubernetes service using a self-service flow in the SDDC console to submit network CIDRs. NSX-T will use these CIDR addresses to create new networks and routes to the TKCs.

After activation is complete, a Supervisor cluster will be deployed on your VMware Cloud on AWS instance.

Note

The service requires a minimum of three hosts in a vSphere cluster for activation.

Tanzu Kubernetes networking

Kubernetes clusters can be deployed through the TKG service. The underlying networking services, such as load balancing and **Network Address Translation (NAT)** rules, are created for applications that have been deployed to Tanzu Kubernetes automatically.

TKG clusters are placed within a namespace segment and **Network Addresses are Translated (NATed)** to other networks in the SDDC. To ensure that NAT pool resources are available for the new network segments, egress and ingress CIDRs will be required during the initial setup.

The **NSX-T Container Plugin (NCP)** creates load balancers for the applications installed in the clusters.

During the initial setup, four different CIDR ranges are required to be able to activate the TKG service:

- **Service CIDR**: For the Supervisor cluster service address space
- **Namespace CIDR**: For network segments created with new namespaces

- **Ingress CIDR**: A pool used to provide ingress access through NSX-T load balancers for workloads

- **Egress CIDR**: A pool used for **Source-NAT** (**SNAT**) of outbound traffic of Kubernetes nodes for workloads

The following diagram describes each of the preceding segments:

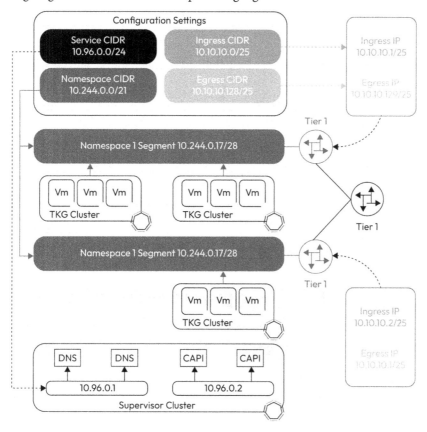

Figure 3.19 – TKG networking segments

The NSX-T container plugin is used to configure network access automatically. Kubernetes operators can use the Kubernetes API for interaction with the VMware Cloud on AWS networking environment. They can also request services of type `LoadBalancer`. NCP will create an NSX-T load balancer and **Virtual IP** (**VIP**) address from the ingress IP pool, and then the organization can access the applications within the clusters.

Tanzu Kubernetes Storage

Tanzu services use vSAN storage to present persistent volumes using **cloud-native storage** (**CNS**).

vSAN integrates and enhances cloud-native storage capabilities, and these integrations are important to delivering cloud-native applications on Kubernetes in vSphere. vSAN supports policy-driven dynamic provisioning of a Kubernetes **persistent volume claim** (**PVC**).

As a storage policy is assigned with a cluster, that cluster will have a Kubernetes StorageClass of the same name. Platform operators can request PVCs from this StorageClass to create persistent volumes. Those volumes will be created in the data store identified by the storage policy, and storage policies are applied to a namespace.

vSphere Admins will view the PVCs created within the Kubernetes cluster, and these PVCs will be visible within the vCenter UI.

The following diagram describes the CNS framework:

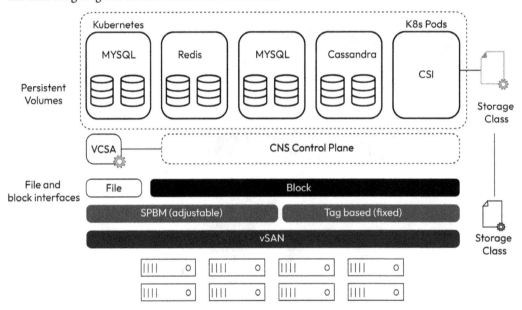

Figure 3.20 – The Tanzu Services CNS framework

In much the same way networking resources are created from a Kubernetes manifest, platform operators can apply manifests to request PVCs right through the Kubernetes API.

The TKC will provision the virtual disk in the vSAN datastore and connect it to the Kubernetes nodes that require that disk.

TMC Essentials

TMC is provided as a **Software as a Service** (**SaaS**) and acts as a global management plane for Kubernetes clusters. TMC gives organizations global visibility, scalable operation, and consistent policy.

TMC enables platform operators to deploy Tanzu Kubernetes Grid clusters using the TMC API, command-line interface, or user interface. The clusters can then be scaled, upgraded, or configured using the same interfaces.

TMC can apply and enforce policy on clusters that are managed. This makes it easy for operators to configure them. Operators can apply security policies and access to a cluster, or group of clusters, for uniform configuration throughout the fleet. This capability is available to more than just Tanzu Kubernetes clusters. TMC can be connected to any Kubernetes cluster that conforms to policy management. This includes managed services, such as Amazon EKS or Azure AKS clusters.

TMC enables a multi-cloud Kubernetes control plane for management, global visibility, a consistent policy for Kubernetes clusters, and enhanced security and governance. The following figure illustrates conceptually the different functions and Kubernetes environments that TMC can apply policy to and manage:

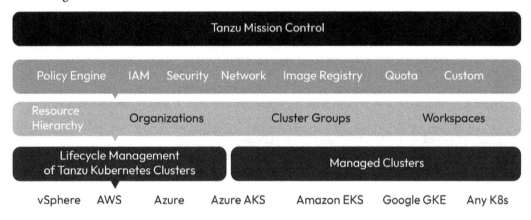

Figure 3.21 – TMC

TMC helps deliver a multi-cloud control plane for Kubernetes clusters to platform operators or SREs using TMC Essentials. TMC provides the provisioning and management of the life cycle of Tanzu Kubernetes clusters centrally and attaches any conformant Kubernetes clusters running anywhere on any cloud for centralized management at scale, increasing security and governance, including deployments of Kubernetes through cloud-native providers.

TMC provides global visibility across clusters and clouds and increases security and governance by automating operational tasks, such as access and security management, at scale.

Developers get access to virtualized infrastructure through Kubernetes APIs without the need to invest time in operations, security, and governance. Meanwhile, IT teams can provision capacity and manage resource quotas to multiple developer teams without managing the underlying infrastructure. The following figure shows conceptually how the different personas of IT admins, developers, and Kubernetes platform operators can all interact with Tanzu services:

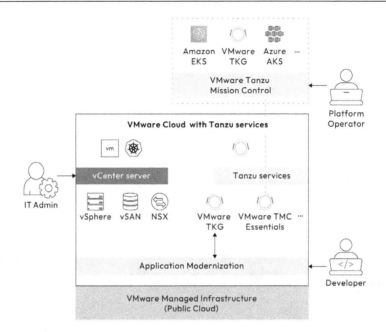

Figure 3.22 – Different users of Tanzu services – platform operators, IT admins, and developers

TMC gives you global visibility across clusters and clouds.

Packaging

The Tanzu service is a subset of the capabilities of the Tanzu Standard packaging.

The following table describes the differences between the included Tanzu services package with VMware Cloud on AWS and the Tanzu Standard separately purchasable add-on. The following figure shows a comparison between the Tanzu services for VMware Cloud on AWS and Tanzu Standard packages:

Key product component	Tanzu services for VMC on AWS	Tanzu Standard (Can be purchased in VMC Console)
Managed Tanzu Kubernetes Grid service (internally known as TKGS) via Cloud Console	✓	✓
Full Tanzu Kubernetes Grid platform for deploying on VMC instances	✓	✓
Full Tanzu Kubernetes Grid platform for public cloud deployment		✓
Full Tanzu Kubernetes Grid platform for deploying on vSphere and VCF on-premises		✓
Tanzu Mission Control Essentials version	✓	
Tanzu Mission Control Standard version		✓

Figure 3.23 – Comparing Tanzu services and Tanzu Standard

The Tanzu service has three major capabilities out of the box – managed TKG Kubernetes services, the TMC Essential version, and a lighter version of TMC.

Compared to Tanzu services, Tanzu Standard offers a few more capabilities. It allows TKG deployment on public clouds and TKG on-premises on vSphere and VCF.

TMC Essentials, compared to TMC Standard and TMC Advanced, offers more policy features, as shown can be seen in the following table. The following figure shows the difference between TMC Essentials, included with the VMware Cloud on AWS edition, and the Tanzu Standard and Advanced add-on editions:

Comparison between Tanzu Mission Control versions

Key Features	TMC Essentials (included in VMC purchases)	TMC Standard (included in Tanzu Standard purchase)	TMC Advanced (need to purchase through salled flow) *can purchase standalone or with Ta Advanced edition
Data Model: Cluster Group, workspaces, managed namespaces	✓	✓	✓
Global visibility on cluster and workload health/metadata/inventory	✓	✓	✓
Cluster lifecycle management	✓	✓	✓
Attach any conformant clusters	✓	✓	✓
TMC Audit logs and TMC events	✓	✓	✓
Federation to customer's IDP	✓	✓	✓
Custom Roles			✓
Access policy	✓	✓	✓
Basic security policy	✓	✓	✓
Custom security policy			✓
Advanced policy types (image registry, networking, quota, and custom policy):			✓
Policy Insights and alerting			✓
Data Protection			✓
Conformance inspection:			✓
CIS security benchmark inspection		✓	✓
TMC Catalog (GA in Q3)		✓	✓
Integration with Tanzu Observability and Tanzu Service Mesh			✓

Figure 3.24 – Comparing TMC versions

The Essentials version includes the multi-cloud life cycle management and visibility portion. The Standard edition is required for data protection and conformance inspections, and the Advanced version is required for the advanced security, networking, and quote policies.

Summary

In this chapter, we reviewed the major integrated services in VMware Cloud on AWS, including the HCX architecture and the different migration options available with HCX (migration using vMotion, bulk migration, replication-assisted vMotion, and OS-assisted migration). We also discussed the capabilities and architecture of Aria Operations for Logs and the Tanzu-managed Kubernetes service.

The next chapter will focus on more hands-on instructions demonstrating the deployment, configuration, and setup of VMware Cloud on AWS SDDCs.

Part 2: Configuration, Maintenance, and Troubleshooting on VMware Cloud on AWS

Part 2 explores deploying a VMware Cloud on AWS **Software-Defined Data Center** (**SDDC**). It covers creating a VMware Cloud organization, implementing **role-based access control** (**RBAC**), and managing identity on vCenter and **Cloud Service Platform** (**CSP**). The chapter addresses VM storage policies, compute policies, and the **Elastic Distributed Resource Scheduler** (**EDRS**) for cluster scaling. SDDC networking and security configurations, extending to day-two operations, are explored. This part details NSX advanced security services, VMware HCX, Aria Operations for Logs, and Tanzu Kubernetes Grid Service, offering crucial insights. It also covers modernizing applications with native AWS services and automating infrastructure management through **Infrastructure as Code** (**IaC**). Additionally, it addresses meeting low-latency, local data-processing requirements, and data sovereignty compliance with VMware Cloud on AWS Outposts.

This part consists of the following chapters:

- *Chapter 4, Getting Started with Your First VMware Cloud on AWS SDDC*

- *Chapter 5, Configuring vCenter, vSAN, and VMC Console*

- *Chapter 6, Understanding Networking and Security Configurations*

- *Chapter 7, Exploring Integrated Services Configuration*

- *Chapter 8, Building Applications and Managing Operations*

- *Chapter 9, Deploying Infrastructure as Code with VMware Cloud*

- *Chapter 10, Identifying Low-Latency Workloads to Run on VMware Cloud on AWS Outposts*

Getting Started with VMware Cloud on AWS SDDC

This chapter will help you navigate through the process of deploying a new VMware Cloud on AWS SDDC.

We will cover the following topics:

- Creating a VMware Cloud Organization
- The VMware Cloud on AWS SDDC provisioning wizard
- Enabling access to vCenter
- RBAC and identity management on vCenter and **Cloud Services Platform** (**CSP**)
- Application deployment example

The first step organizations take to start using VMware Cloud on AWS services and get onboarded is to create an Organization. Let's have a quick recap of the concept of Organizations.

VMware Cloud on AWS service accounts are created within an Organization.

Organizations are the common construct used in all VMware Cloud service offerings. They act as an **Identity and Access Management** (**IAM**) tools within the Cloud Services Console.

To get initial access to the platform, users must create a new **My VMware** account or use an existing one. They should link pre-purchased credits called **SPP credits** or funds to the Organization's **VMware Customer Connect** (formerly **MyVMware** portal).

VMware Cloud allows users to be associated with multiple Organizations and hold different roles per Organization. Organization owners are given the **Organization Owner** role and they can invite new users and view billing information. The second role is Organization Member. Both roles allow access to all resources, services, and information of the Organization.

Creating a VMware Organization

The organization's administrator will receive an invite via email to create an Organization. This is done either after a purchase order has been processed through VMware or AWS, or once a self-service flow with a credit card has been completed.

> **Note**
> The link for the creation of an Organization is unique and can be used only one time.

Once the link has been clicked on, a My VMware login prompt will appear, as shown in the following screenshot:

Figure 4.1 – Organization creation initial login with a My VMware account

Once the user credentials are entered, the Organization creation process will start.

First, provide the Organization's name, agree to the terms of service, and click on **CREATE ORGANIZATION AND COMPLETE SIGN-UP**, as shown in the following screenshot:

Figure 4.2 – Set up an Organization

After that, administrators will have access to CSP and, from there, can review the information available on the Launchpad and access the inventory of services available within CSP. As seen in the screenshot that follows, on the left-hand side is a navigation pane, which we'll explore in further detail later, and at the top right-hand side is the newly created Organization name with the user account created based on the My VMware credentials used in the login process.

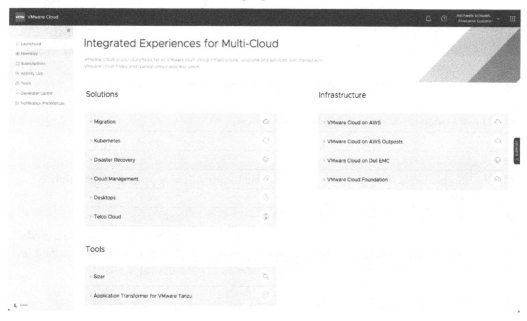

Figure 4.3 – VMware Cloud Launchpad

Click on the upper-right corner of the screen to finalize the account details setup, click on the username and Organization name on the upper-right side, and click on **View Organization**, as shown in the following screenshot:

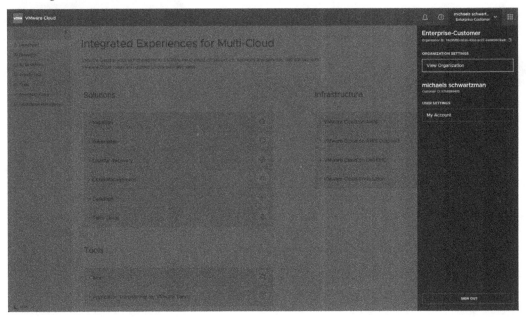

Figure 4.4 – CSP View Organization dropdown

Next, fill in and confirm the correct Organization address.

> **Note**
>
> Missing information in this phase may potentially fail the provisioning process or subscription creation process.

Link a fund (you must use the My VMware account designated as the fund owner) or add a credit card. There could be several funds associated with a single Organization, but only a single default or active fund at a given time needs to be selected, as illustrated in the following screenshot:

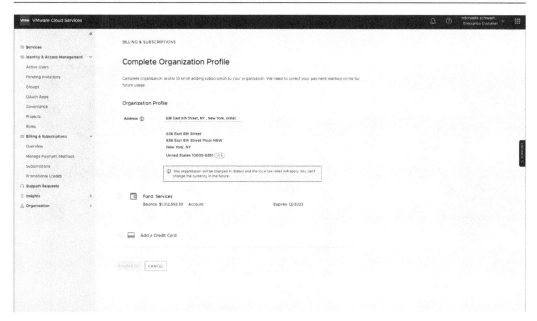

Figure 4.5 – CSP fund selection

Reserved Instances subscription creation

When you purchase VMware Cloud on AWS capacity, you can select between **Reserved Instances** (**RIs**) with a term commitment for one or three years or opt to consume the service based on the on-demand rate. RIs purchased based on the term commitment are normally more cost-efficient compared to the on-demand rate. If you opt to use RIs for your VMware Cloud on AWS deployment, you must create a host subscription in your Organization. It's important to create the subscription *before* deploying the SDDC – VMware Cloud on AWS will apply an on-demand rate to your SDDC if no subscription has been created.

After selecting the fund, create the host subscriptions: click on the nine-dot grid on the upper right-hand side to see the list of services and click on **VMware Cloud**, as seen in the following screenshot:

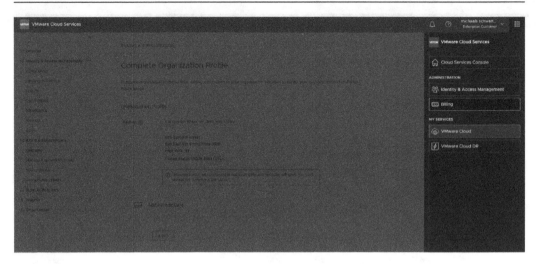

Figure 4.6 – Navigate to VMware Cloud

Once you have funds associated with the Organization, you can proceed to the next step.

Click on **Subscriptions** in the **VMware Cloud** Services Console and create a term commitment, as seen in the following screenshot:

Figure 4.7 – Navigate to Subscriptions in VMware Cloud Services Console

Now, in the subscription workflow, click on **Host Capacity**. The other subscription options are for SRM/VSR DRaaS, and the **NSX Advanced Firewall** paid add-on services:

‹ Create Subscription

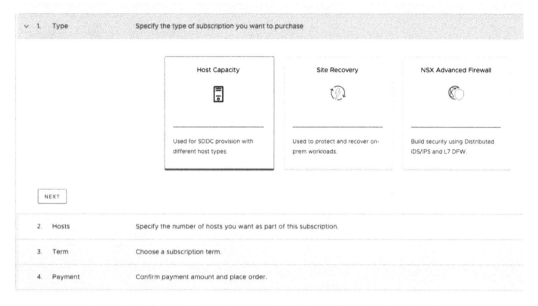

Figure 4.8 – Create Subscription wizard in VMware Cloud Services Console

In the subscription details, we'll need to fill in the relevant subscription region.

> **Note**
>
> Please note that prices in AWS change per region and, once selected, the region and the host type cannot be changed unless a Flexible Subscription is used.

Afterward, for the **Host Type** option, select the host type you chose during the sales process. In this example, we have selected the default I3 hosts.

For the **Number of Hosts** option, select the number of hosts the subscription is to cover. In our example, we have selected an amount that will cover a minimal cluster size of 2 hosts, as seen in the following screenshot:

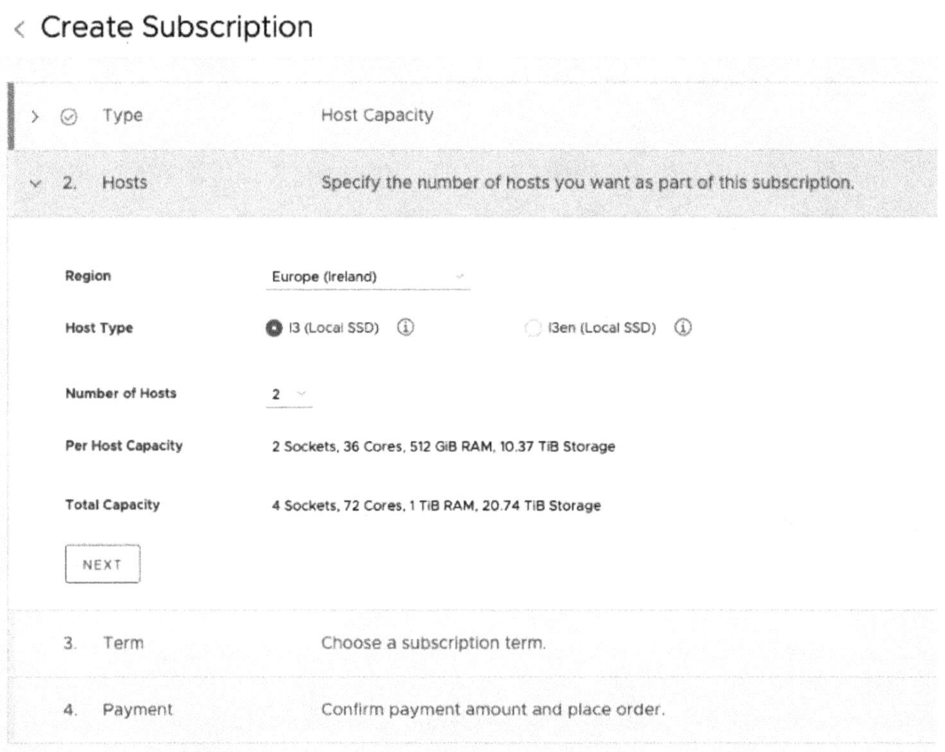

< Create Subscription

		Type	Host Capacity
>	⊘	Type	Host Capacity

	2.	Hosts	Specify the number of hosts you want as part of this subscription.
∨	2.	Hosts	Specify the number of hosts you want as part of this subscription.

Region   Europe (Ireland)

Host Type   ● I3 (Local SSD) ⓘ   ○ I3en (Local SSD) ⓘ

Number of Hosts   2 ∨

Per Host Capacity   2 Sockets, 36 Cores, 512 GiB RAM, 10.37 TiB Storage

Total Capacity   4 Sockets, 72 Cores, 1 TiB RAM, 20.74 TiB Storage

[NEXT]

3. Term   Choose a subscription term.

4. Payment   Confirm payment amount and place order.

Figure 4.9 – Create Subscription – select Host Type and Region

> **Note**
> A subscription can be created in increments of 1. For instance, when a organization wants to increase its cluster size from 2 to 3 hosts, another subscription with 1 host can be created to cover the extra, third host.

Defining the subscription term is an important part of the subscription creation – you should reflect the term in your sales contract.

Subscription flexibility is such that you can either opt to use a fixed subscription (defining the host type, duration, and AWS region) or a flexible subscription. With a flexible subscription, you can change the host type and AWS region later, giving you more flexibility with the deployment. However, there is a trade-off associated with a flexible subscription – the price of RIs is normally higher with a flexible subscription.

For the subscription duration, you can choose between a 1-year and a 3-year contract. A 3-year contract is the most cost-effective option; however, it might limit your flexibility in moving workloads to another AWS region or changing the host type.

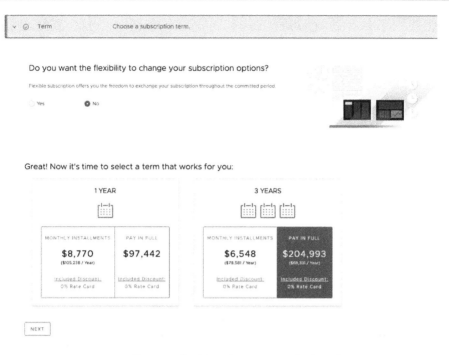

Figure 4.10 – Choose a Flexible Subscription and select the term

In our example, we have selected the **3 YEARS** and **PAY IN FULL** options. Next, the organization's administrator will need to confirm the order. Once the process is completed successfully, you will see the subscription created with an **Activated** status, as seen in the following screenshot:

Figure 4.11 – Subscription creation confirmation

> **Note**
>
> The activation of the subscription may take several minutes. It's normal to see the status as pending. Please refresh after several minutes; otherwise, contact the VMware customer success team.

VMware Cloud on AWS SDDC provisioning wizard

To initiate the SDDC provisioning wizard, on the left-hand side, select **Inventory** and click on **CREATE SDDC**, as seen in the following screenshot:

Figure 4.12 – Create SDDC

> **Information**
>
> When selecting the host type and the region, it's important to match the subscription. The SDDC wizard does not validate the selection with the subscription option. If the subscription does not cover the selected region and host type, on-demand rates will be applied.

The SDDC name is the logical name of the SDDC. You can change the name afterward.

A single-host deployment option is available for **Proof-of-Concepts (PoCs)** and limited to 60 days. The single-host SDDC has no SLA.

The **Stretched Cluster** option will create a cluster stretched between two **Availability Zones (AZs)** in the same region, providing higher redundancy and an uptime SLA of up to 99.99%. **Stretched Cluster** is a unique option of VMware Cloud on AWS, enabling you to provide resiliency to your applications on the infrastructure level. This infrastructure option is transparent to applications and does not require architecture design changes, helping you to save on EC2 instances and additional service costs and drastically reducing the time it takes to migrate line of business applications to the cloud.

In our example, we have selected a multi-host deployment model with 2 x I4 hosts, the minimal number of hosts for a production cluster, as seen in the following screenshot:

< Create Software-Defined Data Center (SDDC)

| ∨ | 1. | SDDC Properties | Give your SDDC a name, choose a size, and specify the AWS region where it will be created. |

SDDC Name	Production SDDC
AWS Region	US West (Oregon)
Deployment	○ Single Host ● Multi-Host ☐ Stretched Cluster ⓘ
Host Type	I4I (Local SSD) ⓘ
Number of Hosts	2
Host Capacity	2 Sockets, 64 Cores, 1 TiB RAM, 19.96 TiB Storage
Total Capacity	4 Sockets, 128 Cores, 2 TiB RAM, 39.96 TiB Storage

SHOW ADVANCED CONFIGURATION

NEXT

Figure 4.13 – Create SDDC configuration

You can use the advanced configuration option to specify the size of the SDDC appliance. By default, all SDDCs are deployed using a medium appliance size. You can opt to increase the size to large if the design includes a large SDDC with multiple cluster and/or you are looking to implement the multi-edge feature to boost network performance.

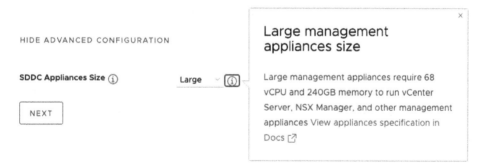

HIDE ADVANCED CONFIGURATION

SDDC Appliances Size ⓘ   Large ⌄ ⓘ

NEXT

Large management appliances size

Large management appliances require 68 vCPU and 240GB memory to run vCenter Server, NSX Manager, and other management appliances View appliances specification in Docs ↗

Figure 4.14 – SDDC Appliances Size configuration

The appliance configuration can be changed after the deployment.

Configuring the connected VPC

VMware Cloud on AWS utilizes AWS account linking and AWS CloudFormation to acquire the necessary permissions to access your AWS account. Once the accounts are linked, VMware Cloud on AWS executes a CloudFormation template, establishing IAM roles and granting permissions to access several VMware accounts to assume certain roles.

The **Connected VPC** serves the purpose of enabling organization to leverage native AWS services in conjunction with VMware Cloud on AWS. Alternatively, a different VPC connected to the SDDC using VMware Transit Connect can also be used to access native AWS services.

To establish a connection between the AWS account containing the connected VPC and the SDDC console, click on **OPEN AWS CONSOLE WITH CLOUD FORMATION TEMPLATE**, as seen in the following screenshot:

Figure 4.15– Creating and setting up an SDDC AWS account

If not already logged in, use the AWS account ID and credentials to log in to the AWS account that has the connected VPC.

In the AWS Management Console, on the right side, let us change the region from the default **US West (Oregon)** region to the **Europe (Ireland)** region in our example, as seen in the following screenshot:

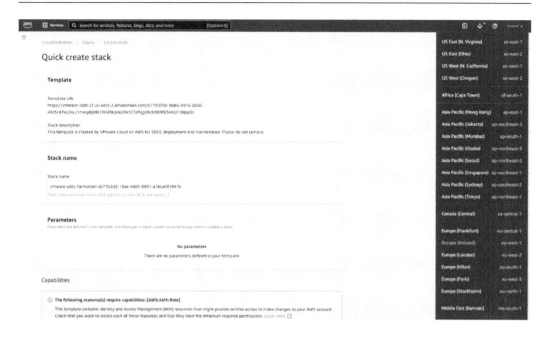

Figure 4.16 – Launch CloudFormation template from AWS Management Console

We can retain or change the CloudFormation stack name. The logged-in user needs to have the appropriate permissions to create an IAM role that updates the VPC routing table through a Lambda function, as seen in the screenshot that follows.

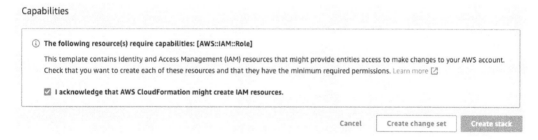

Figure 4.17 – Create CloudFormation Stack from AWS Management Console

Acknowledge the checkbox and click **Create stack**.

The stack creation process may take several minutes, and when provisioning is completed, the progress can be seen on the left-hand side with the **CREATE_COMPLETE** status, as seen in the following screenshot:

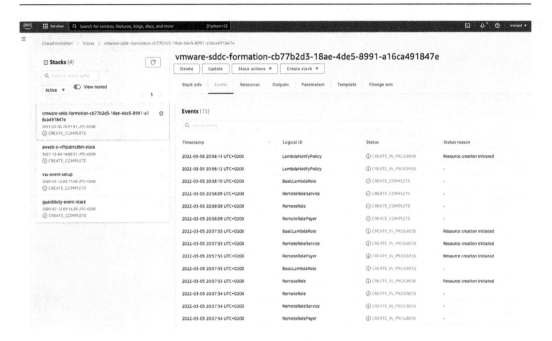

Figure 4.18 – AWS Management Console – Create stack confirmation

> **Note**
>
> VMware Cloud Adminstrators need to make sure the function is not blocked by AWS features such as Control Tower guardrails or **Service Control Policies** (**SCPs**). The minimal required permissions can be found in the VMware documentation (`https://docs.vmware.com/en/VMware-Cloud-on-AWS/services/com.vmware.vmc-aws-operations/GUID-DE8E80A3-5EED-474C-AECD-D30534926615.html`).

AWS VPC and networking prerequisites

Next, link the SDDC to an AWS native account that contains the associated connected VPC and subnets. It is essential that the AWS account contains a VPC and a subnet in the required **Availability Zone** (**AZ**) and Region.

Start by creating a subnet in every AZ in the AWS Region where the SDDC will be created. It will help you identify all AZs where instance (i4i/i3/i3en) capacity is currently available and can be deployed. Select the AZ that corresponds to your SDDC placement criteria, considering AZ affinity for proximity with AWS workloads or AZ anti-affinity for isolating AWS workloads. Additional factors such as latency and cross-AZ data transfer costs should be considered.

> **Note**
>
> Two connected VPC subnets in separate AZs must be available and selected in a stretched cluster deployment.
>
> Intra-AZ traffic does not incur egress traffic costs; inter-AZ traffic, inter-region, and internet traffic does incur egress costs.

The Amazon VPC defines subnets that should be uniquely routable in the organization's network. These subnets must be no smaller than /27 and larger subnets such as /26 or greater are recommended for scalability reasons.

After the SDDC is created with the selected subnet, it's important not to delete or modify the subnets. The following figure depicts the SDDC and connected VPC subnet architecture:

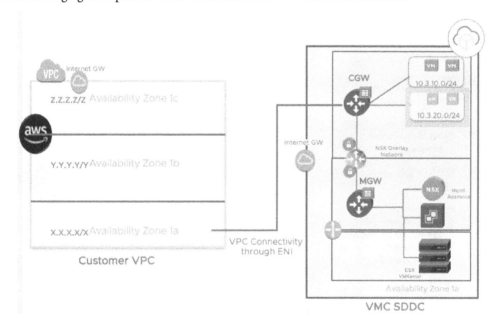

Figure 4.19 – Create SDDC connected VPC topology

Next, let us go through the creation of the VPC and subnets on the AWS side. We need to confirm that the prerequisite VPC subnets have been created in AWS, as described.

Let's go to the VPC service in the AWS Management Console and click on **Your VPCs** | **Create VPC**, as seen in the following screenshot:

Figure 4.20 – AWS Management Console – navigate to VPC

Let's provide a name tag and an IPv4 CIDR subnet from which the subnets will be divided, as seen in the following screenshot:

Figure 4.21 – AWS Management Console – Create VPC

Retain the default configurations of **IPv4 CIDR manual input**. The tenancy can remain as the default. Next, let's click **Create VPC**.

Once provisioning is completed, a summary page with the VPC details will appear, as seen in the following screenshot:

Figure 4.22 – AWS Management Console VPC summary

Next, let's select **Subnets** on the left-hand side, and select **Create subnet**.

In the subnet creation wizard, we'll select the newly created VPC, provide a name for the subnet, and select a specific availability zone, as seen in the following screenshot:

Figure 4.23 – AWS Management Console – create subnet per AZ

Let's create two additional subnets with a unique CIDR and availability zones.

Click on **Create subnet**, and this is what the summary should look like:

Figure 4.24 – AWS Management Console subnet creation summary

This completes the prerequisites on the AWS native side. Now let's come back to the VMware Cloud Services Console.

Finalizing the SDDC creation

Once you have finished the AWS configuration, all necessary details are reflected in the VMware Cloud SDDC console, as seen in the following screenshot:

Figure 4.25 – VMware Cloud SDDC console connected AWS account dropdown

Click on **NEXT** in the wizard and view the VPC and subnets we have created in the AWS Management Console in the previous steps. Let's select a single AZ in our deployment and click on **NEXT**, as seen in the following screenshot:

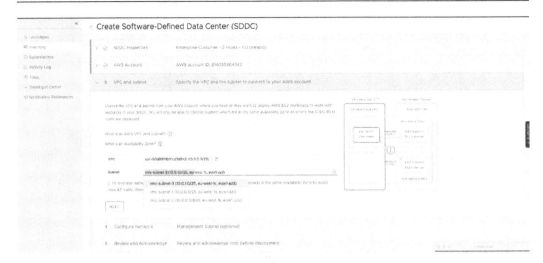

Figure 4.26 – SDDC creation – select VPC and subnet

In this step, we configure the SDDC management network CIDR. There are several important considerations to be made while selecting the SDDC management network:

- The management network CIDR defines the IP address space for all internal components of the SDDC, such as the management and vMotion interfaces of ESXi hosts, vCenter Server, and any managed add-on components deployed in the SDDC.

- You can select the /16, /20, or /23 subnet mask. The /23 subnet mask is recommended only for small deployments.

- A /23 network supports only 27 ESXi hosts. A /20 network can support 251, and a /16 can support up to 4,091 ESXi hosts.

> **Note**
> The actual number of usable hosts is fewer than what is specified above. Two hosts per SDDC, plus one per cluster are reserved for maintenance operations and host failure remediation purposes, meaning a /23 network SDDC with one cluster will have a usable host number of 24 instead of the specified 27.

This network can't be modified after it has been deployed. It is better to use /23 only for testing or SDDCs with a specific purpose that are not likely to grow in capacity.

The management CIDR cannot contain network 192.168.1.0/24 because this network is used as a default compute network. The networks 10.0.0.0/15 (10.0.0.0->10.1.255.255), 172.18.0.0/16, and 172.31.0.0/16 are also reserved, and the management CIDR cannot overlap any of these ranges.

If you have plans to build a hybrid environment or connect multiple SDDCs together, the management CIDR cannot overlap.

We need to provide the selected CIDR in the wizard and the rest will be done automatically by the service.

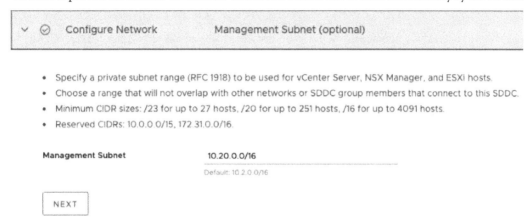

Figure 4.27 – Management Subnet VMware Cloud on AWS SDDC creation

In the preceding step, we confirm our understanding that prices are associated with the SDDC provisioning per host. We will click on **Deploy SDDC**. The deployment process of the SDDC takes up to 120 minutes, and we will be able to see the progress in the VMware Cloud SDDC console:

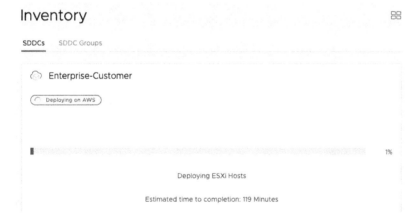

Figure 4.28 – SDDC creation progress

Dedicated bare-metal hosts are allocated to each SDDC, followed by the deployment of the VMware SDDC stack that includes vSphere, vSAN, and NSX. At the end of the process, you will have a fully functional SDDC ready to run workloads. However, before deploying your first VM, you will need to get access to vCenter Server.

Enabling access to vCenter Server

To be able to successfully manage the SDDC, you need to enable access to vCenter Server. vCenter Server can be accessed from the internet or a private address accessible from the VPN, DX, or AWS VPC connected to the SDDC. By default, the NSX firewalls block access to the vCenter Server from the internet. In the upper-right corner of the VMware Cloud SDDC console, click on **OPEN VCENTER** and a pop-up message with the following options will appear. Let's click on **FIREWALL RULE**, as seen in the following screenshot:

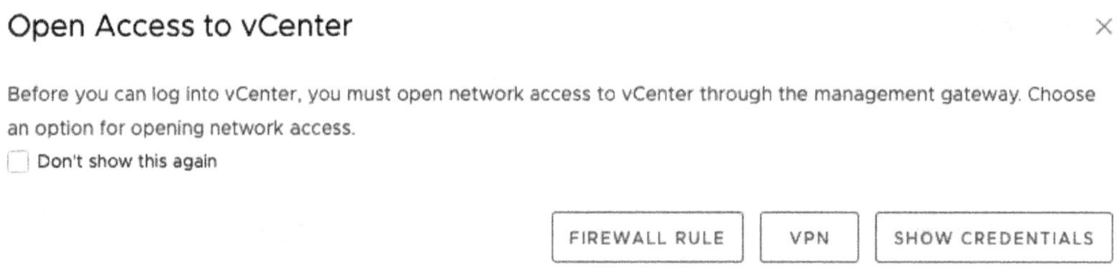

Figure 4.29 – Open vCenter with access credentials

Now let's enable access to vCenter from remote public IPs. By default, internet access to vCenter is blocked by the Management Gateway firewall. Navigate to the **Networking & Security** tab, and open the **Gateway Firewall** section, as seen in the following screenshot:

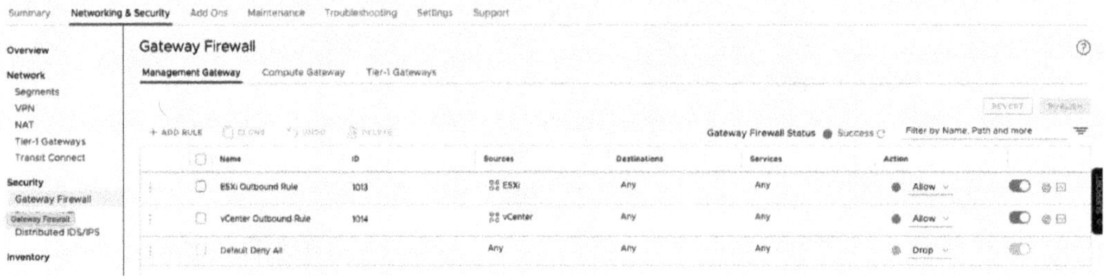

Figure 4.30 – Networking & Security – Gateway Firewall

The default NSX firewall ruleset does not allow access to vCenter from external IP addresses. Only outbound communication from vCenter or the ESXi hosts is allowed. First, let's create a new rule allowing vCenter access from a specific IP address. Click on the + **ADD RULE** button and a new rule configuration will appear. Provide a descriptive name for the rule and click on the source **Edit** button, as seen in the following screenshot:

Figure 4.31 – Creating firewall rules

Here, we'll create a *user defined group* that will represent connecting source IP addresses. After providing a descriptive name for the group, we'll click on **Set Members**, as seen in the following screenshot:

Figure 4.32 – Creating a user defined group

In the new window, we'll enter the source IP address to initiate the communication toward the vCenter Server. Multiple addresses and address ranges can be provided, as seen in the following screenshot:

Figure 4.33 – Define source IP addresses

First, make sure to click on **SAVE** to save the group (*1*), and check the steps are marked in the right order, and only then click **APPLY** (*2*), as shown in the following screenshot:

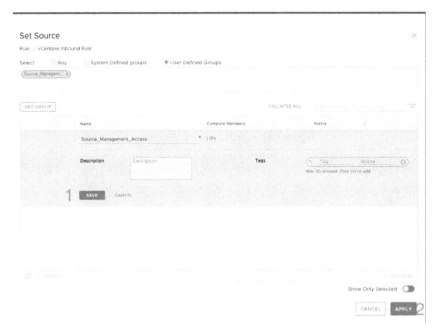

Figure 4.34 – Defining source IP addresses and saving the configuration

Lastly, it is important to select the destination and services we wish to enable. The destination field should be modified by selecting the predefined vCenter *system defined group*. Additionally, there are system-defined services that are predefined during the provisioning process. The service can be selected under **Services** | **HTTPS** and **Allow** under **Actions**, as shown in *Figure 4.35*.

Figure 4.35 – Publishing a rule

Do not forget to publish the rule on the upper right-hand side of the screen, otherwise, the configuration will not be applied.

> **Tip**
> Even though external public access to vCenter Server is supported, it is required to limit it to a specific IP address or range. Most enterprise organizations, for security reasons, prefer accessing the vCenter Server using private IP address access over a Site-to-Site VPN or AWS Direct Connect. Using **Any** as a source for the vCenter Server is not supported for security reasons.

After configuring the firewall rule, go back to the **OPEN VCENTER** button in the VMware Cloud SDDC console and click on **SHOW CREDENTIALS**.

The cloud admin credentials and the **OPEN VCENTER** button will appear. The credentials are predefined during the provisioning process and cannot be changed. Administrators and Operators can copy-paste the credentials from here.

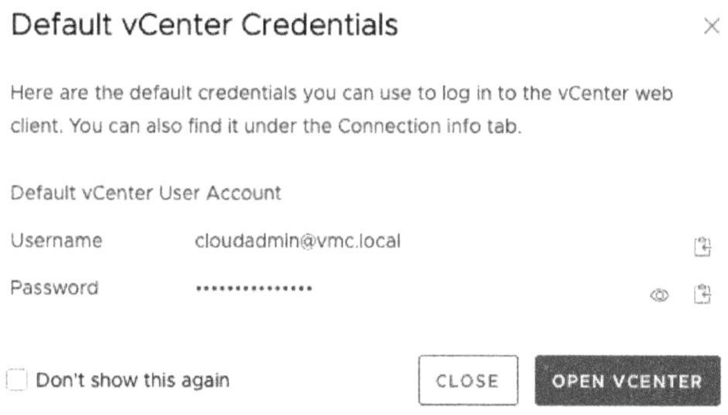

Figure 4.36 – OPEN VCENTER

Let's click on the **OPEN VCENTER** button and enter the credentials in the newly opened tab. The vSphere Web Client will open, as seen in the following screenshot:

Figure 4.37 – First vCenter access

The vCenter Server UI is no different from on-premises vCenter Server and uses the latest publicly available version of the vCenter software (for a greenfield SDDC).

Managing the vCenter FQDN

The vCenter FQDN is a sub-domain of `vmwarevmc.com` and is managed by VMware, including its certificates. By default, the FQDN is set to resolve to a public IP address to facilitate initial access to vCenter Server via the vSphere Web Client. If you are looking to build a hybrid environment and interconnect with on-premises vSphere environment, you may want to change the resolution of the vCenter FQDN to a private IP. This IP is only accessible via VPN, DX, or connected VPC and requires valid **Border Gateway Protocol** (**BGP**) configurations to be able to advertise the management network. We recommend setting up the connectivity before changing the vCenter IP.

You will be able to change the FQDN resolution for vCenter Server using the **Settings** tab in the SDDC console.

Figure 4.38 – Change the vCenter FQDN to resolve to a private IP

Now that we can access the vCenter Server, we'll set up basic **Role-Based Access Control** (**RBAC**) and add additional users to vCenter and **Cloud Services Platform** (CSP).

RBAC and identity management on vCenter and CSP

VMware Cloud on AWS service access has two authentication domains: the CSP authentication domain and the vCenter authentication domain. With the new version 1.22 release, it is possible to configure federated SSO between CSP and vCenter: when this feature is enabled, a user authenticated through CSP will get access to vCenter Server without additional authentication. Before a user will be able to log in, an appropriate vCenter role must be assigned using the `cloudadmin` account.

VMware Cloud on AWS uses a restricted operation model to manage access to vCenter Server. The default administrator user – `cloudadmin@vmc.local` – does not have full administrator rights compared to the `administrator@vsphere.local` account. This is expected for a managed service and prevents users from accidentally changing the settings having an impact on SLA or environment stability. The permission set available to the `cloudadmin` account and the corresponding

CloudAdmin role includes the maximum level of permissions available for users on VMware Cloud on AWS and cannot be increased.

> **Note**
>
> The creation of local users or groups on the `vmc.local` domain is not supported.

To authenticate using a user or a member of a group other than the `cloudadmin@vmc.local` user, we have a couple of options:

- Use federated login with CSP (version 1.22 onward): `https://vmc.techzone.vmware.com/resource/feature-brief-vcenter-federated-login-vmware-cloud-aws`.

- Use **Cloud Gateway Appliance** (**CGA**) and configure **Hybrid Linked Mode** (**HLM**) with the on-premises vCenter SSO domain. You can check the process at `https://docs.vmware.com/en/VMware-Cloud/services/vmware-cloud-gateway-administration/GUID-91C57891-4D61-4F4C-B580-74F3000B831D.html`.

- Configure an external identity source such as an LDAP AD.

In this book, we will illustrate the third option as the first two options are adequately covered in the service documentation.

Let us go through the configuration of an external identity source in vCenter:

1. To start, we need to log in to the vCenter Web Client using the `cloudadmin` account and navigate to the **Administration** section on the left-hand menu, as seen in the following screenshot:

Figure 4.39 – vCenter Administration section

2. Afterward, go to **Single Sign-On | Configuration** and **Identity Sources**. Here, we can click on **ADD** and configure another LDAP identity source, as seen in the following screenshot:

Figure 4.40 – Identity sources under the vCenter Administration section

The configurations corresponding with this managed AD service can be seen in the following screenshot:

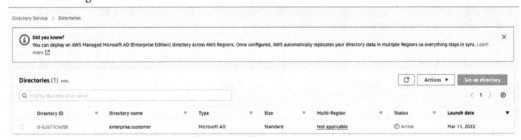

Figure 4.41 – AWS managed AD setup

The preconfigured AD has the domain name of enterprise.customer, with an admin account of admin and two endpoints – one on each AZ for redundancy purposes. The vCenter configuration is reflected in the following screenshot:

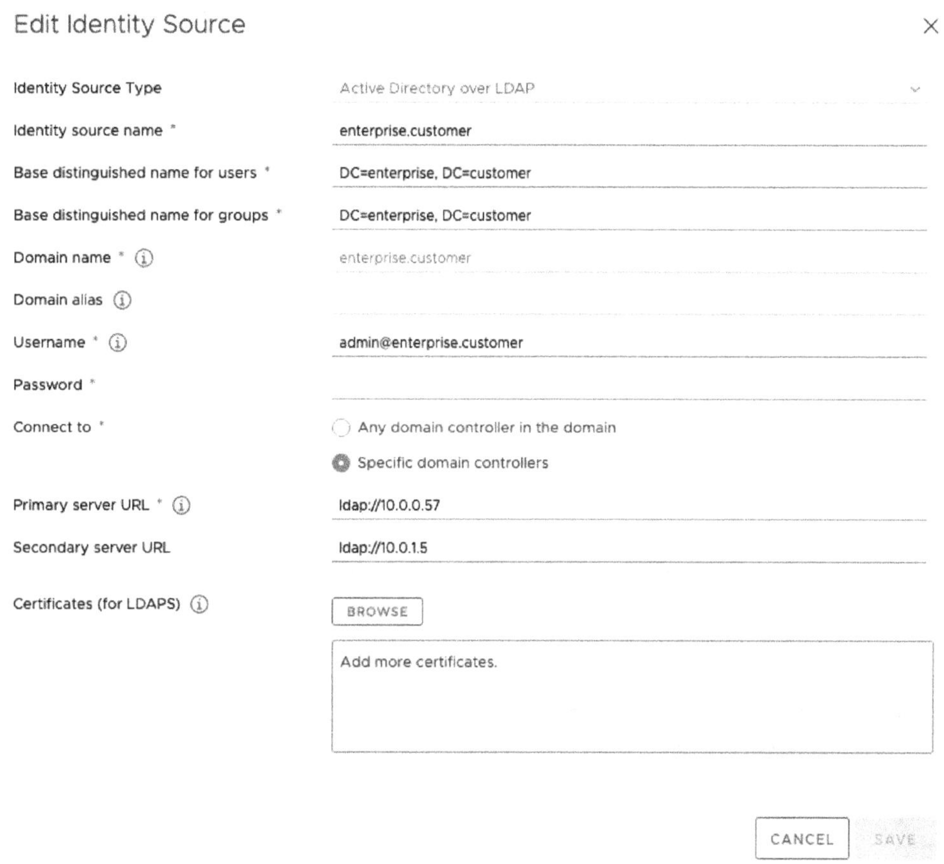

Edit Identity Source   ✕

Identity Source Type	Active Directory over LDAP
Identity source name *	enterprise.customer
Base distinguished name for users *	DC=enterprise, DC=customer
Base distinguished name for groups *	DC=enterprise, DC=customer
Domain name * ⓘ	enterprise.customer
Domain alias ⓘ	
Username * ⓘ	admin@enterprise.customer
Password *	
Connect to *	◯ Any domain controller in the domain
	◉ Specific domain controllers
Primary server URL * ⓘ	ldap://10.0.0.57
Secondary server URL	ldap://10.0.1.5
Certificates (for LDAPS) ⓘ	BROWSE

Add more certificates.

CANCEL   SAVE

Figure 4.42 – Identity source AD details – vCenter

In the following example, we associate the admin user with the CloudAdmin role and click on **Propagate to children** to apply this on the entire vCenter hierarchy of objects, as seen in the following screenshot:

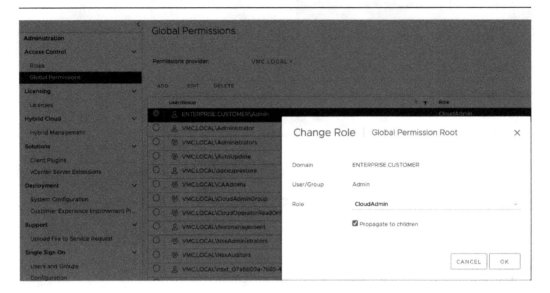

Figure 4.43 – Global permission association in vCenter

Next, with the configurations in the previous steps completed, log in to vCenter with the **ENTERPRISE. CUSTOMER** *Admin* domain user. In the following screenshot, you can see that the login is successful, and the user can view the vCenter hierarchy with the **CloudAdmin** role:

Figure 4.44 – vCenter login with the enterprise.customer admin user

RBAC and identity management on CSP

CSP leverages a different authentication flow. The CSP default identity source is the My VMware accounts. Administrators who require access to the VMware Cloud Services Console need to hold a My VMware account and be invited to the Organization. The IAM is managed from the CSP portal under **Identity & Access Management**, under the **Active Users** section. We can add new users and assign them their corresponding roles and permissions. In the following example, we add a new user to the VMware Cloud service with the **Administrator** and **NSX Cloud Admin** roles:

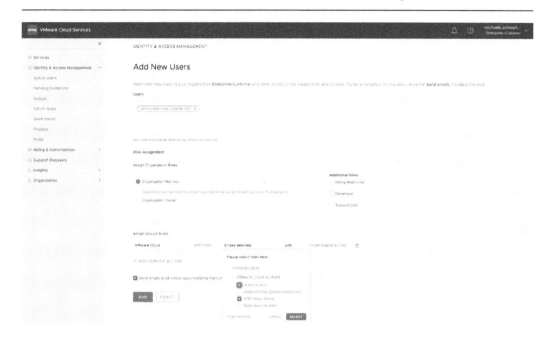

Figure 4.45 – CSP adding new users to the VMware Cloud service

Once we click on **ADD**, the administrator will receive an invite email to the service. Our example will be visible in the **Pending Invitations** tab because the administrators does not have an active My VMware account and will need to create one to use the invite, as seen in the screenshot:

Figure 4.46 – CSP adding new users to VMware Cloud pending invitations

Another authentication flow is to federate CSP with an external IDP identity provider such as Azure AD or Okta and leverage the existing corporate domain authentication infrastructure.

To start the federation process, administrators need to go to their CSP Organization and click on **SET UP** to start the process, as seen in the following screenshot:

Figure 4.47 – Initiate enterprise federation from CSP

> **Information**
>
> The federation provisioning process creates a new federated Organization. Starting with version 1.22 of SDDC, you can federate CSP and vCenter and leverage accounts from the federated domains to authenticate to vCenter.

You can access VMware Cloud resources through their corporate credentials without storing them on CSP and leveraging MFA authentication procedures. The full configuration of the IDP federation is beyond the scope of this chapter.

Application deployment example

The following section describes how to deploy VM templates in vCenter and enable network connectivity. First, to deploy an application on vCenter, we'll need to upload templates and images to vCenter. In our example, we'll use the content library mechanism:

1. Log in to vCenter, navigate to the left-hand menu, and click on **CREATE**, as seen in the following screenshot:

Figure 4.48 – Content Libraries

2. Create a content library and specify the name:

Figure 4.49 – Create a content library

3. In our example, we'll choose **Subscribed content library** instead of hosting a local content library to sync an existing content library uploaded to S3. Using a master content library helps to manage the subscribed content library with corporate templates and quickly enables the distribution of required sources to start the deployment:

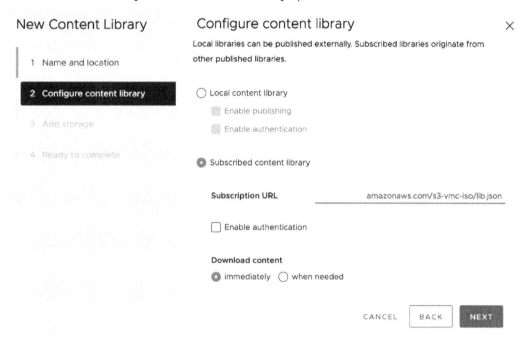

Figure 4.50 – Sync content library from S3

By default, the content library sync deployment will fail because of the connected VPC S3 endpoint redirect feature in VMware Cloud on AWS, as seen in the following screenshot:

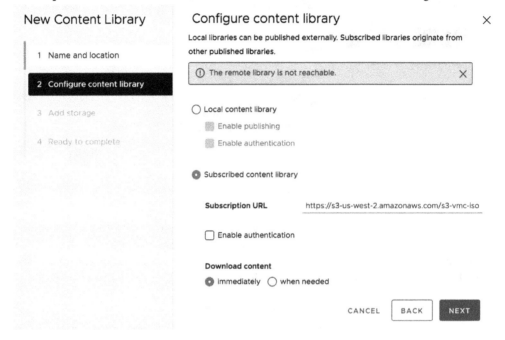

Figure 4.51 – Sync content library from S3 error

The preceding error will appear unless we turn the S3 redirect off or the connected VPC has an S3 endpoint terminated.

4. To disable the S3 redirect, navigate to the NSX Manager UI, select **Networking**, choose **Connected VPC** under **Cloud Services**, and confirm the **S3** radio button is disabled.

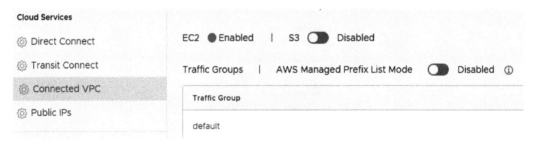

Figure 4.52 – Connected VPC

5. Afterward, continue with the S3 content library sync and click on **Next**.

6. To configure storage, select **WorkloadDatastore** to place the content library in the vSAN datastore. You can also add an NFS datastore and use it to store the content library:

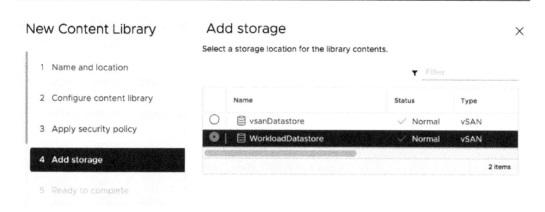

Figure 4.53 – Select the storage target datastore

7. Review the summary of the content library configuration, and click on **FINISH** to proceed, as seen in the following screenshot:

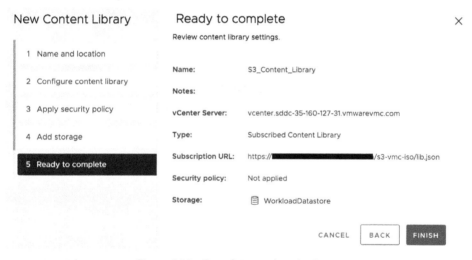

Figure 4.54 – Complete synchronizations

8. Once we have the content library synced to vCenter (this can take time, depending on the size and the number of templates), we can now deploy our first application, using an existing template, with MySQL, which resides in the content library:

Figure 4.55 – Deploy Windows Server from the content library

9. Right-click the template and start the deployment of a Windows DB server. Select the virtual
    machine name, specify the folder in vCenter, and click **NEXT**, as seen in the following screenshot:

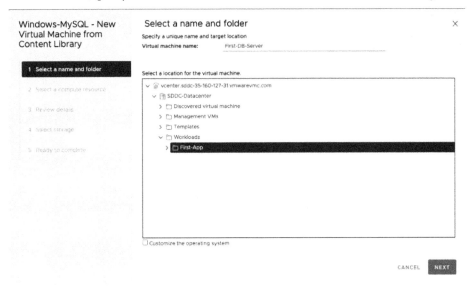

Figure 4.56 – Template deployment folder selection

> **Note**
>
> The **CloudAdmin** role doesn't have the permissions to create a VM in the `Discovered virtual machine` or `Management VMs` folders.

10. In the **Select a compute resource** section, select **Compute-ResourcePool**, as seen in the following screenshot:

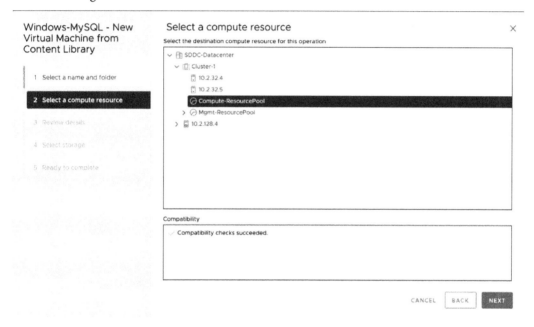

Figure 4.57 – VM deployment resource pool

> **Note**
>
> The **CloudAdmin** role doesn't have the permissions to create a VM in the **Mgmt-ResourcePool** resource.

11. In the **Select storage** section, select **WorkloadDatastore**, and the default VM storage policy will apply. We will discuss storage policies in the next chapter. Click on **NEXT**:

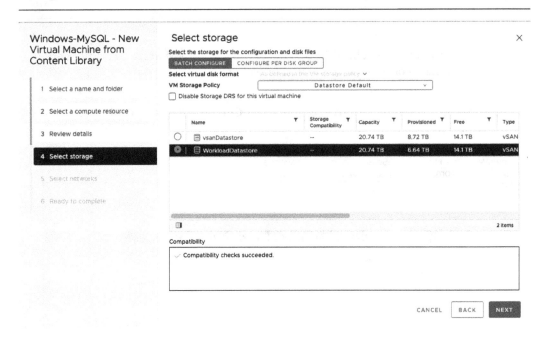

Figure 4.58 – Select storage datastore

> **Note**
>
> The **CloudAdmin** role doesn't have the permissions to create a VM on **vsanDatastore**.

12. In the **Select networks** section, we'll select a pre-provisioned network segment – **DB-Segment**:

Figure 4.59 – Select networks

13. Let's review the **Segments** section from the VMware Cloud SDDC console's **Networking and Security** tab. The segment is already preconfigured in our example, as seen in the following screenshot:

Figure 4.60 – Segment List

14. Review the summary of the VM deployment and click on the **FINISH** button to deploy the VM, as seen in the following screenshot:

Figure 4.61 – Confirm deployment details

Follow the same deployment process to deploy a web-app server VM and power on both VMs, as seen in the following screenshot:

Figure 4.62 – vCenter applications view

We have the application VMs turned on now. By default, VMs can communicate with each other inside the same segment but are not allowed to receive connections from any external networks. Now let us enable external connectivity to the web server VM. To do that, we will configure firewall rules using the Gateway Firewall and we will configure the following:

- Allow access from the web server VM to all external destinations
- Allow access from the internet to the website hosted on the web server VM

Two new rules are created to allow the VMs residing on the web segment to access all destinations and ingress access for the HTTPS service (port 443), applying the rules on the internet interface, as seen in the following screenshot:

Figure 4.63 – Connected VPC

Now let us enable external internet access through destination NAT toward the web-app server VM to make the website available for users:

1. First, we'll request a new public **Elastic IP (EIP)** in the **Public IPs** section and assign it a descriptive name, as seen in the following screenshot:

Figure 4.64 – Connected VPC

2. Second, create a destination NAT rule in the **Internet** NAT rules section, and the rule will map the internal IP address of the web-app VM to the EIP and forward port 443 traffic toward it:

Figure 4.65 – Connected VPC

Now the application will be accessible from the internet using the EIP.

Summary

In this chapter, you got familiar with the steps required to start consuming VMware Cloud on AWS, including onboarding to the CSP portal, provisioning your first SDDC, providing access to the SDDC management components, and deploying your first application.

In the next chapter, you will learn how to manage a **Software Defined Data Center** (**SDDC**), VM storage policies, compute policies, and the **Elastic Distributed Resource Scheduler** (**EDRS**) mechanism for automatically scaling the cluster based on resource usage through the VMware Cloud Services Console.

You will also learn about the essential management of workloads, vSAN storage, and hosts and clusters required for day-to-day operations.

5
Configuring vCenter, vSAN, and VMware Cloud Console

This chapter focuses on how to manage a **Software-Defined Data Center** (**SDDC**), VM Storage Policies, compute policies, and the **Elastic Distributed Resource Scheduler** (**Elastic DRS**) mechanism for automatically scaling the cluster based on resource usage through the **VMware Cloud** (**VMC**) console.

You will learn about the essential management of workloads, vSAN storage, and hosts and clusters required for day-to-day operations.

The following are the topics to be covered in this chapter:

- Managing VMware Cloud on AWS
- vSAN storage policies
- Compute policies
- Contacting VMware for support and maintenance

Managing VMware Cloud on AWS

VMware Cloud on AWS management and operations are possible using several management consoles, including the following:

- The familiar VMware vSphere Web Client to manage workloads (VMs) in your deployment
- An SDDC console to manage capacity, activate add-ons, and configure advanced options for your deployment
- A separate standalone NSX UI to manage networking in your SDDC, including creating workload segments, external connectivity, firewall configuration, and troubleshooting

In this chapter, we cover the functionality of the SDDC console. In the first section, we'll go through the various aspects of the configuration of an SDDC.

SDDC console overview

Once the VMware Cloud on AWS SDDC is deployed in a VMware Cloud Organization, you will use the central **Cloud Services Portal** (**CSP**) under the VMware Cloud service to manage your SDDC deployment. The following screenshot shows a VMware Cloud SDDC console view:

Figure 5.1 – VMware Cloud on AWS SDDC console view

> **Information**
> Here is the SDDC console URL: `https://vmc.vmware.com/console`.

The SDDC console features the following configuration elements (tabs):

- **Summary**
- **Networking & Security**
- **Storage**
- **Elasticity**
- **Integrated Services**
- **Maintenance**
- **Troubleshooting**
- **Settings**
- **Support**

Summary tab

In the **Summary** tab, you will find the aggregated count of the total number of clusters, hosts, CPU, memory, and raw storage resources. Additionally, this tab also shows the applied cluster Elastic DRS policy, Tanzu Kubernetes Grid activation status, and Microsoft **Services Provider License Agreement** (**SPLA**) licenses activation status.

> **Information**
>
> Tanzu Kubernetes Grid activation and management will be covered in *Chapter 7*.

Networking & Security tab

The **Networking & Security** tab now features a set of dashboards that help monitor the network configuration and status. This dashboard replaces the legacy **Networking & Security** tab functionality, improving SDDC console performance and providing a single view of the network configuration. To manage networking in your SDDC, you will use the standalone NSX Manager UI.

Storage tab

The **Storage** tab has been recently introduced to the SDDC console. This tab enables the workflow to map an external NFS datastore to your SDDC.

> **Note**
>
> Attaching a datastore to the SDDC is only available via the SDDC console. You cannot run this workflow through the vSphere Web Client.

Elasticity tab

The recently added **Elasticity** tab (available on all SDDCs starting from version 1.18) simplifies managing Elastic DRS configuration, enhances visibility into Elastic DRS settings, and enables the creation of custom Elastic DRS policies. There will be more on the Elastic DRS later in this chapter.

Integrated Services tab

The **Integrated Services** tab (previously called the **Add-On** tab) lists the available services and provides a way to activate service deployment. Currently available add-ons are shown in *Figure 5.2*.

> **Note**
>
> Some services (such as VMware HCX) are available free of charge, and some (such as NSX Advanced Firewall) require separate subscriptions. The list of services included with a VMware Cloud on AWS subscription is constantly changing. Please check the VMware documentation for the latest updates.

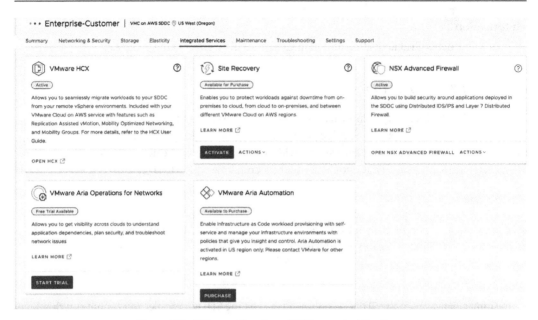

Figure 5.2 – VMware Cloud on AWS Integrated Services

Maintenance tab

VMware manages the life cycle of your SDDC, including security patches, version updates, and other service activities. The **Maintenance** tab improves visibility into service operations and allows customers to request a maintenance operation or postpone a planned upgrade. Check this tab regularly to ensure that you are prepared for upcoming maintenance in your SDDC.

Troubleshooting tab

The **Troubleshooting** tab provides access to a set of automatic networking tests, helping customers establish **hybrid-linked mode** (**HLM**) and check connectivity with on-premises management services such as Active Directory, DNS, and vCenter. It is recommended to run these tests on hybrid cloud deployments after establishing connectivity with the on-premises vSphere environment using a VPN or AWS Direct Connect.

Settings tab

The **Settings** tab allows access to different SDDC advanced configuration settings, including SDDC appliance size, vCenter information, FQDN resolution, default vCenter user credentials, PowerCLI connection endpoint, and NSX information, to list a few. Note the changed location for some settings compared to the previous version of SDDC.

The SDDC appliance size can be upgraded from **Medium** to **Large** for SDDCs with more than four hosts, which is a prerequisite for the multi-edge feature that is used to improve the network throughput of NSX Edge.

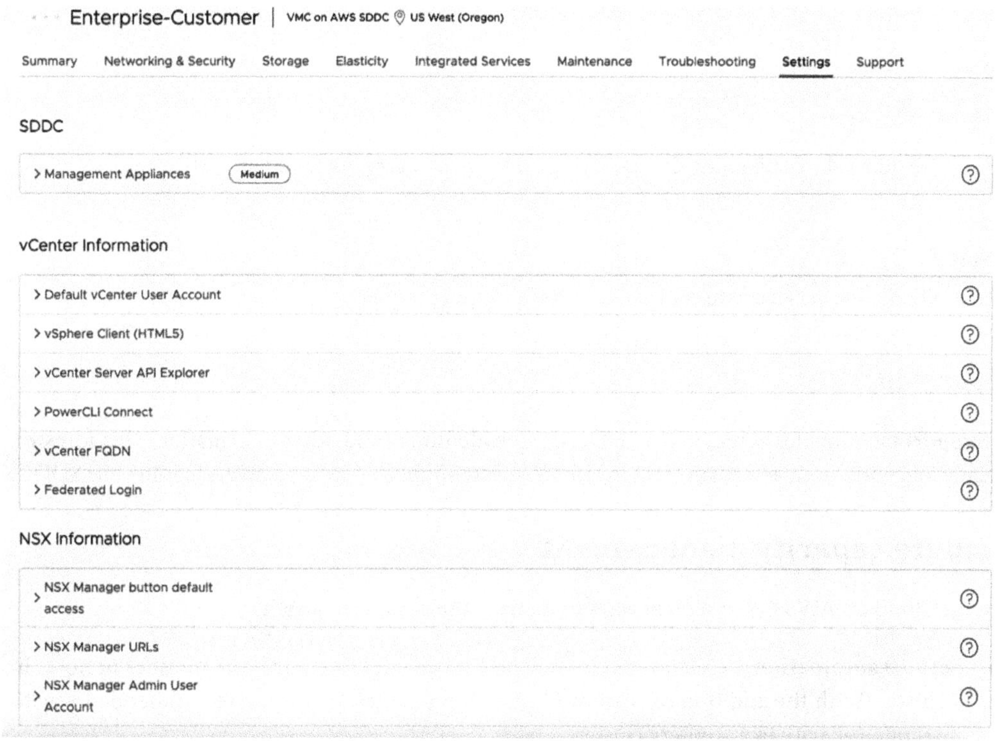

Figure 5.3 – VMware Cloud on AWS configuration Settings tab

Compliance Hardening

VMware Cloud on AWS supports several regulatory compliance attestations, including **Payment Card Industry Data Security Standard** (**PCI DSS**). Some of the compliance certifications (such as PCI DCC) have a special set of requirements, both on the Organization and the SDDC level. While VMware performs Organization-level hardening upon request (with a prerequisite of a new Organization without an SDDC), customers are responsible for the SDDC configuration. Depending on the compliance requirement, you may be required to disable access to **Network & Security Tab Access**, HCX Service, Site Recovery Service v8.4 compatibility (versions earlier than 8.5), and Federated Login Feature. You can disable them in the Compliance Hardening section of the **Settings** tab.

Figure 5.4 – Configuring Compliance Hardening for a VMware Cloud on AWS SDDC

> **Note**
>
> To re-enable the service, you may need to file a support request.

Support tab

The **Support** tab provides access to the SDDC unique identifiers and other information (IP addresses, currently logged-in user, and so on) required for VMware support to help resolve issues in your SDDC.

Compute capacity management

VMware Cloud on AWS offers several ways to manage the compute capacity:

- **Service automation** – Customers can rely on Elastic DRS to control the number of hosts in a cluster. With the addition of custom Elastic DRS policies, this is the recommended way to maintain capacity in a vSphere cluster.

- **External automation using APIs** – Customers can use the automation tools of their choice (such as Terraform) to control the capacity of the SDDC. In this case, we recommend using the default Elastic DRS Baseline policy to avoid possible conflicts between different automation tools.

- **Manual** – Through the SDDC console, customers can initiate cluster scale-in and scale-out, add a cluster to an existing SDDC, or create a new SDDC. Manually controlling the number of hosts in a cluster is possible but not recommended since it may lead to underutilization of the capacity or unnecessary billing of compute resources before the workload consumes these resources. However, in several use cases, you might want to add hosts either manually or using Elastic DRS, such as before migrating critical workloads to make sure that the SDDC is scaled out ahead of time in anticipation of intense workloads.

Adding hosts to a cluster (scale-up)

To expand an existing cluster, click on the SDDC tile, and then click **Add Host** on the corresponding **Cluster-1** tile; A warning pops up indicating that Elastic DRS is enabled on the cluster, which would ideally handle additional compute or storage demands by triggering the addition of one or more hosts to the cluster. Select **CONTINUE** to manually increase the capacity of the cluster, as seen in the following screenshot:

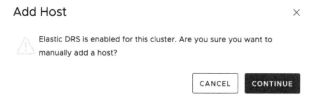

Figure 5.5 – Cluster Add Host operation Elastic DRS warning

Next, select the number of hosts you would like to add to the cluster from the drop-down list. We have selected two hosts, and we'll review a summary of the total capacity about to be added to the cluster, as can be seen in the following screenshot:

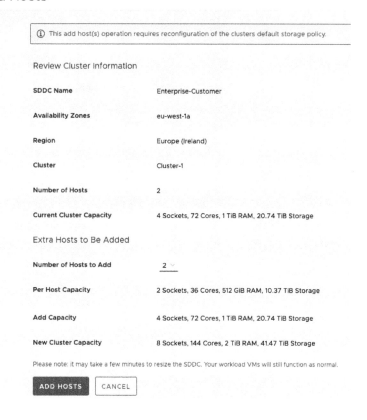

Figure 5.6 – Cluster Add Hosts configuration

> **Information**
>
> You cannot mix different host types in the same vSphere cluster – for example, i3 and i3en.

Click on **ADD HOSTS**, and the capacity expansion process immediately starts. It takes approximately 15 minutes to add a host to an existing cluster.

> **Information**
>
> The expansion of single-host or two-host clusters takes longer than multi-host cluster expansions because of the conversion process that mandates a change in the cluster topology and redundancy configurations.

At the end of the process, the cluster CPU, memory, and storage resources will increase, the host-related networking will be automatically configured, and the progress notification will appear in the console until the operation is completed, as seen in the following screenshot:

Figure 5.7 – Adding host(s) task in progress notification

When manually scaling your SDDC in or out, the following limitations apply:

- Clusters can contain up to 16 hosts. The minimal cluster size is two hosts for a production SDDC.
- A cluster cannot be scaled back to a single host SDDC.
- Manual host additions/removals might not work if Elastic DRS operation is in progress.
- Host addition or deletion operations may temporarily disable some SDDC operations until completion.

Removing hosts from a cluster

A cluster can scale down to two hosts. The workloads must fit the scaled-down cluster from the perspective of the storage capacity.

> **Information**
>
> Host removal operation takes longer than adding a host, as workloads must be evacuated from the removed host before removing it from the cluster. Also, sufficient storage capacity must be available on the remaining cluster for a successful removal operation.

Adding clusters

Another method for adding capacity to an SDDC is to create a new cluster. To do this, click the **ADD CLUSTER** button on the SDDC console. A single SDDC can have one or more clusters with different host types. For example, you can deploy the first cluster using i4i and the second using i3en host types to accommodate both general-purpose workloads and storage-bound workloads.

Note that only the first cluster can host the management components of the SDDC. The capacity of all additional clusters is fully available for customer workloads. Furthermore, the SDDC features listed below are NOT available on the first cluster of the SDDC; they are only available on the additional clusters:

- Custom CPU Core Count: This allows organizations to run a reduced number of CPU cores to run per host compared to the number of physical cores on the host.

- Full Capacity Compute and Storage: The management workloads (vCenter, NSX, HCX, SRM, etc.) consume a certain amount of compute and storage from the first cluster of every SDDC. The additional clusters do not have management workloads running on them.

Also currently, it is possible to provision only one 2-host cluster per SDDC. Additionally, the 2-host cluster is restricted to being the initial cluster created within the SDDC. The additional clusters will have to run a minimum of three host configurations.

The following screenshot shows the details of the **Add Cluster** operation where the custom core count is defined:

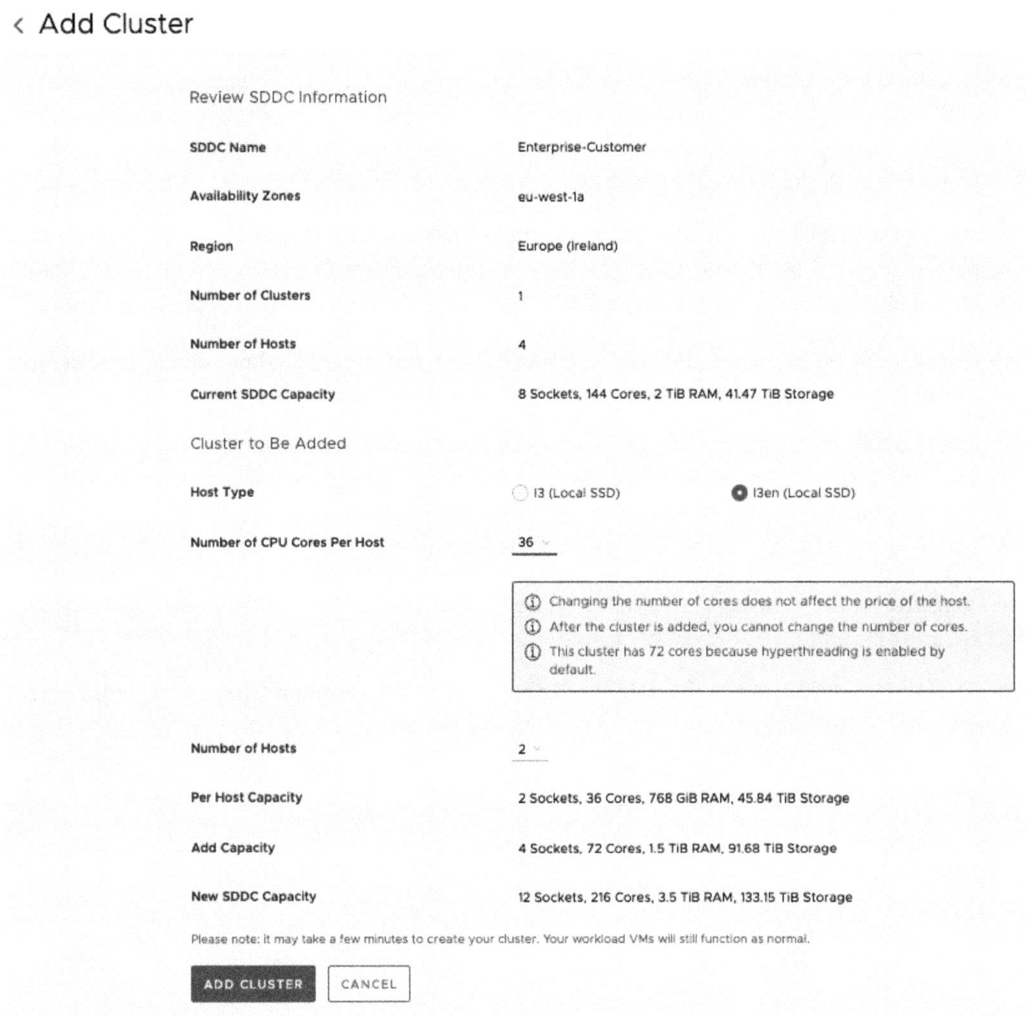

< Add Cluster

Review SDDC Information

SDDC Name	Enterprise-Customer
Availability Zones	eu-west-1a
Region	Europe (Ireland)
Number of Clusters	1
Number of Hosts	4
Current SDDC Capacity	8 Sockets, 144 Cores, 2 TiB RAM, 41.47 TiB Storage

Cluster to Be Added

Host Type	○ I3 (Local SSD) ● I3en (Local SSD)
Number of CPU Cores Per Host	36 ⌄

> ⓘ Changing the number of cores does not affect the price of the host.
> ⓘ After the cluster is added, you cannot change the number of cores.
> ⓘ This cluster has 72 cores because hyperthreading is enabled by default.

Number of Hosts	2 ⌄
Per Host Capacity	2 Sockets, 36 Cores, 768 GiB RAM, 45.84 TiB Storage
Add Capacity	4 Sockets, 72 Cores, 1.5 TiB RAM, 91.68 TiB Storage
New SDDC Capacity	12 Sockets, 216 Cores, 3.5 TiB RAM, 133.15 TiB Storage

Please note: it may take a few minutes to create your cluster. Your workload VMs will still function as normal.

ADD CLUSTER   CANCEL

Figure 5.8 – Adding a cluster with two i3en hosts

Here are some design considerations when configuring a custom CPU core:

- The host price is not affected by reducing the number of cores.

- The CPU custom cores per host cannot be modified on the first cluster but can on additional clusters. After creating a cluster, the CPU core count cannot be changed.

- The custom CPU core count is applied to all hosts in the cluster. If you add additional hosts to an existing cluster, all the newly added hosts will inherit the custom core count.

After the operation is completed, we will see two separate clusters in the SDDC console, as seen in the following screenshot:

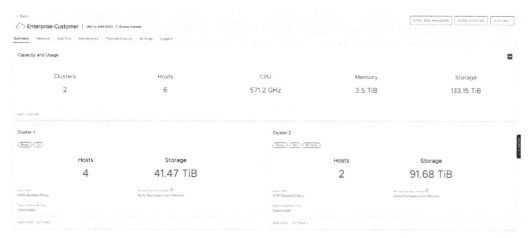

Figure 5.9 – VMware Cloud on AWS SDDC console view with multiple clusters

Delete cluster

Customers can remove any additional clusters in an SDDC except for the initial cluster, which is named **Cluster-1** by default. The **Delete Cluster** operation can be executed from the SDDC console under the cluster's **ACTIONS** drop-down menu, as seen in the following screenshot:

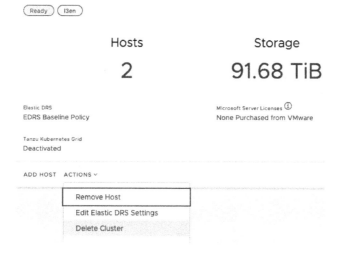

Figure 5.10 – Delete Cluster action

> **Information**
>
> The **Delete Cluster** operation does not evacuate data from the cluster but instead deletes all data immediately. Before deleting a cluster, either back up any VMs you want to retain or migrate VMs to another cluster. You cannot roll back a cluster deletion process.

Here are some considerations to take into account when deleting a cluster:

- All workload VMs in the cluster are immediately terminated, and all the data and cluster configuration will be deleted
- Public IP addresses associated with VMs in the cluster are released

A warning details the consequences of deleting the cluster. The cluster will be deleted once you acknowledge the consequences by checking the boxes and then press the **DELETE CLUSTER** button to confirm the operation, as seen in the following screenshot:

Delete Cluster-2   ✕

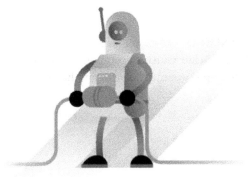

This action cannot be undone. Please confirm that you are aware of the consequences of deleting your cluster.

☑ All workloads in this cluster will be terminated.
☑ You will lose all data and configuration settings in this cluster.
☑ You will lose all UI and API access to this cluster.
☑ All public IP addresses for this cluster will be released.

CANCEL   DELETE CLUSTER

Figure 5.11 – Delete Cluster-2 confirmation

Managing compute capacity with Elastic DRS

The Elastic DRS is a unique differentiator capability of VMware Cloud on AWS. The Elastic DRS service combines the functionality of vSphere DRS with the elastic capacity of public clouds. By constantly monitoring host and storage utilization in the vSphere cluster, Elastic DRS prevents capacity and performance shortages and automatically accommodates the increase in capacity. It is also capable of scaling in a cluster to control costs.

The Elastic DRS algorithm runs every five minutes and can account for random utilization spikes. Additionally, there is a 30-minute delay for a scale-up and a 3-hour wait for subsequent scale-in events.

Elastic DRS settings are applied per cluster. Control over Elastic DRS configuration has now moved to the **Elasticity** tab, as outlined previously.

Figure 5.12 – Managing custom Elastic DRS policies

Each cluster has a default Elastic DRS baseline policy assigned upon creation. The default baseline policy only monitors for storage and initiates the expansion of the cluster only once the storage utilization reaches 80%.

> **Note**
> Disabling Elastic DRS at the cluster level is not supported. Furthermore, it is not possible to adjust the upper threshold for storage utilization beyond 80%.

VMware Cloud on AWS provides flexible configurations for Elastic DRS to accommodate the specific design requirements of your workload while meeting performance, capacity, and cost considerations. You have the option to configure Elastic DRS using predefined policies, although the defined thresholds within these policies cannot be modified. Alternatively, you can create custom Elastic DRS policies to tailor the configuration according to your specific needs.

Please be aware that when using custom or predefined Elastic DRS policies, a scale-out action will only be triggered if *any* of the defined thresholds are reached. In contrast, the scale-in action will only be triggered if *all* the defined metrics drop below their respective thresholds. It's important to note that all metrics are monitored at the host level.

Elastic DRS baseline policy

By default, this policy is enabled and cannot be disabled. When the vSAN utilization reaches 80%, Elastic DRS will automatically trigger a process to add a host. This proactive measure guarantees that there is sufficient available *slack* storage in the vSAN to accommodate the growth of the applications' storage requirements.

> **Information**
>
> VMware mandates a minimum of 20% of unused space, known as **slack space**, to be maintained within the vSAN datastore, in order to ensure smooth operation of the SDDC. It is crucial to have sufficient slack space in the vSAN datastore for its proper utilization. In the event that the free storage space reaches or falls below 25%, there is a risk that the customer may lose the ability to use the SDDC, rendering the environment inoperable. To prevent any harm to the SDDC, if the unused space in an SDDC vSAN datastore drops to 30% or below, VMware will automatically add hosts to the SDDC.

Optimize for Best Performance policy

To ensure a consistent application performance, it is recommended to enable this policy. Once the cluster utilization of CPU, memory, or storage reaches the defined threshold, Elastic DRS will initiate a scale-out action. This proactive measure guarantees a consistent performance of the underlying compute infrastructure. You can check the policy configuration in the following figure:

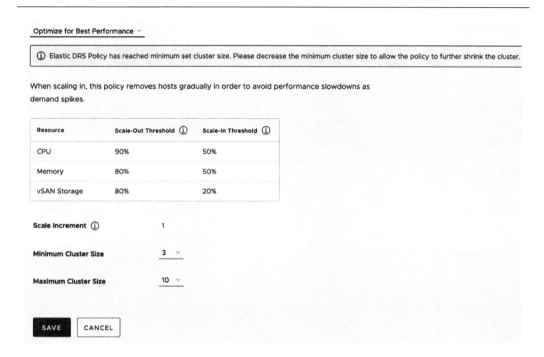

Figure 5.13 – Optimize for Best Performance Elastic DRS policy settings

Optimize for Lowest Cost policy

This policy applies the same high threshold as the previous one, but it features significantly more aggressive lower thresholds. Utilizing this policy can result in a considerably higher VM density per host. You can check the policy configuration in the following figure:

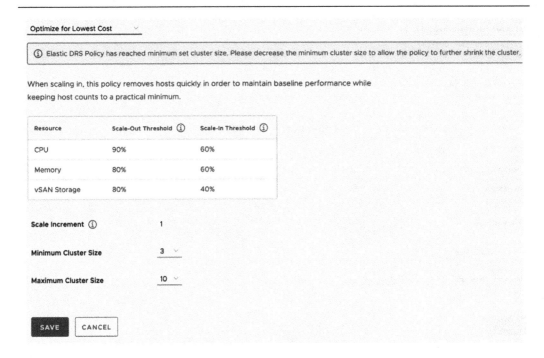

Figure 5.14 – Optimize for Lowest Cost Elastic DRS policy settings

Rapid Scaling policy

All Elastic DRS policies are set up to scale out clusters incrementally, adding one host at a time. However, the Rapid Scaling policy offers a faster response by adding hosts in parallel, making it more convenient to quickly scale out. With this policy, you have the option to add multiple hosts simultaneously, choosing between 4, 8, or 12 hosts. Please note that adding 12 hosts to a cluster may take up to 40 minutes. You can check the policy configuration in the following figure:

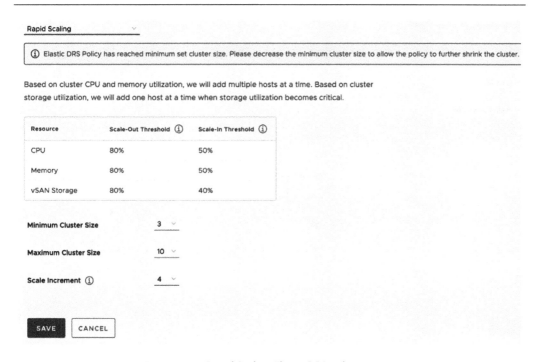

Figure 5.15 – Rapid Scaling Elastic DRS policy settings

Rapid Scaling is the policy of your choice for **Disaster Recovery** (**DR**) or **Virtual Desktop Infrastructure** (**VDI**) use cases.

Custom Managed Elastic DRS policy

In addition to the default Elastic DRS policies, VMware Cloud on AWS provides customers with the capability to create custom Elastic DRS policies that are specifically designed to meet their unique requirements. The following settings can be customized:

- Minimum and maximum cluster size

- Scale increment (up to 6 hosts, with 12 hosts available only with Rapid Scaling)

- Definitions of scale-out and scale-in thresholds for CPU, memory, and storage (note: the upper threshold for storage cannot exceed 80%)

- Option to enable or disable scale-in functionality

The following figure shows the different configuration options that are available to you when creating a custom Elastic DRS policy:

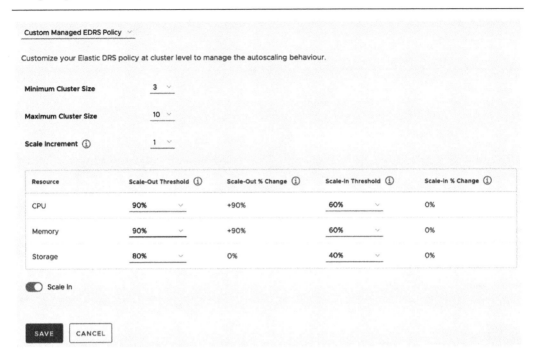

Figure 5.16 – Custom Managed Elastic DRS policy configuration

Custom Elastic DRS policies provide a flexible means to manage capacity within your SDDC. However, we strongly advise conducting thorough testing on all settings, particularly the high and low thresholds. This ensures that you avoid potential performance issues resulting from overly aggressive scale-in thresholds, while also preventing unnecessary costs due to scale-out thresholds that are too lenient. It is crucial to strike the right balance by carefully assessing and fine-tuning these settings.

Elastic DRS notifications

When a scaling event takes place, various types of notifications are generated, and these can be viewed in the **Activity Log** tab within the SDDC console. You can refer to the following screenshot to see an example of how these notifications are displayed:

Figure 5.17 – VMware Cloud on AWS SDDC Activity Log Elastic DRS provisioning of ESX host

In addition, members of the organization receive email notifications regarding Elastic DRS events. An example of an Elastic DRS notification email is shown in the following screenshot:

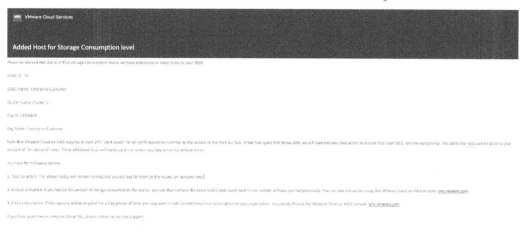

Figure 5.18 – Elastic DRS email notification

Customers can manage their email notifications in the VMware Cloud on AWS console by accessing the **Notification Preferences** tab, as shown in the following screenshot:

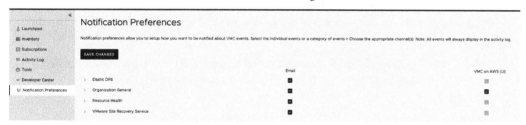

Figure 5.19 – VMware Cloud on AWS Notification Preferences settings

Users will receive a notification on the VMware Cloud console to stay informed about Elastic DRS events.

Microsoft licensing

Licensing Microsoft software in public cloud environments can be a complex task, as it involves considering different terms and conditions associated with various licensing agreements. While this book does not aim to serve as a comprehensive licensing guide, it offers guidelines and an approach to licensing Microsoft software (specifically Windows Server and Microsoft SQL Server) when deploying on or migrating to VMware Cloud on AWS.

Customers may have the option to bring their own Microsoft licenses (BYOL) and leverage their existing licensing agreements. The eligibility to bring licenses is determined by the License Mobility benefit of Software Assurance and the specific agreements in place. It is strongly recommended to obtain the license agreement with Microsoft and consult with vendors (such as VMware, AWS, and Microsoft) to confirm the terms and conditions, as they can vary significantly between customers and product families.

Customers who are unable to utilize their existing licenses have the option to purchase licenses directly through VMware. Specifically, they can acquire licenses for two types of software: Windows Server and SQL Server.

When activating Microsoft licenses provided by VMware, there are several important design considerations to keep in mind:

- Activation is done per cluster, meaning that all hosts within a cluster must be licensed.

- Customers are not charged for maintenance hosts during remediation and upgrade tasks.

- Once the cluster has been licensed, there are no restrictions on the number of Windows Server or SQL Server installations per cluster.

- To optimize licensing costs, it can be advantageous to allocate a dedicated cluster within the infrastructure for running Microsoft workloads, especially when there is a mixture of Windows and non-Windows workloads. Segregating Microsoft workloads in their own cluster allows for better management of licensing requirements and potential cost savings.

- SQL Server and Windows Server have distinct terms, conditions, and pricing. Customers have the option to purchase licenses for Windows Server, SQL Server, or both, based on their specific requirements.

- The Custom CPU Core Count feature of the SDDC does not reduce the number of licenses required. Customers will be billed for the full number of cores associated with the selected host type.

- It is important to exercise caution when enabling the Microsoft licensing provided by VMware, as billing will commence even if there are no VMs with Windows Server or SQL Server deployed or running in the cluster.

Taking these considerations into account will help ensure a smooth and optimized utilization of Microsoft licenses within the VMware environment.

> **Information**
>
> More comprehensive information regarding **Service Provider License Agreement (SPLA)** licensing can be found in VMware's documentation or on the official VMware website at `https://docs.vmware.com/en/VMware-Cloud-on-AWS/services/com.vmware.vmc-aws-operations/GUID-86284D4F-18E8-4659-B7D4-E7B483D5625C.html`.

In order to utilize Microsoft licenses provided by VMware, it is necessary to activate them on a specific cluster within the SDDC. To activate the licenses, follow these steps:

1. Click on the **Edit Microsoft Server Licenses** option.

2. On the subsequent screen, select the desired license types, such as **Windows Server License** and **SQL Server License**.

3. Click on the **SAVE** button to confirm the activation.

    Please note that billing for the licenses will commence immediately upon clicking the **SAVE** button.

Figure 5.20 – Microsoft Server Licenses confirmation

Upon successful activation, the cluster card in the SDDC console will reflect the updated licensing information for Microsoft server licenses. If needed, it is possible to deactivate Microsoft server licenses at any time. However, please note that to do so, you must remove all instances of Windows Server and SQL Server software from the vSphere cluster before the end of the calendar month. You can view the SPLA status in the cluster settings, as shown in the following screenshot:

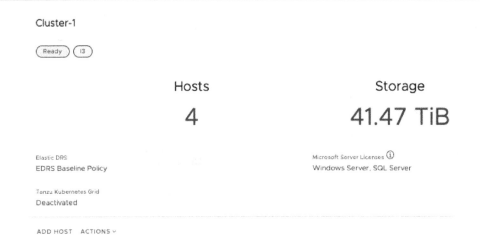

Figure 5.21 – Microsoft Server Licenses activation view

As we are exploring VMware Cloud on AWS configuration, it's time to start with the storage.

vSAN storage policies

Virtual SAN (vSAN) is a key component of VMware Cloud on AWS, providing software-defined storage capabilities. All the ESXi hosts in a cluster establish communication through a dedicated vSAN network. By combining their disk groups, the hosts are consolidated into the vSAN datastore, which employs a **non-volatile memory express (NVMe)** all-flash configuration for cache and capacity tiers.

Datastores serve as logical storage containers for storing VM files. They provide a standardized approach to storing VM files, abstracting the underlying storage system details. Additionally, datastores are useful for housing content libraries containing ISO images and VM templates.

The vSAN **Object Store Filesystem (OSFS)** allows the combination of **Virtual Machine File System (VMFS)** volumes from each host into a single datastore, enabling streamlined management.

To leverage the capabilities of vSAN, customers can configure **VM Storage Policies** tailored to their workload's availability, performance requirements, and adherence to VMware Cloud on AWS **service-level agreement (SLA)** requirements.

VM Storage Policies establish the specific storage requirements for your VMs and VMDK files, ensuring that your VMs receive the necessary level of service based on the vSAN storage policy applied. Key capabilities of storage policies are as follows:

- The configuration of VM Storage Policies is determined by the cluster architecture, such as the number of hosts or the presence of a stretch cluster configuration
- When deploying a VM, specific policies can be assigned to meet its storage requirements

- Customers have the flexibility to modify policies for a VM even after it has been deployed
- By default, a VM is assigned the default datastore VM storage policy unless an alternative policy is specified during the provisioning process

The default vSAN policy operates according to the following principles:

- Tolerance represents the minimum threshold of failures that can be withstood while still complying with the VMware Cloud on AWS SLA
- Each object is configured with a single disk stripe
- The storage space reservation is set to thin-provisioned

The following diagram shows a representation of how a storage policy is applied to a VM or VMDK file in a vSAN cluster:

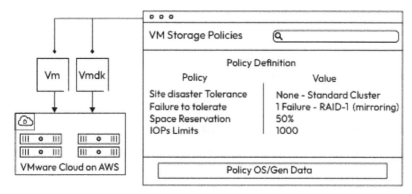

Figure 5.22 – VM Storage Policies

To manage the VM Storage Policies from **vSphere Client**, navigate to **Policies and Profiles** and select **VM Storage Policies**. This will display a list of preconfigured policies, as shown in the following screenshot:

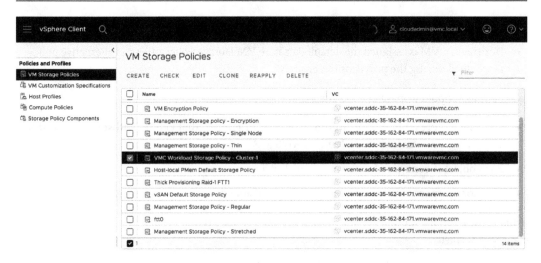

Figure 5.23 – VM Storage Policies in vSphere Client

The first parameter that customers need to configure for a vSAN policy is **failures to tolerate** (**FTT**). The available options to choose from include the following:

- No failures: **No data redundancy**
- One failure: **RAID-1 (Mirroring)** – the default value
- One failure: **RAID-5 (Erasure Coding)**
- Two failures: **RAID-1 (Mirroring)**
- Two failures: **RAID-6 (Erasure Coding)**
- Three failures: **RAID-1 (Mirroring)**

The policy combines the FTT and the RAID methods. In the case of stretched clusters, there is protection against a single availability zone failure. The **Site disaster tolerance** parameter is used to define stretched clusters, as shown in the following screenshot:

Figure 5.24 – VM Storage Policies vSAN Availability parameters

In the **Advanced Policy Rules** tab, the configuration includes space reservation options such as thin or thick provisioning and IOPS throttling settings. When provisioning VMs, each datastore is assigned a default VM storage policy. The configuration of the default policy can be viewed and modified by clicking on the storage datastore and then the **Configure** tab and the **General** option.

For the first cluster, the default policy will be named **VMC Workload Storage Policy - Cluster-1**, as shown in the following screenshot:

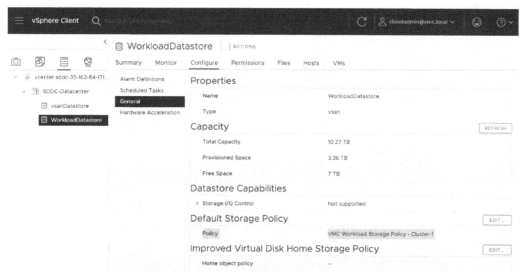

Figure 5.25 – VM Default Storage Policy

Information

While it is not recommended, the default cluster policy can be modified by using the **EDIT** button.

When creating a new VM, the default policy will be automatically selected, and it can be changed in the **Select storage** section, as shown in the following screenshot:

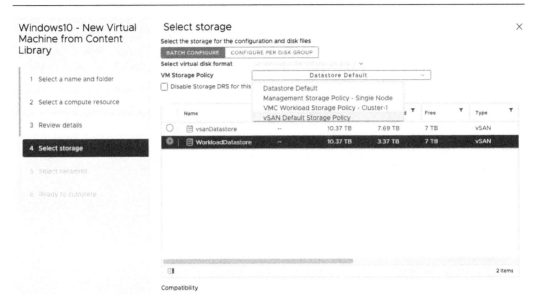

Figure 5.26 – New VM provisioning

To verify and modify the VM policy applied to an existing provisioned VM, you can right-click on the VM and choose **VM Policies**, then select **Edit VM Storage Policies…**, as shown in the following screenshot:

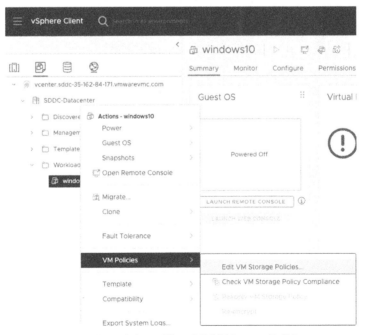

Figure 5.27 – vSphere Client Edit VM Storage Policies

After clicking on **Edit VM Storage Policies…**, you will be able to view the consumed space per VM and disk in this section. Furthermore, you can simulate the impact on storage consumption by modifying the VM policy, such as transitioning from thin provisioning to thick provisioning, as shown in the following screenshot:

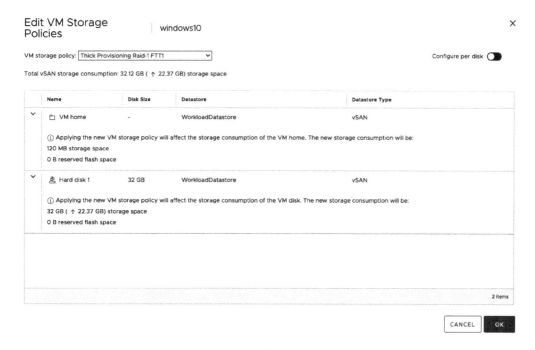

Figure 5.28 – Modifying the VM policy

Alternatively, the VM storage policy can also be changed by editing the **Hard Disk** configuration of a VM from the VM settings.

Information

When designing the storage sizing for VMs in the vSAN datastore, it is crucial to take into account the storage implications of RAID policies. For instance, the default RAID-1 policy applied to a 10 GB VM disk will utilize 20 GB of storage in the vSAN datastore.

When changing VM Storage Policies for multiple VMs, it is advisable to perform these changes gradually rather than all at once. The process of converting policies can temporarily increase storage capacity and performance utilization, which may trigger events such as the Elastic DRS adding hosts or performance degradation.

Management Storage Policies

Unlike the on-premises vSAN, the VMware Cloud on AWS service introduces the concept of Management Storage Policies that cannot be customized by the SDDC's cloudadmin role. The sizes allocated for each management appliance remain consistent regardless of the storage policy applied:

- vCenter Server: 940 GB

- NSX Manager: 3 x 300 GB

- NSX Edge: 2 x 200 GB

Information

With the exception of the single-host storage policy, all storage policies for management appliances in VMware Cloud on AWS utilize thick provisioning (upfront reservation) and RAID-1. It's important to note that the storage reservation values may vary over time with the release of new versions of the SDDC.

In a VMware Cloud on AWS SDDC, the storage utilization of the management appliance is determined by both the size of the cluster and the chosen vSAN storage policy. There are four vSAN storage policies available for management appliances, as follows:

- **Management Storage Policy - Large**: This policy is designed for large-sized clusters consisting of six hosts and above. It provides tolerance for two host failures using **RAID-1 (Mirroring)**.

- **Management Storage Policy - Regular**: This policy is suitable for regular-sized clusters and can tolerate one host failure through **RAID-1 (Mirroring)**.

- **Management Storage Policy - Single Node**: This policy is specifically used in a single-host **proof-of-concept** (**PoC**) SDDC and is not configured for data redundancy.

- **Management Storage Policy - Stretched**: This policy offers the ability to tolerate one host failure using **RAID-1 (Mirroring)**. It can also be configured to tolerate the failure of an entire availability zone.

Information

When performing workload sizing in a small cluster, such as one with only two hosts, it is crucial to consider the overhead of the management appliances. This is because the storage consumption of the management appliance can constitute a significant portion of the overall vSAN storage utilization.

Storage capacity monitoring

Customers can monitor the utilization of their vSAN cluster by navigating to the cluster's **Monitor** tab in the vSphere Client and selecting the **vSAN | Capacity** submenu, as shown in the following screenshot:

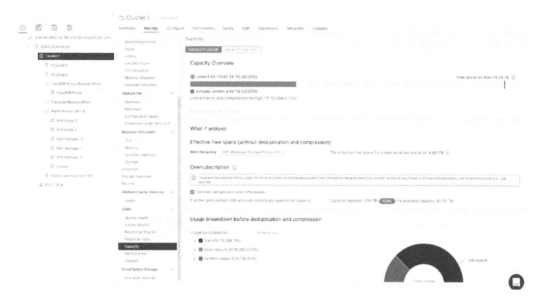

Figure 5.29 – vSphere Client vSAN cluster capacity monitoring

In the previous section, we discussed various VM Storage Policies. In the next section, we will explore the configuration of DRS rules using **Compute Policies**.

Compute Policies

VMware Cloud on AWS comes with DRS automatically enabled. The DRS parameters at the cluster level are controlled by VMware and cannot be adjusted by the `cloudadmin` role. However, customers have the ability to create compute policies that incorporate affinity or anti-affinity rules using vSphere categories and tags within the SDDC. These policies help govern workload placement and influence DRS behavior.

There are several types of **Compute Policies** available:

- **VM-host affinity rules**: These rules ensure that VMs are placed on the same host to optimize performance. For example, they can be used to isolate intra-VM communication on a single host or allocate important workloads to underutilized hosts to prevent resource contention.

- **VM-host anti-affinity rules**: These rules maximize workload availability by running applications on separate hosts, reducing the impact of host failures.

- **Disable DRS vMotion**: Compute policies can be used to prevent workloads from being migrated to different hosts unless the current host is experiencing failure or undergoing maintenance by VMware.

To configure a compute policy, customers first need to create vSphere tags and categories and assign them to the relevant hosts and VMs that they want to include in a compute policy. The compute policy can be configured from **vSphere Client** by navigating to **Tags & Custom Attributes**, as shown in the following screenshot:

Figure 5.30 – vSphere Client Tags & Custom Attributes

To begin, we will create two new categories, one for the host and another for the VM, as shown in the following screenshot:

Figure 5.31 – Creating two new categories in the vSphere Client

Next, we will proceed to create two tags: one for the VM and another for the host. Each tag will be associated with the respective category we created in the previous step. The following screenshot shows a visual representation of this process:

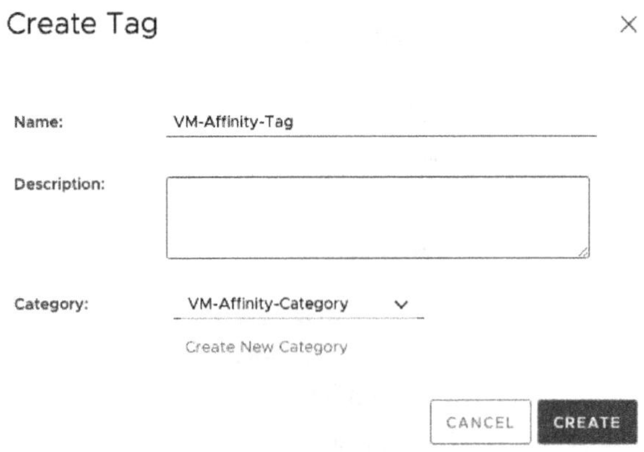

Create Tag   ×

Name: VM-Affinity-Tag

Description:

Category: VM-Affinity-Category   ∨

                Create New Category

                                    CANCEL   **CREATE**

Figure 5.32 – Creating new tags in the vSphere Client

Next, we will proceed to assign the tags to the VMs and hosts. To do this, right-click on the desired object (VM or host) – for example, a host – and select **Tags & Custom Attributes**, followed by **Assign Tag…**. The following screenshot shows a visual representation of this process:

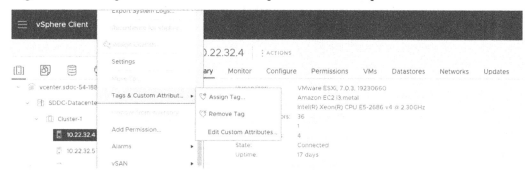

Figure 5.33 – vSphere Client Assign Tag option

Subsequently, select the host tag that was created earlier and assign it to the selected host. Please refer to the following screenshot for a visual representation of this step:

Figure 5.34 – vSphere Client Assign Tag configuration

Finally, we need to assign tags to the VMs to which we want to apply the compute policy rule. To configure the compute policy in **vSphere Client**, go to the **Policies and Profiles** section and select **Compute Policies**, as shown in the following screenshot. Click on the **ADD** button to continue.

Figure 5.35 – Creating a compute policy in the vSphere Client

To finalize the configuration in this example, create a VM-host affinity rule by selecting **VM-Host affinity** from the **Policy type** drop-down menu. Enter a name and description for the policy. Next, choose the appropriate options under the created VM and host tags and categories, and click on the **CREATE** button. Please refer to the following screenshot for visual guidance:

Figure 5.36 – New Compute Policy

The compute policy rules are designed to maintain specific host placements for VMs, ensuring the proximity of VMs for optimal workload performance.

Contacting VMware for support assistance

VMware Cloud on AWS is a service provided by VMware, which means that VMware offers direct support and manages the VMware infrastructure. In cases where a **Managed Service Provider** (**MSP**) delivers the service, the MSP takes ownership of the customer relationship and provides Tier-1 support. However, VMware remains responsible for managing the AWS infrastructure of VMware Cloud on AWS in both models. This includes continuous monitoring and proactive alerting by the VMware **site reliability engineering** (**SRE**) team. The VMware SRE team is tasked with maintaining the infrastructure stack, which involves upgrades and life cycle management of every SDDC deployed on the platform.

For backend support, the VMware SRE team handles all production problems to ensure the availability of the service. However, customers cannot directly access the VMware SRE team. Instead, any VMware Cloud on AWS issues can be addressed through the dedicated support group in the VMware **Global Support Services** (**GSS**) Organization. Support can be obtained by accessing the VMware Cloud console, where an integrated live chat window is available. Opening a support ticket through the live chat is typically the fastest way to engage with support.

Please note that the information provided is based on general practices and may vary depending on specific service agreements or arrangements with VMware.

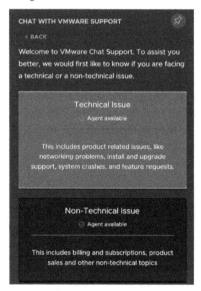

Figure 5.37 – VMware Chat Support

Telephone support is also available for VMware Cloud on AWS. The response time SLA is determined by the severity of the problem. To open a support ticket, the SDDC **Support** tab in the VMware Cloud on AWS console provides valuable information such as the organization ID and SDDC ID.

In addition, support tickets can be created in the **Cloud Service Provider** (**CSP**) platform, which will then redirect to the VMware Customer Connect website. The process for creating support tickets through the CSP is depicted in the following screenshot.

It's important to note that specific procedures and interfaces for support ticket creation may vary based on the CSP and any customized arrangements with VMware.

Figure 5.38 – Support Requests to open a support ticket

Information

For more information on how to get support, you can refer to `https://docs.vmware.com/en/VMware-Cloud-services/services/Using-VMware-Cloud-Services/GUID-E4DC731F-C039-4FB2-949E-9A61584CD5BF.html` and `https://kb.vmware.com/s/article/2006985`.

The following table provides the service severity levels and their corresponding response time SLAs:

Service Levels, Severities and Hours of Operation

Production Support		Initial Response Targets	Severity Definition Guidelines
Response Times	Sev 1	Within 30 minutes	Production down, no work around available
	Sev 2	Within 4 bus hours	Major functionality impaired, although restricted, operations can continue. Workaround Available.
	Sev 3	Within 8 bus hours	Partial, non-critical loss of functionality. Impaired options of some components, but users can use the software
	Sev 4	Within 12 bus hours	General Usage questions, cosmetic issues including errors in documentation
Hours of Coverage	Sev 1	24 x 7	All routed directly to in region Engineers
	Sev 2, 3 & 4	10 x 5 (M-F Local Business Hours 8am – 6pm)	

Figure 5.39 – Support SLA per severity

Information

The severity levels and SLA can be found at `https://www.vmware.com/content/dam/digitalmarketing/vmware/en/pdf/support/vmware-severity-definitions-response-time-business-hours-datasheet.pdf`.

Maintenance model

VMware Cloud on AWS regularly updates customers' SDDCs to deliver new features and bug fixes. These updates ensure that all SDDCs in the fleet have the same software versions. When an SDDC upgrade is scheduled, VMware will send customers an email notification. Typically, this email is sent 7 days prior to a regular update and 1–2 days before an emergency update.

> **Information**
>
> All SDDCs are upgraded to even-numbered software releases, such as VMware Cloud on AWS version 1.20 and 1.22. Odd-numbered versions, such as 1.11 and 1.13, are only available for new SDDC deployments and cannot be used as upgrade targets. For more detailed information, please refer to the provided resource at `https://docs.vmware.com/en/VMware-Cloud-on-AWS/services/com.vmware.vmc-aws-operations/GUID-EE89B216-BE93-4A1A-9280-8F20E2A5266F.html`.
>
> You can ask to postpone a scheduled maintenance window by contacting their customer success or account team representative.

To ensure that customers receive important notifications regarding maintenance activities, it is recommended to whitelist the email addresses `donotreply@vmware.com` and `noreply@vmware-services.io`. Customers will receive email notifications before, during, and after maintenance events.

For more details about the maintenance schedule and information on different upgrade phases and their impact, customers can refer to the **Maintenance** tab in the SDDC console. A screenshot of the console is provided for reference:

Figure 5.40 – SDDC console showing scheduled maintenance

> **Information**
>
> For more detailed information about the upgrade process and its various phases, customers can visit the following URL: `https://docs.vmware.com/en/VMware-Cloud-on-AWS/services/com.vmware.vmc-aws-operations/GUID-EE89B216-BE93-4A1A-9280-8F20E2A5266F.html`.
>
> In the event of an unplanned availability issue or incident with the VMware Cloud on AWS service, customers will receive an incident report via email. The notification will be sent from the email address `noreply@vmware-services.io`.

Summary

In this chapter, we have covered various aspects of capacity management, including adding hosts and clusters, managing vSphere with restricted permissions, and configuring compute and VM Storage Policies. We also discussed the Elastic DRS policy for scaling out and scaling in. Additionally, we explored how to engage with VMware Cloud on AWS support and understand the maintenance and upgrade process in a managed environment.

In the next chapter, we will delve into the intriguing subject of NSX networking and security configurations.

6

Understanding Networking and Security Configurations

This chapter focuses on the practical basics of SDDC networking and security functionality, starting from basic networking and security features, including NSX Micro-Segmentation, and Day 2 operations.

You will learn the networking and security configuration essentials required for day-to-day work.

The following topics are covered in this chapter:

- VMware Cloud on AWS NSX configuration overview
- Managing SDDC networking
- Virtual private network
- Connected VPC
- Direct Connect
- Transit Connect
- NSX security basic configuration
- NSX day two operations
- IPFIX
- Port mirroring
- NSX Micro-Segmentation

Before moving forward to the configurations, let's summarize the NSX environment concept. You can find a detailed overview of VMware Cloud on AWS networking in *Chapter 2*.

VMware Cloud on AWS NSX configuration overview

VMWare Cloud for AWS leverages VMware NSX functionality for network communication and security.

VMware Cloud on AWS utilizes NSX capabilities to create a logical network overlay on top of AWS VPC and SDDC constructs. It provides all switching, routing, and security services (including a firewall service with Micro-segmentation for ingress/egress traffic) required for the customer environment.

NSX has two layers of routing. One layer is the Tier-0 Edge Router, which serves as a North/South gateway to the traffic flowing in and out of the SDDC.

The second layer consists of the Tier-1 Gateways: the **Management Gateway** (**MGW**) and the **Compute Gateway** (**CGW**), which serve as North/South gateways to the SDDC networks. The management networks served by the MGW are used exclusively for the SDDC infrastructure management components. The default CGW acts as a default router for all networks used by the customer workloads.

A recently released network enhancement enables administrators to create multiple Tier-1 gateways serving workloads in addition to the default CGW; we'll explore it in further detail in this chapter.

Managing SDDC networking

VMware Cloud on AWS is a constantly evolving service that influences the way customers access, manage, and troubleshoot SDDC networking and security configurations. On the initial launch of the service, all networking configuration elements were exposed directly through the VMware Cloud Console on the **Networking & Security** tab. However, as the number of networking features grows, a decision has been made to transfer the configuration portion of the SDDC network to the NSX Manager web interface. The **Networking & Security** tab remains but now contains a set of view-only dashboards that help SDDC admin to quickly identify vital parts of the networking configuration.

> **Note**
>
> At the time of writing, it is still possible to revert to the legacy **Networking & Security** view by toggling a **Legacy view** radio button. However, this is temporary, and the **Networking & Security** view will be removed in a future release (as indicated in the following screenshot).

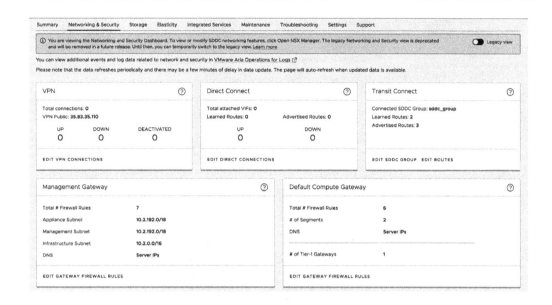

Figure 6.1 – VMWare Cloud Console Networking & Security tab

The NSX Manager web interface (NSX UI) is now the primary (and soon will be the only) way to configure networking settings for your SDDC.

> **Note**
> All the interface steps and screenshots in this chapter refer to the NSX Manager web interface.

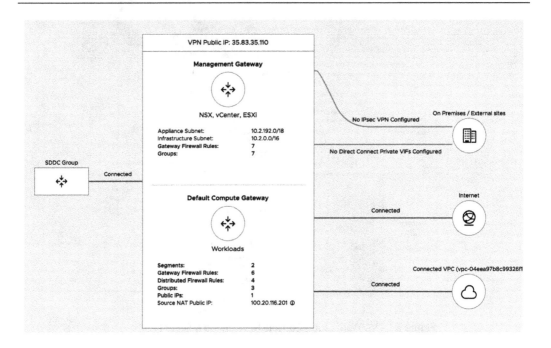

Figure 6.2 – VMware Cloud on AWS SDDC networking overview

You can access the NSX UI through the **OPEN NSX Manager** button in the SDDC Console. By default, when accessing the NSX UI through the **Open NSX Manager** button, the connection over the internet will be used. CSP will pass the credentials to the NSX Manager.

> **Information**
>
> To view and edit the networking configuration for your SDDC, the NSX Cloud Admin or NSX Cloud Auditor CSP role is required.

For enhanced security, we recommend changing the NSX Manager URL resolution to a private IP address and using a VPN or DX to access it. If you choose to do so, you will need to explicitly authenticate within the NSX Manager.

The local `cloud_admin` credentials, the password to the NSX manager, and the URL can be found in the SDDC console under **Settings | NSX Manager URLs | URL to access via an internal network** (log in through NSX Manager credentials), as seen in the following screenshot:

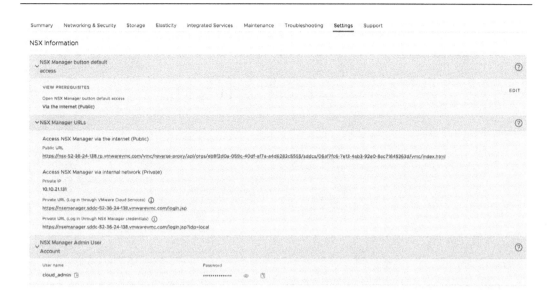

Figure 6.3 – Access NSX Manager through a private IP

When using the NSX Manager `cloud_admin` credentials for authentication, customers can add an external LDAP as an authentication source for the NSX Manager.

Network segments

Customers are responsible for provisioning NSX network segments and deploying workloads.

Segments are equivalent to AWS subnets and VMware virtual switch port groups; virtual machines have their **virtual network interface card** (**vNIC**) connected to network segments provisioned in the NSX Manager.

Users can create routed, extended, or disconnected networks and associate them with a Tier-1 Gateway:

- *Routed* segments are automatically connected to the Tier-1 Gateway and, as the name implies, externally routed

- *Disconnected* segments do not have an uplink to the tier-1 gateway and are not routed

- *Extended* (Layer 2) segments used by NSX L2 VPNs are not routed

To create a new segment, navigate from **Networking** to the **Segments** section, as seen in the following screenshot:

Figure 6.4 – Create a new segment

On the **Segments** pane, in the **NSX** tab, click on **ADD SEGMENT** and provide a segment name (the name will be reflected as an available segment in the vSphere Web Client), under the **Connected Gateway** field, select **Segments** as **Routed,** and in the **Subnets** field, specify the default gateway IP address of the CIDR to be used for the segment (e.g., 10.22.12.2/23 as shown in the following screenshot):

Figure 6.5 – Create a new routed segment

Click on **SAVE**, and when asked to continue configuring the segment parameters, such as the DHCP options, choose **NO** (we'll review DHCP configurations later in this chapter):

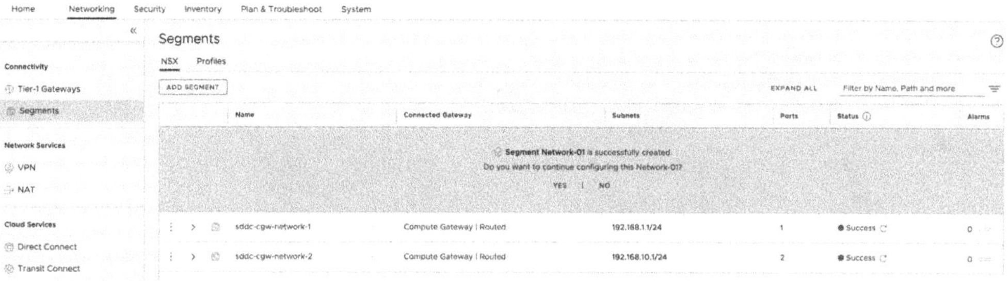

Figure 6.6 – Continue configuring a segment

Next, we'll create a *disconnected* segment. In the **Connected Gateway** section, select **Disconnected**. This configuration means the segment will be disconnected from the tier-1 gateway, and it can be useful for isolated testing purposes and security appliances, or for customer-managed appliance use cases. The rest of the steps are the same as creating a routed segment, as seen in the following screenshot:

Figure 6.7 – Create a disconnected segment

The third segment type is an *extended* segment. Click **ADD SEGMENT** and select **Extended**. Unlike a **Routed Segment** where the default gateway resides on a Tier-1 logical router on the SDDC, the default gateway for **Extended Segments** remains on-premises. This is why the subnet field is disabled or grayed out. The Layer 2 VPN tunnel ID used to extend the segment from on-premises needs to be specified in the **VPN Tunnel ID** field (as shown in *Figure 6.8*).

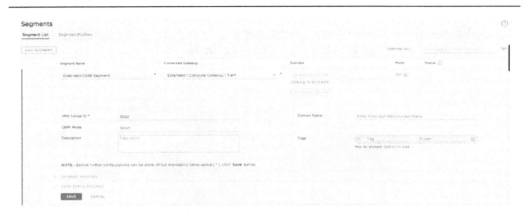

Figure 6.8 – Create an extended segment

If a Layer 2 VPN tunnel has not been established, it will not be possible to save the segment configuration, and a message prompting to create one will appear as in the following screenshot:

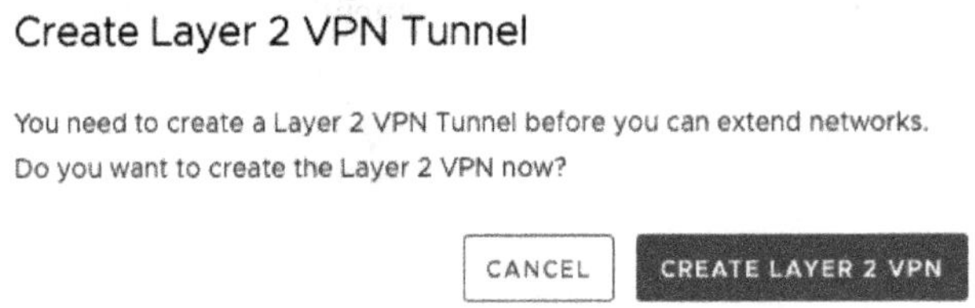

Create Layer 2 VPN Tunnel

You need to create a Layer 2 VPN Tunnel before you can extend networks.
Do you want to create the Layer 2 VPN now?

CANCEL   CREATE LAYER 2 VPN

Figure 6.9 – Create Layer 2 VPN Tunnel message

> **Note**
> This process of creating an extended segment applies to a configuration where the Layer 2 VPN is established using NSX Edge. If you use HCX to extend the network, you do not need to create an extended segment – segments will be created by HCX automatically.

Multiple Tier-1 Gateways

Customers can create multiple tier-1 gateways in addition to the default CGW, thus creating a topology that can support workload isolation and multitenant topologies, as seen in the following diagram:

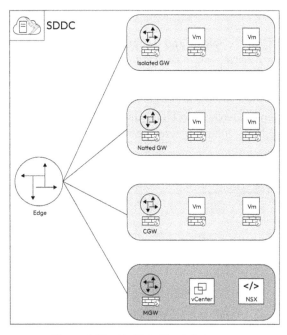

Figure 6.10 – Multiple Tier-1 Gateways

Additional gateways beyond the CGW have the following configuration options:

- **Routed Compute Gateways** are connected to the SDDC's NSX overlay networks. Segments running behind routed CGWs can communicate with workloads running behind other CGWs, including the default CGW. Additionally, these VMs can access the internet through **Elastic IP (EIP)**.

- **NATted Compute Gateways** require NAT configurations to establish connectivity with the SDDC's NSX overlay networks. Network segments behind a NATted CGW are not advertised, allowing the creation of segments with overlapping CIDR blocks within the SDDC. This allows for organizations to create multi-tenant environments, or complex designs with overlapping IP addresses. Segments behind NATted CGWs can communicate with external networks using route aggregation.

- **Isolated Compute Gateways** are disconnected from the SDDC's NSX overlay. Network segments behind an isolated CGW are neither advertised not NATted. However, network segments behind an isolated CGW can communicate with each other, but would not be able to connect with segments behind other CGWs or external networks. Isolated CGWs can be used for advanced use cases such as **Disaster Recovery (DR)** testing using isolated networks.

> **Information**
>
> For further details on CMA topology and design, please refer to the Tech Zone design at https://vmc.techzone.vmware.com/resource/designlet-vmware-cloud-aws-static-routing-multiple-cgws-t1s#section3.

To create a new tier-1 gateway, let's navigate to **Tier-1 Gateways** under **Networking** and click on **ADD TIER-1 GATEWAY**, as seen in the following screenshot:

Figure 6.11 – Tier-1 Gateways view

Next, enter the name for **Tier-1 Gateway Name**. The name will appear later when we associate segments with the gateway and set the gateway type as **Routed**, as seen in the following screenshot:

Figure 6.12 – Create a new Tier-1 Gateway

The other option types for gateways are **NATted** and **Isolated**. The type is selected during the provisioning process but can be edited after the creation.

By default, there are no segments associated with the newly provisioned gateways. This can be viewed in the **#Linked Segments** column, as seen in the following screenshot:

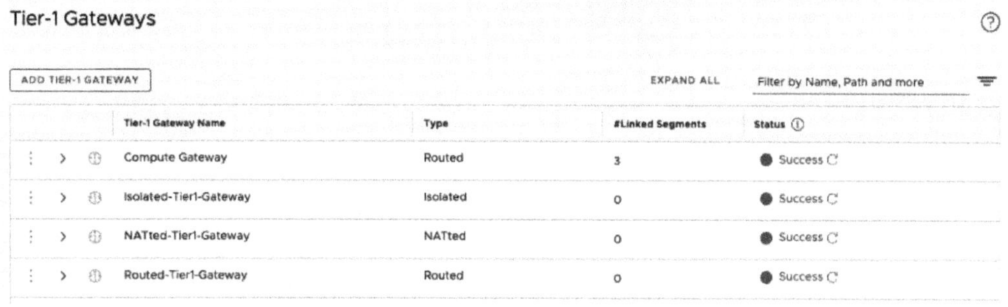

Tier-1 Gateways

			Tier-1 Gateway Name	Type	#Linked Segments	Status ⓘ
⋮	›	⊞	Compute Gateway	Routed	3	● Success ↻
⋮	›	⊞	Isolated-Tier1-Gateway	Isolated	0	● Success ↻
⋮	›	⊞	NATted-Tier1-Gateway	NATted	0	● Success ↻
⋮	›	⊞	Routed-Tier1-Gateway	Routed	0	● Success ↻

ADD TIER-1 GATEWAY   EXPAND ALL   Filter by Name, Path and more

Figure 6.13 – Multiple Tier-1 Gateways provisioned

To associate segments to created tier-1 gateways, we'll navigate back to the **Segments** section under **Networking**. Once we create a new segment in the **Connected Gateway** section, we'll be able to select the newly created Tier-1 gateways and create an overlapping CIDR segment associated with a new NATted tier-1 gateway. In this example, `10.22.12.2/23` is tied to **Routed-Gateway**, when there is another segment with the same CIDR connected to **Compute Gateway**, as seen in the screenshot:

Figure 6.14 – Associating a segment to a new tier-1 gateway

To overcome the overlapping CIDR segment communication IP collision problem, we'll create a **Destination Network Address Translation** (**DNAT**) rule for communications targeted toward the overlapping CIDR segment and a **Source NAT** (**SNAT**) rule for communications originating from the overlapping CIDR segment within the SDDC.

To create the NAT rules for the NATted gateway, navigate to the **NAT** section under **Networking** and select the NATted tier-1 gateway, as seen in the following screenshot:

Figure 6.15 – Create a NAT rule for overlapping segments

Afterward, click on **ADD NAT RULE**, provide it with a name, and under **Action**, select **DNAT**. The **Match Source** field can remain empty, the **Destination** field will be a unique non-overlapping CIDR 192.168.2.0/24, and the **Translated** field will be the duplicated segment address of 10.22.12.0/24. Then click on **SAVE**, as seen in the following screenshot:

Figure 6.16 – Create a DNAT rule for overlapping segments

To create a SNAT rule, click on **ADD NAT RULE** under **Action**, select **SNAT** in the **Match Source** field, and add the duplicated CIDR segment 10.22.12.0/24. The **Destination** field can remain empty, and the **Translated** field will be the unique non-overlapping CIDR 192.168.2.0/24. The configuration is a mirror of the DNAT rules. Click on **SAVE** to complete the configuration, as seen in the following screenshot:

Figure 6.17 – Create a SNAT rule for overlapping segments

After the creation of the rules, the following configuration should appear under **NATted-Tier-1 -Gateway**, which will allow communication to and from the duplicate CIDR subnet, as seen in the following screenshot:

Figure 6.18 – NAT configuration summary

Internet NAT

Source NAT (SNAT) is automatically configured for all SDDC and tier-1 gateway workloads. SNAT is configured for translating the source IP of the VM into the internet public IP address assigned by the VMware Cloud on AWS SDDC. Therefore, customers do not need to create NAT rules for outbound traffic. The console does not present the default source NAT policy. The default translated IP address is visible in the **Overview** section, on the **Home** tab. It is labeled as **Source NAT Public IP**, as seen in the following screenshot:

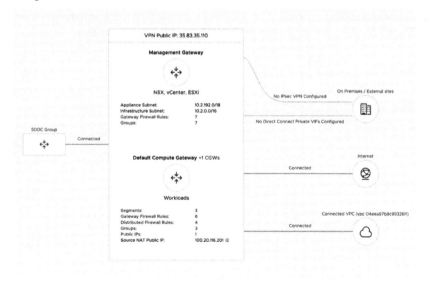

Figure 6.19 – Summary overview SNAT public IP address

The workload's firewall blocks all communication to the internet to provide a secure environment by default. These workloads must be allowed to access the internet through this firewall.

A 1:1 NAT or DNAT is also possible for workloads running in VMware Cloud on AWS that must be exposed to the internet (for example, web servers). It's necessary to request a public IP address from the VMware Cloud on AWS Management console. You will use the **Public IPs** section on the **Networking** tab, as seen in the following screenshot:

Figure 6.20 – Public IP request

> **Information**
>
> Public IPs are metered and charged, and customers are charged the standard AWS fee for a public IP. The VMware Cloud On AWS bill shows the public IP address fees.

Once the public IP has been assigned, it can be connected via NAT to a private IP for the VM. The configuration is in the **NAT** section on the **Networking & Security** tab. According to the policy in the example, all traffic towards port 80 from the internet will be translated into 10.22.23.45, as seen in the following screenshot:

Figure 6.21 – Internet DNAT rule to the web server

Customers need to configure a firewall rule that allows internet access to the private IP addresses of the VM. As NAT is performed before inbound firewalling, the default firewall rule should refer to the private address.

For multiple tier-1 gateway configuration, the VM's workloads could communicate with one another inside the SDDC and from the outside world.

However, we'll need to configure route aggregation to enable a segment behind a tier-1 gateway to communicate to external resources over DX, vTGW, or to the SDDC's Management segment.

Route aggregation is not required for internet access via an Internet Gateway (IGW).

Route aggregation

To configure route aggregation, select the **Networking** tab and navigate to **Global Configuration**, as seen in the following screenshot:

Figure 6.22 – NSX Manager standalone UI networking global configuration

In the upper - left corner, select **Route Aggregation**, and under **Route Configurations**, select **ADD ROUTE CONFIGURATION**, enter a description under **Name,** and select **INTRANET** under **Connectivity Endpoint**.

Figure 6.23 – Create a new route aggregation prefix list

Afterward, a pop-up message will appear for the **Set Prefixes** configuration. Click on **ADD PREFIX** and configure the unique non-overlapping CIDR 192.168.2.0/24 that we used for the **NATted** segment. In the event of multiple contiguous CIDRs, it is possible to summarize all the routes using a larger supernet route. Click on **ADD** and **APPLY**, as seen in the following screenshot:

Figure 6.24 – Creating a prefix list for route aggregation

Afterward, provide a name and click on **SAVE**, as seen in the following screenshot:

Create Aggregation Prefix List   ✕

Name	Prefixes
Route-Aggregation *	1 *

CANCEL   SAVE

Figure 6.25 – Saving the aggregation prefix list configuration

After saving the configuration, we can confirm routes are being advertised to external entities by looking at the routing table under **Advertised Routes**. The **Advertised Routes** tab is visible under **Transit Connect** if it is in use. The configured prefix list of 192.168.2.0/24 advertised routes will appear with the **Aggregated** tag, as seen in the following screenshot:

Figure 6.26 – Aggregated advertised routes under Transit Connect

> **Information**
>
> The Transit Connect routes will appear if an SDDC group has been configured. There will be more on SDDC groups later in this chapter.

DHCP

DHCP can be turned on for each segment during the provisioning process. On a new tier-1 gateway, DHCP can't be configured until the DHCP profile is set on it. To enable DHCP on a newly created Tier-1 gateway, edit the **Tier-1 gateway** configurations under **Networking** and **Tier-1 Gateways**. Then click on the three dots on the left-hand side of the tier-1 gateway, click on **Edit**, and then click on **Set DHCP Configuration**, as seen in the following screenshot:

Figure 6.27 – Enabling DHCP configuration on a tier-1 gateway

Next, select the default DHCP server profile, and click on **SAVE**. This profile is preconfigured on a hidden segment of 10.96.0.1/30 and cannot be edited. However, a new profile with a different configuration can be added, as seen in the following screenshot:

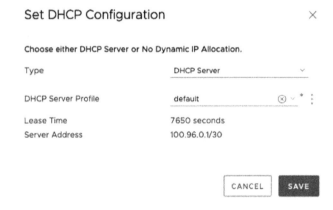

Figure 6.28 – Select DHCP Server Profile under DHCP Configurations

After the profile has been activated on the Tier-1 gateway, DHCP needs to be configured per segment. DHCP functionality is disabled by default in new network segments. Customers can use static IPs for workloads if they want to, and they can also combine static IPs and DHCP, but in this case, static IPs should remain outside the DHCP IP range.

To configure and enable DHCP on the segment, navigate back to the **Segments** section under **Networking**, click on the three dots near the segment, and click on **Edit**, as seen in the following screenshot:

Figure 6.29 – DHCP configuration per segment

Afterward, select **SET DHCP CONFIG**, and a new window will appear by default with the **Gateway DHCP Server** option and the default DHCP profile selected. The **DHCP Config** option needs to be toggled on, and the **DHCP Ranges** value needs to be configured as part of the selected subnet. In the example shown, a network segment 10.22.12.0/23 with a default gateway of 10.22.12.1/23 and a DHCP range of 10.22.12.100-10.22.12.200 is configured. Additionally, **Lease Time** and **DNS Servers** have to be configured; as seen in *Figure 6.30*. The next section explores the DNS configurations.

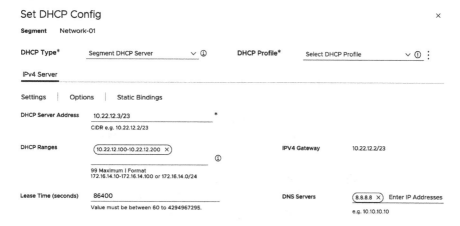

Figure 6.30 – DHCP configuration per segment

Other configuration options for DHCP settings are **Local DHCP Server** for configuring a dedicated DHCP server in the segment that is not shared and **DHCP Relay** for using an external DHCP server.

Domain Name System (DNS)

VMware Cloud on AWS provides DNS services for the **Management Gateway** (**MGW**), **Compute Gateway** (**CGW**), and custom Tier-1 CGWs. Within the SDDC, default DNS zones are integrated for both the Management Gateway and Compute Gateway. Each zone is equipped with a preconfigured DNS forwarding service. The DNS servers set up under the (MGW) DNS Forwarder are utilized by management components such as vCenter to resolve on-premises **Fully Qualified Domain Names** (**FQDNs**). Meanwhile, the DNS servers configured under the CGW DNS forwarder serve the purpose of resolving FQDNs for workload VMs connected to the built-in NSX DHCP-enabled segments.

Organizations can use the **DNS Services** tab on the **DNS Services** page to enable, disable, or update properties for the default zone. Organizations can also create multiple DNS zones or customize additional properties for DNS forwarders in any zone.

The DNS configuration can be found under **Networking | DNS**. It displays the default DNS configuration for the different gateways, as seen in the following screenshot:

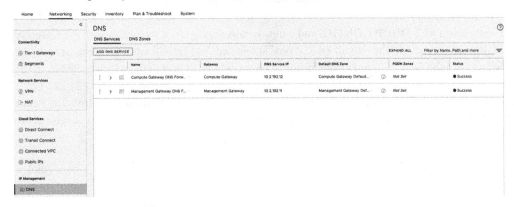

Figure 6.31 – DNS configuration

The default DNS zone configuration is using Google DNS servers 8.8.8.8 and 8.8.4.4 for resolving DNS queries. This can be edited by clicking the three dots on the left side of the DNS service and clicking on **Edit**.

A thorough understanding of DNS configuration is required to set up a fully functional hybrid cloud environment. Organizations can change the default DNS servers of the Management Gateway DNS zone by pointing it to an on-premises DNS server, after which workloads running on VMware Cloud on AWS SDDC should be able to resolve on-premises DNS entries.

> **Note**
>
> For more information, please consult the VMware documentation `https://docs.vmware.com/en/VMware-Cloud-on-AWS/solutions/GUID-25B7F9346825C50F67BF60403CCCAE21.html`.

Virtual private network

You can use a **Virtual Private Network** (**VPN**) to establish connections between on-premises vSphere environments and other SDDCs, or between other cloud environments and VMware Cloud on AWS SDDCs. You can choose between policy-based and route-based VPN connectivity.

When using default Tier-1 routers, your VPN connection is terminated on the Tier-0 Gateway. For custom gateways, the VPN terminates directly on the custom gateway.

Route-based VPNs

Route-based VPNs support dynamic routing and simplify routing configuration in complex network environments. Route-based VPNs utilize BGP over a VPN tunnel. Customers can establish the tunnel using a private connection such as a Direct Connect private **virtual interface** (**VIF**) or public internet.

To configure the VPN connection, navigate to the **Networking** tab and click on the **VPN** section. Select **SDDC** and choose **Route Based**.

Provide the VPN connection name and specify the route-based VPN public IP endpoint in the **Local IP Address** drop - down field. Customers can choose between a private IP (Direct Connect) or a public IP address. The **Remote Public IP** value is the public IP address of the on-premises or remote VPN endpoint.

When configuring a route-based VPN connection you must specify the BGP configuration. In most configurations, you will configure the BGP peering using a pair of IP addresses belonging to the same subnet. It's a best practice to limit the subnet size to just two IP addresses (the /30 subnet) to prevent possible misuse of the remaining IP space.

You configure the **BGP Local IP/Prefix Length** value to match the **BGP Remote IP** value. You may need to consult your network administrator to obtain a subnet and BGP configuration parameters, including the **BGP Neighbor ASN** value:

Figure 6.32 – Route-based VPN configuration

Additional VPN parameters, such as the IKE profile and the IPsec profile, must match on both sides for the session to be established. Click on **SAVE**. Once the VPN has been configured successfully, both the status and the BGP remote IP should have the up and green status, as seen in the following screenshot:

Figure 6.33 – Route-based VPN status

To view further details on the session, you can click on **VIEW STATISTICS** located on the right side of the tunnel to display traffic statistics, as seen in the following screenshot:

Figure 6.34 – Route-based VPN statistics

The view routes and download routes are available for detailed information on advertised and learned routes, as seen in the following screenshot:

Advertised Routes   Learned Routes

Total: 19

Network	Next Hop	LocPrf	MED	AS Path
172.30.111.0/24	0.0.0.0	100	0	
172.30.118.0/24	0.0.0.0	100	0	
10.1.2.0/24	0.0.0.0	100	0	
172.30.120.0/24	0.0.0.0	100	0	
172.30.115.0/24	0.0.0.0	100	0	

CLOSE

Figure 6.35 – Route-based advertised routes

A route-based VPN has several advantages:

- Networks can be automatically advertised and learned between the VMware Cloud on AWS SDDC and the on-premises or remote VPN endpoint. This reduces errors and simplifies operations. No manual configuration is required when networks are added and removed from the environment.

- A route-based VPN provides redundancy. Multiple VPN tunnels can be established in an active/standby or active/active configuration using the ECMP protocol. eBGP metric advertisements are used to determine the on-premises or remote VPN endpoint BGP neighbor behavior in an active/active configuration.

- You can configure a route-based VPN connection as a backup for your DX connectivity. You activate this option in the **Direct Connect** menu. See the following screenshot for more details:

Figure 6.36 – Activating a route-based VPN as a backup to Direct Connect

> **Note**
>
> A number of prerequisites apply when using a route-based VPN as a backup – all advertised routes should exactly match in both connections.

Policy-based VPN

With a policy-based VPN, there is no routing protocol such as BGP, so the initial setup of the VPN connection is easier. However, administrators must manually update the routing tables on both ends of the network when new routes are added.

From the VMware Cloud Console, navigate to **Inventory > SDDCs** and select the **SDDC** and click **View Details.** Then click **Open NSX Manager** to log in to the NSX Manager. In the NSX Manager UI, under **VPN**, select **SDDC** and choose **Policy Based**. Customers choose their local IP address in the same way as with route-based VPNs, either a private or public endpoint, enter their remote peer IP address, and choose the local and remote segments that should be reachable from a drop - down box, as seen in the following screenshot:

Figure 6.37 – Policy-based VPN configuration

A few design considerations are important to remember when using a policy-based VPN connection:

- The policy-based VPN is applied globally. If there is a match between source and destination traffic, then the policy-based VPN path will be used. This is done before a route table lookup.

- You must manually update the policy-based VPN configuration every time a new segment or a new subnet is defined. The configuration must be adjusted on both sides of the tunnel.

> **Information**
>
> Further configuration details can be found at `https://vmc-onboarding.com/guide/2.-connect-sddc/vpn/policy-based/`.

Layer 2 VPN

VMware Cloud on AWS **Layer 2 Virtual Private Network (L2 VPN)** is capable of extending on-premises networks into the VMware Cloud on AWS SDDC. This extended network is a single subnet with a single broadcast domain. Customers can use it to migrate VMs to and from the VMware Cloud on AWS SDDC without having to change IP addresses. In addition to data center migration, you can use an extended L2VPN network for disaster recovery, or data center extension use cases.

The L2VPN feature in VMware Cloud on AWS enables the extension of VLAN-backed VM networks, specifically designed for carrying workload traffic. A key requirement for a network to be extended using L2VPN is that it must be VLAN backed. Consequently, it is feasible to extend a network between an on-premises environment and VMware Cloud on AWS. However, extending a network between two distinct VMware Cloud on AWS SDDCs is not possible because VMware Cloud on AWS SDDC networks are not backed by VLANs.

The L2VPN feature in VMware Cloud on AWS enables the extension of VLAN-backed VM networks, specifically designed for carrying workload traffic. A key requirement for a network to be extended using L2VPN is that it must be VLAN-backed. Consequently, it is feasible to extend a network between an on-premises environment and VMware Cloud on AWS. However, extending a network between two distinct VMware Cloud on AWS SDDCs is not possible because VMware Cloud SDDC networks are not backed by VLANs.

> **Note**
>
> If you plan to extend subnets using HCX, you do not need to configure L2VPN connectivity separately. HCX will create all required connections automatically.

To configure a Layer 2 VPN, on the NSX Manager UI, navigate to the **VPN** section and select **Layer 2** under **SDDC**.

You need to provide the local IP address (either a public or private endpoint) and provide the remote public or private IP, as seen in the following screenshot:

Figure 6.38 – L2VPN configuration

After saving the configuration, customers will be prompted to download a standalone NSX autonomous edge that will serve as an on-premises client for the Layer 2 tunnel in case customers do not have an on-premises NSX deployment. Alternatively, a managed NSX Edge can be utilized to establish the L2VPN.

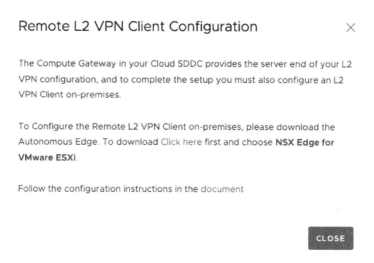

Figure 6.39 – Download an NSX autonomous edge

After saving and establishing the L2VPN, you can specify a segment to be extended. You configure the VPN tunnel ID to match the VLAN ID of the extended network:

Figure 6.40 – L2VPN segment configuration

Multiple Tier-1 Gateway VPNs

Tier-1 gateways can terminate VPNs for multi-tenancy environments, where direct connectivity over the VPN is required by a tenant, as seen in the following architecture diagram:

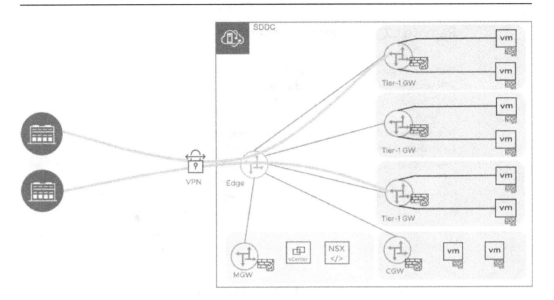

Figure 6.41 – Tier-1 gateway VPN termination diagram

The configuration is available at **Networking | VPN | Tier-1 VPN Services**, as seen in the following screenshot:

Figure 6.42 – Tier-1 gateway VPN termination

> **Information**
>
> Route-based VPNs terminating on Tier-1 Gateways do not support BGP; they support static routes instead.
>
> Further configuration details can be found in the user guide at `https://docs.vmware.com/en/VMware-Cloud-on-AWS/services/com.vmware.vmc-aws-networking-security/GUID-5AF45CE6-FA53-45C0-83E5-25F8E3A055E9.html`.

Connected VPC

Each VMware Cloud on AWS SDDC must be linked to an organization's customer-managed AWS account. Inside the AWS account, organizations must create a VPC with subnets and connect it to the SDDC. This is referred to as the **connected VPC**.

The connected VPC setup is done during the SDDC provisioning process. You can review the configuration using the **Connected VPC** section in the **Networking** tab – the connection details of the AWS account will appear, including **AWS Account ID**, **VPC ID**, and **VPC Subnet**.

Figure 6.43 – Reviewing connected Amazon VPC information

Aggregation Prefixes Lists enables Route aggregation are used to create aggregate prefixes behind customer-configured Tier-1 gateways. The routes part of the Aggregated Prefix Lists will be advertised either on the **INTRANET** endpoint or the **SERVICES** endpoint. As shown in *Figure 6.44*, an Aggregation Prefix List named **Connected - VPC** with aggregated prefixes that include the 10.12.0.0/22 and 10.12.4.0/22 CIDRs is created and advertised over the **SERVICES** endpoint.

Figure 6.44 – Connected VPC route aggregation configuration

The **Advertised** tab in **Connected Amazon VPC** shows the same aggregated routes have been advertised. This can be seen in *Figure 6.45*:

Figure 6.45 – Aggregated routes created using prefix lists advertised to connected VPC

Now that we have reviewed the connected VPC connectivity options, let's review how to configure a Direct Connect connection in the SDDC.

Direct Connect

The VMware NSX version available with VMware Cloud on AWS has a number of features that were specifically developed for the service and are not available on any other NSX deployment. One of the most important is the ability to attach a DX **Virtual Interface** (**VIF**) directly from the NSX web interface.

While a thoughtful discussion about different DX design and deployment configurations is outside of the scope of this book, we still would like to mention a few important things to consider when using DX connectivity with a VMware Cloud on AWS SDDC:

- Both public and private VIFs are supported. However, only a private VIF can be used for hybrid cloud connectivity
- Attachment to a DX gateway through Transit Connect is supported
- You can use AWS-provided DX connectivity or opt for a cloud connectivity provider
- DX information is located on the **Networking** tab in the **Direct Connect** menu item:

Figure 6.46 – Direct Connect configuration

The creation of a VIF should be performed in the AWS Management Console. You must export a VIF to the AWS account associated with the SDDC. You can find this account in the **AWS Account ID** field in the **Direct Connect** menu item.

> **Information**
>
> You can find further technical information on the VMware Cloud Tech Zone at `https://vmc.techzone.vmware.com/resource/designlet-vmware-cloud-aws-sddc-connectivity-direct-connect-private-vif`.

Transit Connect

VMware Transit Connect is a **VMware Managed Transit Gateway** (**vTGW**), which enables complex network topology, including inter- and intra-Region SDDC connectivity, AWS VPC connection, and much more.

You deploy vTGW from the SDDC console through the SDDC groups feature, which lets customers manage multiple SDDCs and external AWS connectivity from one logical entity. SDDC groups are required to enable VMware Transit Connect. You can add just a single SDDC to a group – this action will trigger the creation of a vTGW.

To configure SDDC groups in the SDDC console, click on **CREATE GROUP**, as seen in the following screenshot:

Figure 6.47 – Creating a new SDDC group

Customers can select the SDDCs that need to be a part of the SDDC group in the wizard. In our example, we'll provide the group with a descriptive name, add `Enterprise-Customer-A` and `Enterprise-Customer-B` SDDCs into the group, acknowledge the additional attachment and data transfer costs, and click on **CREATE GROUP** to continue with the group creation, as seen in the following screenshot:

Figure 6.48 – New SDDC group configuration

Information

All SDDCs must have non-overlapping management subnets to form an SDDC group. SDDCs can be located in different regions or in the same region when leveraging SDDC groups. For further details on data transfer costs and attachment costs, see `https://aws.amazon.com/transit-gateway/pricing/`.

After the provisioning process is completed, **Connectivity Status** will show **CONNECTED**, as seen in the following screenshot:

Figure 6.49 – SDDC group configuration

Now the two SDDCs can route to one another through vTGW. You can view the routing table, including advertised and learned routes, in the **Transit Connect** section of the **Networking** tab:

Figure 6.50 – Transit Connect routing table

After the configuration has been done, routing between the SDDC subnets will automatically propagate through vTGW. However, firewall rules need to be opened to allow communication.

VMware Transit Connect has additional capabilities, such as connectivity to AWS VPC, TGW, and Direct Connect attachments; however, they are beyond the scope of this chapter.

> **Information**
>
> You can find further technical information on the VMware Cloud Tech Zone at `https://vmc.techzone.vmware.com/resource/introduction-vmware-transit-gateway-vmware-cloud-aws#sddc-to-on-premises-alternate-design`.

NSX security basic configuration

The NSX Edge firewall, also known as the **Gateway Firewall** in VMware Cloud on AWS, provides security for North/South traffic. There are two default Edge firewalls: the MGW firewall, and the CGW firewall. In addition, as we have seen in this chapter, each Tier-1 gateway manages its own firewall rules.

Management Gateway firewall

The Management Gateway firewall protects access to management components such vCenter and NSX.

There are two types of management groups: **predefined management groups** and **user-defined management groups**. When choosing a source or destination for a management firewall rule, there are three choices: **Any**, **System-Defined**, and **User-Defined**.

System-defined groups simplify the creation of common Management Gateway firewall rules. User-defined groups allow the creation of custom groups based only on an IP address. Such groups are commonly used to provide remote administrators access to management components.

You manage the groups' configuration on the **Inventory** tab in the **Management Groups** section, as seen in the following screenshot:

Figure 6.51 – System-Defined Groups Management Gateway

You cannot use any notation or `0.0.0.0/0` as a source for MGW firewall rules – you need to explicitly specify all the sources requiring access to management components by using IP addresses.

Compute Gateway firewall rules

The Compute Gateway firewall protects access to workloads placed behind the CGW. Compute Gateway firewall rules use grouping objects based on various matching criteria, such as IP address, VM instance, VM name, and security tag.

Default security groups are automatically created and include definitions such as the connected VPC prefixes, or S3 prefixes, and they can be used in a CGW firewall rule source or destination, as seen in the following screenshot:

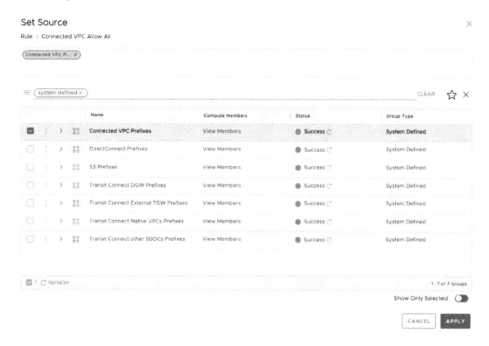

Figure 6.52 – Connected VPC System Defined security group

Customers can manage customized compute groups, under **Groups** in the **Inventory** tab, as seen in the following screenshot:

Figure 6.53 – Compute groups

CGW firewall rules are configured in the **Gateway Firewall** section on the **Security** tab, as seen in the following screenshot:

Figure 6.54 – Gateway Firewall settings

> **Information**
>
> Further details on how to create firewall rules can be found at `https://docs.vmware.com/en/VMware-Cloud-on-AWS/services/com.vmware.vmc-aws-networking-security/GUID-2D31A9A6-4A80-4B5B-A382-2C5B591F6AEB.html`.

Compute firewall rules may be applied selectively to specific interfaces, such as internet, intranet, VPN tunnel, or VPC.

> **Information**
>
> The difference between interfaces can be found at `https://docs.vmware.com/en/VMware-Cloud-on-AWS/services/com.vmware.vmc-aws-networking-security/GUID-A5114A98-C885-4244-809B-151068D6A7D7.html`.

Tier-1 Gateways are managed on the **Tier-1 Gateways** tab in the **Gateway Firewall** section of the **Security** tab, as seen in the following screenshot:

Figure 6.55 – Tier-1 Gateway firewall configuration

After reviewing the NSX firewall configurations, let's review how to discover and troubleshoot networking and security configurations in the SDDC.

NSX day two operations

Network administrators and security personnel often need to review network and security logs. This is often required for auditing or troubleshooting as well as security analysis.

VMware Cloud on AWS integrates all its logs in VMware Aria Operations for Logs.

This capability allows customers to analyze and troubleshoot their application flows using the visibility of packets corresponding to specific NSX firewall rules and have visibility of the connectivity establishment of VPNs. Once a firewall rule has been created on one of the gateways or the DFW firewall, logging can then be turned on directly from the rule by clicking on the right-hand side of the cogwheel and enabling **Logging**, as seen in the following screenshot:

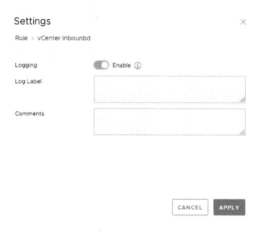

Figure 6.56 – NSX-T firewall rule logging enabled

The rule ID can be seen in the **ID** field. In this example it is **1017**, as seen in the following screenshot:

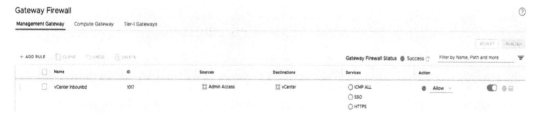

Figure 6.57 – Rule ID Gateway Firewall

This rule ID can be used to filter log results later in VMware Aria Operations for Logs, as seen in the following screenshot:

Figure 6.58 – vRealize Log Insight Cloud

When looking at these logs, customers can drill down to see the specific packet-level details. Traffic can be allowed through the firewall action (pass).

We'll explore more VMware Aria Operations for Logs configuration options in the next chapter.

IPFIX

Security and network administrators use **Internet Protocol Flow Information Export** (**IPFIX**) and its predecessor, NetFlow, for troubleshooting and auditing. IPFIX, a modern IETF standard protocol for exporting traffic flow information, is based on NetFlow.

A flow is a sequence of packets sent in a given time slot and sharing the same 5-tuple values of source IP address, source port, destination IP address, destination port, and protocol. The flow information can include properties such as timestamps, packet/byte counts, input/output protocols, TCP flags, and encrypted flow information.

An IPFIX specification requires the identification of exporters and network entities that monitor traffic and export it in the IPFIX model. Collectors are systems that collect the traffic.

If there is IP connectivity from VMware Cloud On AWS, an IPFIX collector can be placed anywhere on the network. It could reside on-premises, within a VMware Cloud on AWS SDDC, or in AWS.

The configuration of the IPFIX collector is done in the **IPFIX** section, on the **Plan & Troubleshoot** tab. IPFIX data can also be sent to as many as four collectors:

Figure 6.59 – IPFIX collector

Many IPFIX settings are customizable; for example, individual network segments can also be selected. The IPFIX collector captures all flows from VMs connected with those network segments.

Customers can adjust the sampling rate or timeout parameters to control how finely customers want data to be captured. If there are many flows, customers can lower the sampling rate. A lower sampling rate will reduce the number of processed packets, which will reduce the load on the customer's underlying platform. This configuration is done in the IPFIX **Switch IPFIX Profiles** section, as seen in the following screenshot:

Figure 6.60 – Switch IPFIX Profiles

Port mirroring

Port mirroring allows us to copy and redirect packets to a destination monitoring device. This is useful for monitoring and analyzing specific traffic in use cases such as the following:

- Copy it to an advanced firewall (IPS/IDS) to inspect traffic
- For troubleshooting purposes, a copy of a traffic flow can be used
- Mirror traffic to a Wireshark packet capture program to analyze application or packet loss issues

Port mirroring configuration includes specifying the traffic to be monitored (referred to as the source) and determining the direction in which the traffic should be monitored–whether it's the source, destination, or both.

Additionally, the configuration includes identifying the location to which the monitored traffic should be sent, which is typically a monitoring system. This system can be either remote or local.

There are different types of port mirroring sessions, which include **Local Switch Port Analyzer (SPAN)**, **Remote SPAN (RSPAN)**, and **Encapsulated Remote SPAN (ERSPAN)**. VMware Cloud on AWS leverages ERSPAN to copy traffic leaving or entering a virtual port.

The copied traffic should ideally be sent to a destination VM – usually, a host, workload, or machine running packet capture software such as Wireshark for security analysis or an IDS/IPS device. VMware Cloud on AWS lets customers select one or more VMs to be a source. Each VM will be added to a session of port mirroring.

> **Information**
>
> To allow traffic to be routed from the ESXi hosts to the destination device, a security rule must be placed on the MGW firewall.

The port mirroring configuration is done in the **Port Mirroring** section on the **Plan & Troubleshoot** tab, as seen in the following screenshot:

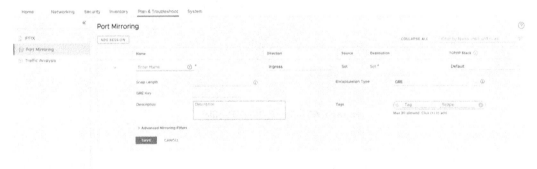

Figure 6.61 – Port mirroring configuration

We have spent some time learning about NSX day two operations, and now we will switch to the NSX distributed firewall feature.

NSX Micro-Segmentation

The **Distributed Firewall** (**DFW**) feature is an integral part of NSX in VMware Cloud. It allows East/West firewalling, also known as micro-segmentation. Micro-segmentation enables customers to segment the network and apply security policies at the vNIC level, allowing the creation of security logic beyond the boundaries of Layer 3 segments.

The NSX DFW provides a contextual view of the virtual data center. Workloads can be secured using meaningful metadata instead of just destination and source IP addresses. For example, a VM instance, name, or security tag can be used for security rules, which allows security policies to be built based on business logic. It helps to reduce the impact of security breaches and meet compliance targets. The NSX DFW has powerful capabilities that allow advanced security use cases such as isolation, multi-tenancy, and DMZ Anywhere.

The DFW configuration is located in the **Distributed Firewall** section on the **Security** tab, as seen in the following screenshot:

Figure 6.62 – Distributed Firewall configuration

The NSX DFW includes four sections for DFW rules: emergency rules, infrastructure rules, environment rules, and application rules. Each section may have multiple policies and rules.

These sections are used to organize policies. Customers may define all rules within one of these sections and are not required to use this structure.

> **Information**
> The default DFW rule permits all traffic.

Rules are processed from the top down. Traffic will see the emergency rules first and application rules last. If no rules have been met, the default rule applies.

Customers can create policies and rules within DFW sections.

Each DFW rule contains a name, source, destination, service (for example, HTTPS), and an action (for example, permit, drop, or refuse). Additionally, Logging can optionally be enabled on each DFW rule. Once enabled, by default, logging is applied in an In-Out (applied to both incoming and outgoing traffic) direction. This can be changed to either In (apply the rule only to incoming traffic) or Out (apply it only to outgoing traffic).

Log entries are sent to the VMware Aria Operations for Logs service (formerly VRealize Log Insight Cloud).

You have now learned the basics of NSX distributed firewall and gained enough knowledge to configure and use NSX capabilities of VMware Cloud on AWS.

Summary

In this chapter, you gained relevant knowledge to be able to design, configure, and operate VMware Cloud on AWS networking based on VMware NSX capabilities. With the recent change in the **Networking & Security** tab in the SDDC console to the new VMware NSX web interface, it's vital for administrators to examine the relevant UI elements and update runbooks and documentation. Cloud and networking architects may practically design recommendations, especially around hybrid cloud connectivity.

You are now prepared to use the full potential of VMware Cloud on AWS networking in your organization.

In the next chapter, we will learn about the new integrated services available with VMware Cloud on AWS.

7

Exploring Integrated Services Configuration

In this chapter, you will gain a comprehensive understanding of the intricacies involved in configuring integrated services. These services encompass the NSX Advanced security service, which offers a Layer 7 firewall and **Intrusion Prevention System/Intrusion Detection System (IPS/IDS)** security features. Additionally, you will explore VMware HCX, VMware Aria Operations for Logs, and the Tanzu Kubernetes Grid Service. By delving into these topics, you will acquire the essential knowledge required for your day-to-day tasks.

Specifically, this chapter covers the following topics:

- Configuring the NSX Advanced Firewall service
- The VMware HCX service
- VMware Aria Operations for Logs
- The Tanzu Kubernetes Grid managed service

Configuring the NSX Advanced Firewall service

The NSX Advanced Firewall service enables the following capabilities:

- A distributed IDS/IPS
- A distributed Firewall with the Layer 7 Application ID
- A distributed Firewall (DFW) with an Active Directory-based user ID – Identity Firewall (IDFW)
- A distributed Firewall with FQDN filtering

The NSX Advanced Firewall service further enhances the capabilities of the integrated distributed firewall, by providing end-to-end visibility and protection for the application traffic. This service protects both east-west and north-south traffic flows and offers additional protection against malware. From an architectural perspective, incorporating the NSX Advanced Firewall service into an SDDC is advisable when your design necessitates stringent compliance and security requirements, mandating end-to-end protection for application traffic. The NSX Advanced Firewall service is a paid service, billed per all the hosts in the SDDC when activated. The service cannot be activated on individual clusters in the SDDC. Organizations can choose between an on-demand rate, or one- or three-year subscriptions.

> **Information**
>
> Pricing information can be found at `https://www.vmware.com/products/nsx-advanced-firewall-for-vmc.html`.

To configure the NSX Advanced Firewall service, you need to perform the following steps:

1. To activate the NSX Advanced Firewall service, navigate in the **SDDC** console to the **Integrated Services** section, and under **NSX Advanced Firewall**, click on **ACTIVATE**, as shown in the following screenshot:

Figure 7.1 – Activating the NSX Advanced Firewall add-on

2. Confirm the activation by clicking the **ACTIVATE** button on the following screen, as shown in the following screenshot:

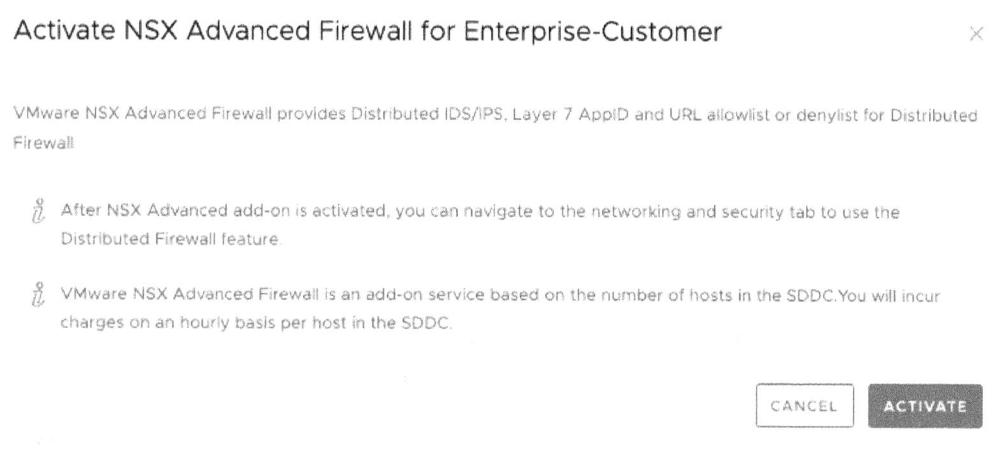

Activate NSX Advanced Firewall for Enterprise-Customer ✕

VMware NSX Advanced Firewall provides Distributed IDS/IPS, Layer 7 AppID and URL allowlist or denylist for Distributed Firewall

ⓘ After NSX Advanced add-on is activated, you can navigate to the networking and security tab to use the Distributed Firewall feature.

ⓘ VMware NSX Advanced Firewall is an add-on service based on the number of hosts in the SDDC. You will incur charges on an hourly basis per host in the SDDC.

CANCEL   **ACTIVATE**

Figure 7.2 – Confirming activation

3. Navigate to the **Distributed IDS/IPS** section under the **Networking & Security** tab to manage the newly activated Advanced Firewall service. On the initial deployment, confirm the steps required for activation by clicking on the **GET STARTED** button, as shown in the following screenshot:

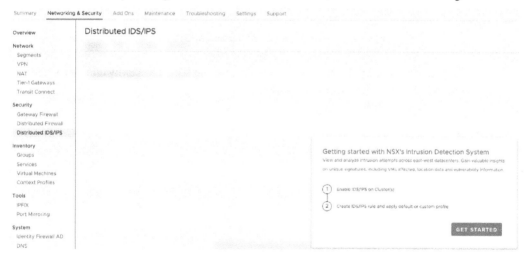

Figure 7.3 – Distributed IDS/IPS

4. Next, open the **Settings** tab, and enable the feature on the SDDC clusters by selecting them and clicking on **ENABLE**, as shown in the following screenshot:

Figure 7.4 – Enabling distributed IDS/IPS on a cluster level

5. Next, to enable the IDS/IPS inspection and prevention, organizations need to create policies and rules under the **Rules** tab. The rules must include an SDDC source or destination, and the rule cannot be just a broad all-encompassing *any-any* rule. The rule can work in **Detect only** mode to only prevent alerts or in **Detect & Prevent** mode to block attacks, as shown in the following screenshot:

Figure 7.5 – Creating an IDS/IPS policy and rule

6. Once the policy has been published, users can monitor the IDS/IPS activity and alerts under the **Events** tab, as shown in the following screenshot:

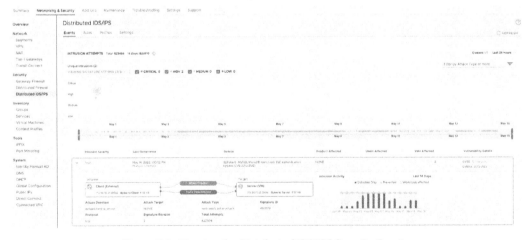

Figure 7.6 – Viewing the Distributed IDS/IPS Security Events

7. FQDN and application-level rule filtering functionality is available upon activation of the service. Those rules are enforced in the **Distributed Firewall** section. To create an FQDN rule, users need to create an *allow DNS snooping* rule with DNS as a service and then add a block rule. The specific FQDN and app IDs are configured under the **Context Profiles** section – for example, with the **Azure-Microsoft** context profile, as shown in the following screenshot:

Figure 7.7 – A DNS FQDN filtering rule

8. The FQDN and App IDs are configured under **Context Profiles**, under the **Networking & Security** tab, as shown in the following screenshot:

Figure 7.8 – FQDN configurations

9. To incorporate attributes into a **Distributed Firewall** (**DFW**), users need to establish a new **Context Profile** and choose the **FQDN** and **App ID** attributes. To accomplish this, navigate to the **Context Profiles** tab, click **ADD CONTEXT PROFILE**, and select **Set Attributes**. Once the attribute is added, users should be able to see entries as shown in *Figure 7.9*:

Figure 7.9 – Context Profiles – ADD ATTRIBUTE

10. An **Active Directory** (**AD**)-based identity firewall is an additional capability of the service, which means that users can create DFW rules based on user identities, such as AD groups, as the source and destination, instead of IP addresses or VM names and tags. Users need to set up an Active Directory/LDAP identity source under **Active Directory**, under the **Identity Firewall AD** tab, as shown in *Figure 7.10*:

Figure 7.10 – Identity Firewall AD

11. After configuring the identity source rules under the **Distributed Firewall** section, you can use **AD Groups** as the source/destination criteria in addition to the standard criteria, as shown in *Figure 7.11*:

Figure 7.11 – Adding AD Group as a member of the Compute Groups

NSX Advanced Firewall is a powerful service, enhancing security and compliance for your application workload deployed on a VMware Cloud on AWS SDDC.

The VMware HCX service

The VMware **Hybrid Cloud Extension** (**HCX**) service enables users to connect and migrate workloads from on-premises to VMware Cloud on AWS and back again, or from VMware Cloud on AWS to/from another VMware Cloud vSphere-based environment. HCX has a number of unique features that help to address the most sophisticated migration use cases, including the ability to schedule a migration, define a migration group, and stretch a Layer 2 network to the cloud.

Deploying and activating the HCX service

The steps to do this are as follows:

1. To activate HCX, navigate to the **SDDC** console and then the **Integrated Services** tab, and select **OPEN HCX**, as shown in the following figure:

Figure 7.12 – The HCX add-on section

2. Next, a new tab will open where we can initiate the HCX deployment on the VMware Cloud side. To do so, click on **DEPLOY HCX**, as shown in the following screenshot:

Figure 7.13 – Deploying the HCX add-on

3. After selecting a deployment, a confirmation message will appear. Select **CONFIRM** to move on, as shown in the following screenshot:

Figure 7.14 – Confirming the HCX activation

4. The deployment process takes about 30 minutes, during which HCX management appliances are provisioned and preconfigured on the SDDC automatically. When the process is complete, users can access the cloud HCX manager by selecting **OPEN HCX**, as shown in the following screenshot:

Figure 7.15 – OPEN HCX – post-deployment

5. Before being able to open the HCX manager, we'll need to allow access to it in the **Management Gateway** firewall section by creating an allow rule with a source management IP address, either private or public, and with the destination set to the **HCX** service, as shown in the following screenshot:

Figure 7.16 – HCX firewall rules on the Management Gateway Firewall

6. HCX management appliance access works like vCenter access; you can access the HCX UI either over the internet or by using a private IP over a VPN/DX. You can change the FQDN resolution to a private or public endpoint in the **SDDC** console under **Settings | HCX Information | HCX FQDN**, as shown in the following screenshot:

Figure 7.17 – The HCX DNS FQDN resolution

7. After configuring the DNS resolution and clicking on **Open HCX**, an authentication window will open. The HCX credentials are the same as the vCenter credentials and can be copied, as shown in the following screenshot:

Figure 7.18 – Opening HCX management

8. The next step is to download the management appliance and deploy it in your pairing environment. In the case of a cloud-to-cloud HCX migration, there is no need to follow this step, as this task is automated on the cloud side. Navigate to **System Updates**, and click on **REQUEST DOWNLOAD LINK**, and the HCX appliance will start downloading, as shown in the following screenshot:

Figure 7.19 – Download the HCX Manager OVA appliance

9. After downloading the HCX Open Virtualization Appliance (**OVA**), deploy it on the on-premises vSphere environment on a vSphere port group that has network connectivity with the local on-premises vCenter Server using a port group that can communicate with the local vCenter and over the WAN.

> **Information**
>
> Further details on how to configure the on-premises side of the HCX appliance can be found at `https://vmc-onboarding.com/guide/4.-deploy-add-ons/hcx-hybrid-cloud-connect/`.

10. Once deployed, users will need to provide an activation key for the on-premises appliance. It can be generated under **Activation Keys** by clicking on **CREATE ACTIVATION KEY**, as shown in the following screenshot:

Figure 7.20 – HCX management license activation

11. The license key confirmation needs to be validated by selecting the system type as **HCX Connector** and clicking on **CONFIRM**, as shown in the following screenshot:

Figure 7.21 – HCX management license activation confirmation

12. In the on-premises HCX Manager appliance, log in to the appliance over port 9443, using the admin credentials entered during the OVA deployment process. In the management UI, users can enter the license key generated on the cloud side, as shown in the following screenshot:

Figure 7.22 – HCX management gateway license activation

13. Additionally, the local vCenter URL and credentials need to be entered under the **vCenter Server** section under the **Configuration** tab to pair with vCenter Server, as shown in the following screenshot:

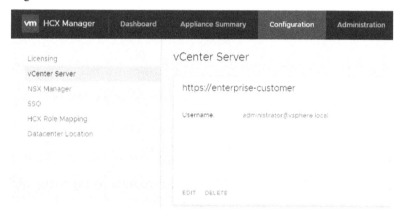

Figure 7.23 – HCX management vCenter configuration

14. After deploying and entering the credentials, the vSphere Client will have a new HCX plugin. The migration and site pairing configurations will be done from the plugin. To access it in the vSphere Client, click on **Menu** and select **HCX**, as shown in the following screenshot:

Figure 7.24 – The HCX plugin vSphere Client

15. In the HCX plugin, the first menu is the dashboard, which shows a summary of the current site pairing configuration, the number of migrated VMs, active migrations, and the number of network extensions, as shown in the following screenshot:

Figure 7.25 – The HCX plugin dashboard

16. To create connectivity between the on-premises HCX manager and the VMware Cloud on AWS side, navigate to **Site Pairing** and click **ADD A SITE PAIRING**. Users will need to add

to the **Remote HCX URL** field the URL of the HCX Manager on the VMware Cloud on AWS side and enter the credentials of the *cloudadmin* user. Then, they need to click on **CONNECT**, as shown in the following screenshot:

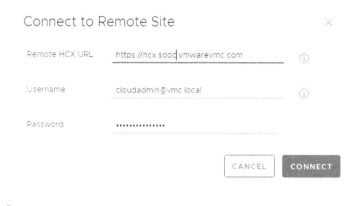

Figure 7.26 – HCX site pairing configuration

17. After creating the site pairing, if the firewall ports are open and the configuration is correct, the site pairing status will appear as green, indicating that it is connected, as shown in the following screenshot:

Figure 7.27 – HCX site pairing success

After creating a site pairing, the next step is to create a *service mesh* that will deploy the **Interconnect (IX)**, **WAN optimization (WO)**, and **Network Extension (NE)** appliances and configure them to enable the migration services. To do so, the user needs to configure the network and compute profiles that define which resources can be used on-premises and where those appliances will be deployed. The network profiles need to include, at a minimum, the management *network profile*, which needs to have access to vCenter/ESXi and the VMware Cloud HCX over the public internet or by a direct connection, and the *vMotion network profile*, which needs to be part of the vMotion network. Optionally, a vSphere replication network can be configured as well. However, mostly, it is part of the management network. The configuration examples can be seen in the following screenshot:

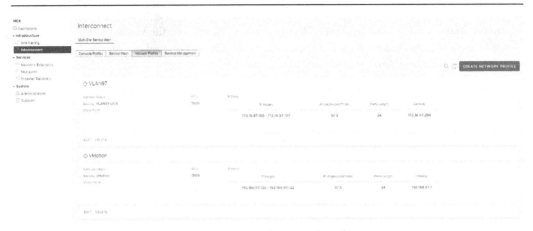

Figure 7.28 – An HCX network profile

18. In addition, the compute profile needs to define where to deploy the appliances and which services to enable. A summary of a configured *compute profile* is shown in the following screenshot:

Figure 7.29 – An HCX compute profile

19. To create a new compute profile, select **CREATE COMPUTE PROFILE**, and a creation wizard will appear. On the first screen, provide the profile with a name and click on **CONTINUE**, as shown in the following screenshot:

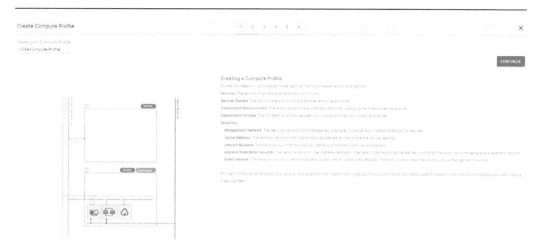

Figure 7.30 – The HCX compute profile creation

20. Next, the user needs to select which services to enable using this compute profile. All services can be enabled except **SRM integration**, which is not part of the VMware Cloud on AWS license at the time of writing. Toggle the services on and click on **CONTINUE**, as shown in the following screenshot:

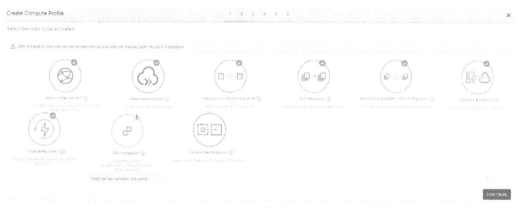

Figure 7.31 – Selecting an HCX compute profile service

21. Now, select the cluster where the HCX services should be deployed, and click on **CONTINUE**, as shown in the following screenshot:

Figure 7.32 – HCX compute profile resource activation

22. Now, we select the specific compute and storage allocation that the appliances will use and where they will be deployed. The folder placement selection is optional, as are the interconnect appliance resource reservations. After selection, click on **CONTINUE**, as shown in the following screenshot:

Figure 7.33 – Select Deployment Resources and Reservations

23. Now, we will select the *management network profile* we previously created and click on **CONTINUE**, as shown in the following screenshot:

Figure 7.34 – Select Management Network Profile

24. Now, select the uplink network profile, which is tied to the same management profile selected in the previous step, and click on **CONTINUE**, as shown in the following screenshot:

Figure 7.35 – Select a vSphere replication profile

> **Note**
>
> It's possible to pair HCX appliances either using the internet or DX. If you would like to leverage DX for pairing, you must preconfigure the cloud-side HCX first using the following resource: `https://vmc.techzone.vmware.com/resource/designlet-vmware-cloud-aws-sddc-connectivity-vmware-hcx-over-direct-connect`.

25. Next, select the vMotion network profile, which we created in the previous step, and click on **CONTINUE**, as shown in the following screenshot:

Figure 7.36 – Select vMotion Network Profile

26. Select the vSphere replication network profile; most users can use the same profile as the management network profile unless a dedicated network is used. After selection, click on **CONTINUE**, as shown in the following screenshot:

Figure 7.37 – Select vSphere Replication Network Profile

27. Choose the network **vSphere Distributed Switch** (**vDS**) used for the Layer 2 network extension service. After selection, click on **CONTINUE**, as shown in the following screenshot:

Figure 7.38 – Select Network Containers Eligible for Network Extension

28. Now, review the network connectivity that will be required. This is useful when needing to coordinate with security teams. Click on **CONTINUE**, as shown on the following screenshot:

Figure 7.39 – Review Connection Rules

29. Now, the user can review the final configuration of the compute profile and click on **FINISH**, as shown in the following screenshot:

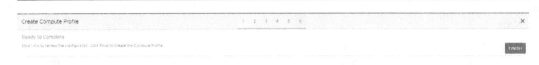

Figure 7.40 – Ready to Complete

30. Now, after we have completed the creation of the compute profile, we will establish a service mesh. To do so, navigate to the **Service Mesh** tab and click on **CREATE SERVICE MESH**, as shown in the following screenshot:

Figure 7.41 – HCX service mesh creation

31. Select the **Source** and **Destination** sites and click **CONTINUE**, as shown in *Figure 7.42*:

Figure 7.42 – Select Sites

32. Now, select the Compute Profile created previously on the on-premises HCX Manager. The Compute Profile on the HCX Cloud Connector on the VMware Cloud on AWS will be preconfigured during the HCX provisioning process. Click on **CONTINUE**, as shown in the following screenshot:

Figure 7.43 – Select Compute Profiles

33. Now, users will need to confirm the services that will be activated with the service mesh. The services are deducted from the configuration previously made on the compute profile. Choose the services you would like to deploy and click on **CONTINUE**, as shown in the following screenshot:

Figure 7.44 – Service mesh service selection

34. Now, select the network uplink profiles. They will be used by the **HCX-Interconnect (HCX-IX)** service and **HCX-Network Extension (HCX-NE)** appliances defined in the previous steps with the management network profile. On the cloud side, select **externalNetwork**. Click on **CONTINUE**, as shown in the following screenshot:

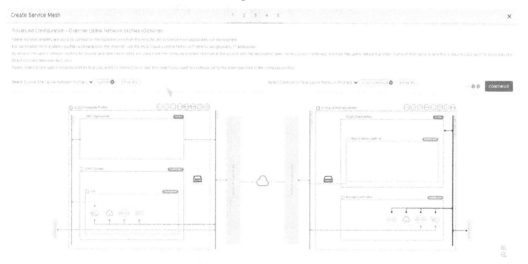

Figure 7.45 – Select an uplink network profile for the HCX service mesh

35. We need to select the **vSphere Distributed Switch (VDS)** or **NSX Virtual Distributed Switch (N-VDS)** on the local side and map it to the remote network container on the cloud side. In

addition, we will need to select the number of appliances deployed on the local side. Each network extension appliance can handle up to seven VLANs. If more VLANs require an extension, it is possible to deploy multiple appliances. Select the number of appliances, and then click on **CONTINUE**, as shown in the following screenshot:

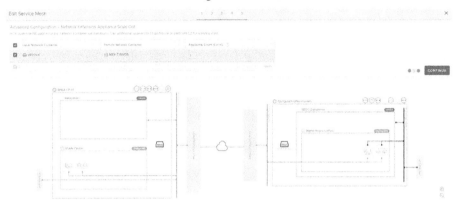

Figure 7.46 – Select the number of network appliances

36. Now, users can select the advanced configurations. Those settings are optional and can be left unchecked. **Application Path Resiliency** is used to create multiple tunnels over the WAN to optimize multiple WAN paths, and **TCP Flow Conditioning** reduces packet fragmentation over WAN. Select the appropriate options, based on your WAN requirements, and click on **CONTINUE**, as shown in the following screenshot:

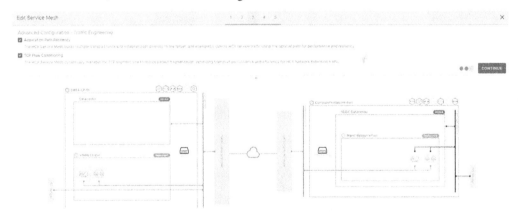

Figure 7.47 – Advanced configuration for the HCX service mesh

37. Next, we review the topology, confirm there are no errors during the selection process, and then click on **CONTINUE**, as shown in the following screenshot:

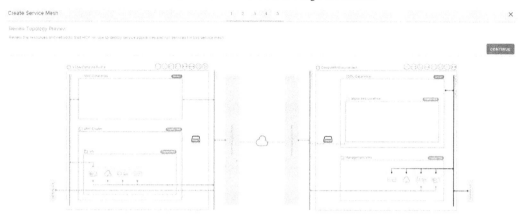

Figure 7.48 – Review Topology Preview

38. Finally, we provide a name for the service mesh and click on **FINISH**, as shown in the following screenshot:

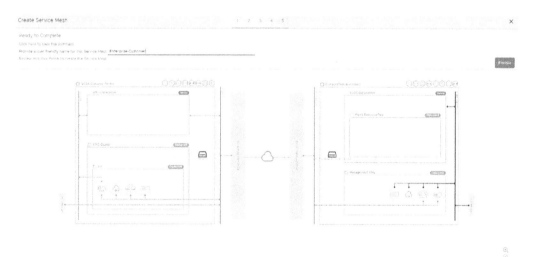

Figure 7.49 – HCX service mesh deployment confirmations

39. After completing the configuration, the service mesh will deploy the appliances. Users can follow the progress through the **Tasks** tab, as shown in the following screenshot:

Figure 7.50 – HCX service mesh deployment

40. Once the service mesh deployment process is completed, a green indication will appear in the **Tasks** tab, as shown in the following screenshot:

Figure 7.51 – HCX service mesh deployment confirmation

The service mesh has now been successfully deployed. Let's configure the network extension in the next section.

Configuring an HCX Layer 2 network extension

After the service mesh has been successfully deployed, users can continue configuring the network extension service.

The Layer 2 extension service is a unique capability of VMware HCX, powering live migration of workloads with uninterrupted network connectivity. A Layer 2 network extension enables you to retain an original IP address by retransmitting ARP protocol broadcast traffic between two disjoin network segments transparently for application workloads. HCX offers you a unique opportunity to configure the service with just a couple of clicks, unprecedented for any network connectivity between clouds.

To configure a Layer 2 network extension, follow these steps:

1. Under **Network Extension**, click on **CREATE A NETWORK EXTENSION**, as shown in the following screenshot:

Figure 7.52 – HCX Network Extension creation

2. Next, users will need to select the VLAN they would like to extend. Note that it is not possible to extend the ESXi management or vMotion VLAN. Select the workload VLAN and click on **NEXT**, as shown in the following screenshot:

Figure 7.53 – Selecting a VLAN for the HCX network extension

3. In this section, users will need to enter the **Gateway IP Address / Prefix Length** value and map it to **Extension Appliance**. The IP configuration should match the current IP scheme implemented for the selected VLAN. Once the details are filled in, they should click on **NEXT**, as shown in the following screenshot:

Figure 7.54 – HCX network extension configuration

> **Note**
>
> The default gateway of the stretched network is *always* located on the source side of the network extension. All north-south traffic sent to or from a VM residing on the extended segment will first traverse a gateway on the source side, even if the destination is within the AWS cloud. The only exception is traffic to other segments within the same SDDC when the **Mobility Optimized Networking** configuration is enabled. **Mobility Optimized Networking** tremendously helps you avoid asymmetric routing and extensive latency, when a VM residing on the extended segment communicates to a VM residing on a different segment within the same SDDC, enabling local routing on the cloud side.

Migrating a workload with HCX

The steps involved to do this are as follows:

1. To migrate workloads, navigate to the **Migration** tab and click on **MIGRATE**, as shown in the following screenshot:

Figure 7.55 – The HCX Migration section

2. Now, we need to create a migration group. First, provide the group with a name under **Group Name**, select the VMs to migrate, and then click on **ADD**, as shown in the following screenshot:

Figure 7.56 – The HCX migration group application selection

3. Next, we will need to fill the fields in green to perform resource mapping on the destination side. These include the compute resource pool, data store, folder, migration type, and the destination port group. Then, click on **GO**, as shown in the following screenshot:

Figure 7.57 – HCX migration resource mapping

Note

HCX supports different migration types beyond **vMotion**. **Bulk Migration** uses vSphere Replication to replicate the VM data and requires a VM restart when switching to the destination. **Replicate-assisted vMotion** uses both vSphere replication for the data transfer and vMotion to switch over the VM, providing both flexibility and increased scalability (compared to just vMotion) and avoiding downtime if combined with a layer 2 VLAN extension.

The following screenshot shows the aforementioned HCX migration types:

Figure 7.58 – HCX migration types

4. You can monitor the migration progress by expanding the migration group and selecting the specific VM that is being migrated, as shown in the following screenshot:

Figure 7.59 – The HCX migration progress

Once the migration is completed, the progress bar will turn green, as shown in the following screenshot:

Figure 7.60 – The HCX migration completed

Now, we will go on to discuss the principles of log management in your VMware Cloud on AWS SDDC.

VMware Aria Operations for Logs

VMware Aria Operations for Logs aggregates logs from all infrastructure-related services in VMware Cloud on AWS, such as vCenter, ESXi, NSX, and the SDDC console. It is automatically preconfigured for all services. From the Cloud Service console, navigate to **Services** and select **VMware Aria Operations for Logs**.

Once inside the service, users can see a flow of all the different log messages and a summary of event types, as shown in the following screenshot:

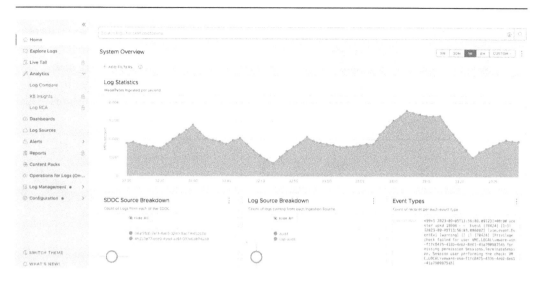

Figure 7.61 – VMware Aria Operations for Logs

Users have the ability to search for specific log messages, such as those associated with VPN events, by utilizing free-form text queries. For instance, entering the query terms `text | Contains | vpn` in the query field and clicking on the search icon will display all log messages in the environment containing the text VPN, as illustrated in *Figure 7.62*:

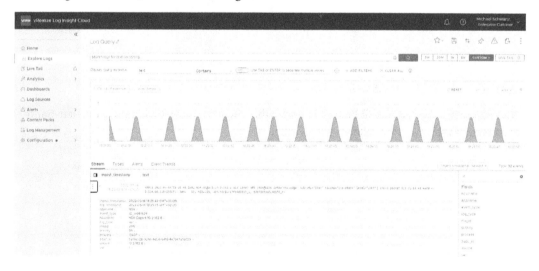

Figure 7.62 – VMware Aria Operations for Logs search

VMware Aria Operations for Logs offers alerting capabilities. The creation of alert definitions is based on search queries. To set up an alert, navigate to **Alert Definitions** on the left-hand side navigation bar and click on **CREATE NEW**. A configuration for the alert will appear. Specify an alert name in the **NAME** field. Once the alert is triggered, it will define a query, similar to our log search. In this instance, we use the keywords vpn and down for the query, with vpn serving as the query name. To throttle alerts, a trigger condition threshold can be defined. In our case, we aim to trigger the alert for every message, so the *threshold is greater than 0*. Finally, click on **SAVE**, as shown in *Figure 7.63*:

Figure 7.63 – A vRealize Log Insight cloud alert definition

Once the alert is triggered, it will be visible under the **Triggered Alerts** section in the left-hand navigation bar, as shown in the following screenshot:

Figure 7.64 – VMware Aria Operations for Logs triggered alerts

Now, it's time to familiarize yourself with the Kubernetes capabilities of VMware Cloud on AWS.

The Tanzu Kubernetes Grid managed service

The **Tanzu Kubernetes Grid** (**TKG**) managed service is included as part of the basic offering of VMware Cloud on AWS. Users can run, deploy, manage, and operate Kubernetes clusters on top of VMware Cloud on AWS, like they can with on-premises vSphere. The SDDC console provides a mechanism to enable TKGs on a selected cluster within an SDDC.

> **Note**
> To enable TKG, a cluster should have at least three hosts.

To activate TKG, you need to open the SDDC console, and inside the specific SDDC under **ACTIONS**, select **Activate Tanzu Kubernetes Grid**. This will initiate the deployment wizard for TKG, as shown in the following screenshot:

Figure 7.65 – Activation of vSphere with Tanzu

On the first screen of the wizard, you will need to fill in the networking details of the service CIDR used within the Tanzu Supervisor Cluster for Kubernetes Services, such as **ClusterAPI** and **etcd**. **Namespace Network CIDR** defines a new vSphere namespace. To support this namespace, a new tier-1 router with a segment from this pool will be created. The Tanzu Kubernetes cluster VM will be attached to it.

Ingress CIDR is used for traffic entering the environment through *DNAT*, and **Egress CIDR** is used for traffic exiting the Kubernetes environment through *SNAT*. Click on **VALIDATE AND PROCEED**, as shown in the following screenshot:

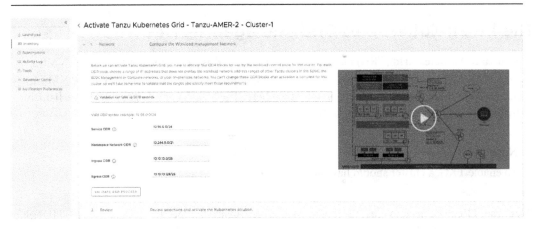

Figure 7.66 – TKG CIDR validation and activation

Now, you will see a summary of the activation parameters entered, as well as a comment that **Tanzu Mission Control** will be enabled together with **Tanzu Kubernetes Grid**; click on **ACTIVATE TANZU KUBERNETES GRID**, as shown in the following screenshot:

Figure 7.67 – TKG and Tanzu Mission Control activation

After service activation is complete in the SDDC console, you can navigate to the vSphere Web Client and validate the creation of a new namespace:

Figure 7.68 – vSphere namespaces

To provision a new vSphere namespace, which is the basis of running Kubernetes workloads, navigate in the vSphere Client to **Workload Management** and click on **CREATE NAMESPACE**, as shown in the following screenshot:

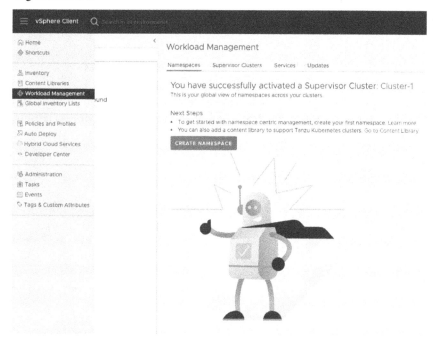

Figure 7.69 – vSphere Workload Management – creating a new namespace

Select the supervisor cluster used to create the vSphere namespaces. In our example, it is **Cluster-1**. In the **Name** section, provide a DNS-compliant name for the cluster, as shown in the following screenshot:

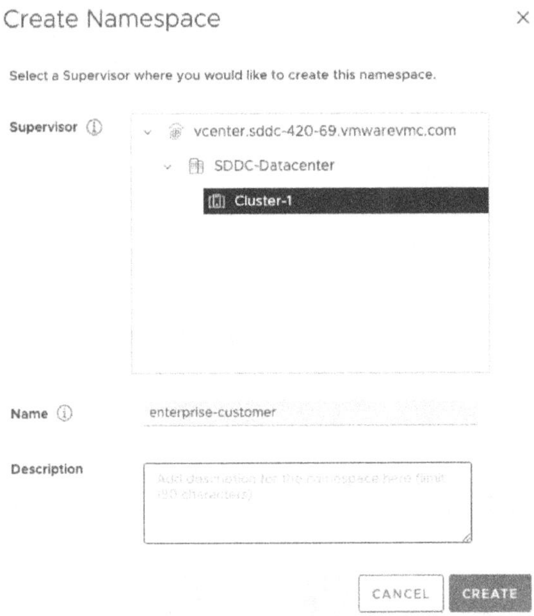

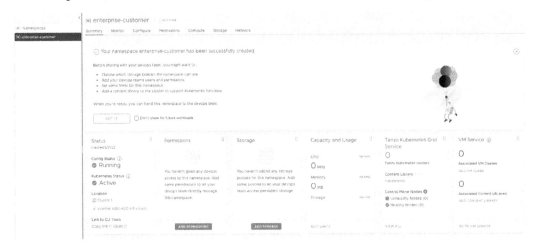

Figure 7.70 – vSphere namespace creation

After the namespace is created, users need to assign the different resources and permissions to it. To start with permissions, click on **ADD PERMISSIONS**, as shown in the following screenshot:

Figure 7.71 – Namespace resource and permission allocation

Unless another LDAP source was configured, the default identity source is **vmc.local** with the `cloudadmin` role, and the best practice would be to perform this configuration with a non-default identity source. We provide the `cloudadmin` user with the **Owner** role, the highest privilege role in our example. Click on **OK** to continue, as shown in the following screenshot:

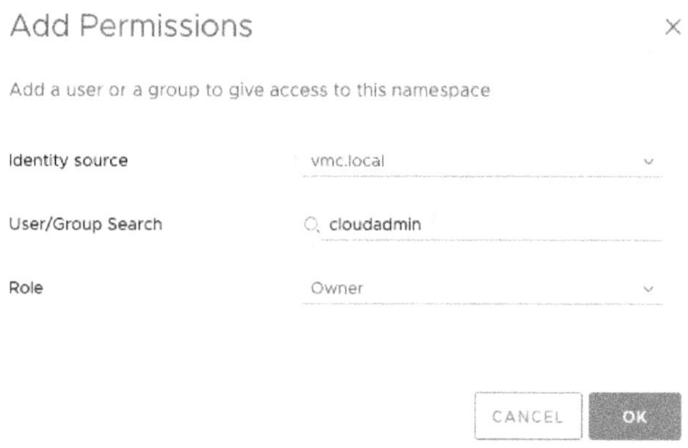

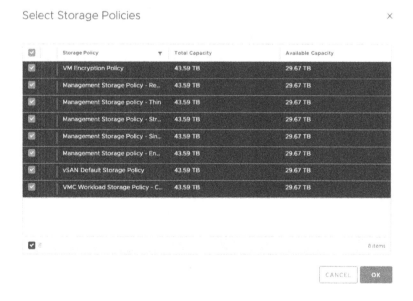

Figure 7.72 – Assigning a namespace permission

Next, click on **ADD Storage**, and add the vSAN storage policies to the namespace for persistent volume claims inside the Kubernetes environment. In our example, we have selected all available vSAN storage policies and clicked on **OK**, as shown in the following screenshot:

Figure 7.73 – vSAN storage policy to Persistent Volume Claim (PVC) mapping

Under **VM Service**, click on **ADD VM CLASS**, and select all of the different VM service t-shirt sizes to be consumed later as a VM service. After selecting them, click on **OK**, as shown in the following screenshot:

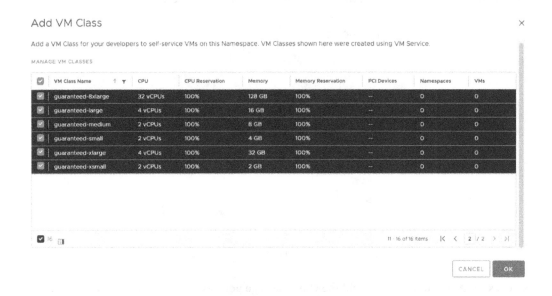

Figure 7.74 – VM service t-shirt size selection

Finally, click on **ADD CONTENT LIBRARY**. On the following screen, we subscribe to a preconfigured content library. It contains the latest Kubernetes software images and will be used when deploying a new Kubernetes cluster. Click on **OK**, as shown in the following screenshot:

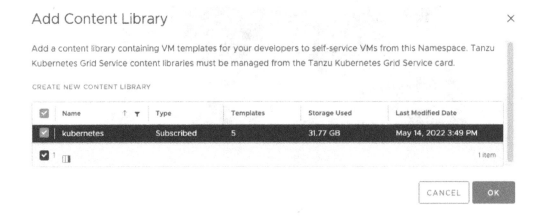

Figure 7.75 – A Kubernetes content library

Now that we have completed the activation process of the vSphere namespaces, we can continue connecting to our Kubernetes cluster and deploying Kubernetes workloads. A well-configured Kubernetes cluster should include all the parameters, as shown in the following screenshot:

Figure 7.76 – A vSphere namespace configuration example

In this section, we described how to activate Tanzu services on VMware Cloud on AWS.

> **Information**
>
> For further instructions on how to deploy workloads in the vSphere environment, visit https://vmc.techzone.vmware.com/tanzu-kubernetes-grid-service-vmware-cloud-aws.

Summary

In this chapter, we reviewed how to configure VMware NSX Advanced Firewall, deploy HCX end to end, implement the different HCX migration methods, navigate and configure alert capabilities in VMware Aria Operations for Logs for VMware Cloud on AWS, and configure vSphere with Tanzu services.

In the following chapter, we'll cover the topic of building applications and managing operations.

8
Building Applications and Managing Operations

Once organizations have deployed or migrated workloads on VMware Cloud on AWS, the next step is modernizing applications using native AWS services. Although AWS offers over 180 services, only a few have been tested and validated to work with VMware Cloud on AWS. This chapter will focus on the modernization aspect of VMware Cloud on AWS and then review day 2 operations, support, troubleshooting, and maintenance.

The following topics will be covered in this chapter:

- Application integration with native AWS services
- VMware Cloud on AWS operations and monitoring
- VMware Cloud on AWS integrated services
- SDDC upgrades and maintenance

Application integration with native AWS services

AWS and VMware have verified a limited number of AWS services capable of integration with workloads running on VMware Cloud on AWS. By incorporating these services as part of their migration and modernization approach, organizations can reduce operational overhead, lower the **Total Cost of Ownership** (**TCO**), and improve the agility and scalability of their workloads

The following diagram illustrates the VMware Cloud on AWS managed service leveraging native AWS services:

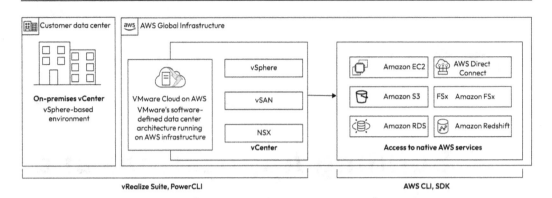

Figure 8.1 – Native AWS services integration with VMware Cloud on AWS

This chapter covers network connectivity between native AWS services and VMware workloads. Once the network connectivity is established, we will explore standard native AWS service integrations, including offloading storage to secondary storage in the AWS cloud, protecting **Virtual Machine** (**VM**) workloads using AWS networking services, and leveraging AWS databases and analytics services with workloads running in the **Software-Defined Data Center** (**SDDC**).

Networking between SDDC and native AWS services

To effectively integrate AWS services, it is critical to establish resilient network connectivity between VMware Cloud on AWS SDDC workloads and AWS services. This section will outline the connectivity required to connect the organization's native AWS account with the VMware Cloud on AWS SDDC.

To set up VMware Cloud on AWS, two AWS accounts are required. The first account is the VMware Cloud on AWS SDDC account (also known as the **shadow account**), which hosts the VMware Cloud on AWS SDDC infrastructure. VMware owns, manages, and operates this AWS account. The second account is an organization's AWS account often referred to as the customer-owned AWS account, owned, operated, and funded directly by the customer based on the consumption of AWS services within it.

The organization's AWS account often referred to as the customer-owned AWS account has an Amazon **Virtual Private Cloud** (**VPC**) designated as the connected VPC. This connected VPC can run several native AWS services, which can be leveraged by the VM workloads running on the VMware Cloud on AWS SDDC.

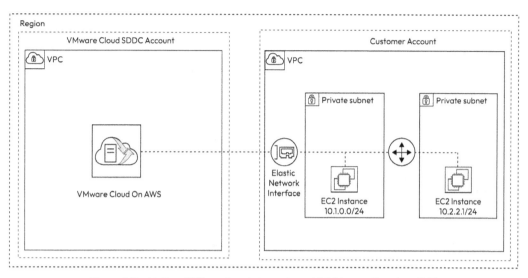

Figure 8.2 – Native AWS services integration with VMware Cloud on AWS

The diagram (*Figure 8.2*) shows an Amazon VPC on the left side, known as the shadow VPC, which operates within the VMware-owned AWS account, referred to as the shadow account. The account and VPC are hidden by the VMware Cloud Services Console, preventing organizations from accessing them. The shadow VPC uses **Cross-Account Elastic Network Interfaces (X-ENIs)** to communicate with an Amazon VPC, known as the connected VPC, on the right side, which runs in a organization's AWS account often referred to as the customer-owned AWS account.

The diagram (*Figure 8.2*) also shows the Amazon **Elastic Compute Cloud (EC2)** instances running in the connected VPC in the organization's AWS account often referred to as the customer-owned AWS account. Several X-ENIs (only one active) provide high-bandwidth and low-latency connectivity to services running in the connected VPC. While the diagram shows only Amazon EC2 instances, various AWS services, such as Amazon S3, Amazon **Elastic File System (EFS)**, Amazon FSx, Amazon RDS, and AWS Backup, can integrate with workloads running in VMware Cloud on AWS. Each VMware Cloud SDDC account can only connect to a single AWS account, often referred to as the customer-owned account, and therefore only one AWS connected VPC can be designated for each VMware Cloud on AWS SDDC. The connected VPC can only be specified during or immediately after SDDC deployment and cannot be changed without destroying and recreating the SDDC.

A single Amazon VPC can serve as the connected VPC for multiple VMware Cloud on AWS SDDCs. However, a VMware Cloud SDDC can be integrated with only one connected VPC. Also, some large enterprise organizations may require access to AWS services across multiple Amazon VPCs from their VMware Cloud on AWS SDDCs. In such cases, they can use SDDC groups and VMware Transit Connect to establish connectivity between the Amazon VPCs and SDDCs. VMware-AWS network connectivity using AWS Transit Gateway and VMware Transit Connect architectures was covered in *Chapter 2*.

Having covered the prerequisites, let us explore some validated and commonly used native AWS service integrations for VMware Cloud on AWS workloads.

Integrating Amazon ELB with VMware Cloud on AWS

AWS **Elastic Load Balancing** (**ELB**) is a service that distributes incoming application traffic to multiple targets and virtual appliances automatically. The targets can be EC2 instances, IP addresses, or lambda functions. When integrating with workloads on VMware Cloud on AWS, the target type is always IP addresses. The **Application Load Balancer** (**ALB**) is used for load-balancing HTTP requests, while the **Network Load Balancer** (**NLB**) is used for load-balancing network/transport protocols (Layer 4 – TCP and UDP requests).

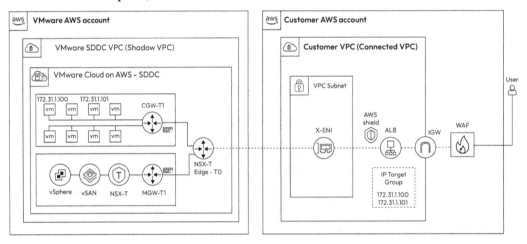

Figure 8.3 – Amazon ELB integration with VMware Cloud on AWS

Figure 8.3 illustrates that the load balancer infrastructure, including Amazon ELB, is hosted on the connected VPC on the right side, while workloads on the VMware Cloud on AWS SDDC are used as IP targets. The ELB public IP is routed by the connected VPC's internet gateway to receive inbound traffic from users anywhere on the internet. The load balancer then distributes requests to VMs based on the IP target group configured on the elastic load balancer. Traffic between the Amazon **Elastic Load Balancer** (**ELB**) and workloads on the VMware Cloud on AWS SDDC are routed through the ENI over the NSX-T Edge T0 router before eventually reaching the VMs on the VMware Cloud SDDC.

Organizations can enhance the security of their Amazon ELB and the workloads behind it by using Amazon's **Web Application Firewall** (**WAF**). WAF enables organizations to monitor the HTTP(S) requests forwarded to their web application resources. It can help protect websites from common attack techniques such as SQL injection and **Cross-Site Scripting** (**XSS**). Organizations can also create rules that block or rate-limit traffic from specific user agents, IP addresses, or requests with certain headers. Organizations can also enable AWS Shield on the elastic load balancer for protection against **Distributed Denial of Service (DDoS)** attacks.

In addition, organizations can leverage Amazon CloudFront (not depicted in *Figure 8.3*), a **Content Delivery Network (CDN)** that improves the delivery of dynamic and static web content to end users by enhancing the reliability and availability of web applications. CloudFront has copies of frequently accessed files cached at various edge locations across the globe. These edge locations comprise a global network of data centers where CloudFront delivers content. When an end user requests content served by CloudFront, the request is sent to the edge location nearest to the end user with the lowest latency.

Integrating Amazon Simple Storage Service

Amazon **Simple Storage Service (S3)** is a cloud-based object storage service that enables organizations to store and retrieve data from anywhere at any time. Using S3, organizations can leverage cloud-native storage that offers high scalability, performance, security, and durability at a low cost to develop a wide range of applications. The following figure illustrates the integration of VMware Cloud on AWS workloads with an Amazon S3 bucket privately using a VPC gateway endpoint.

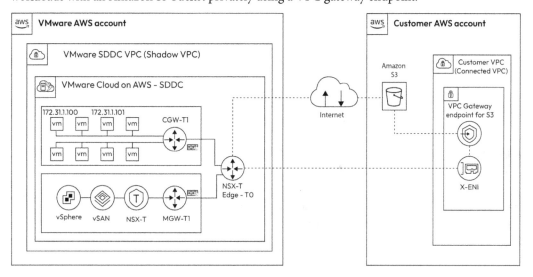

Figure 8.4 – Amazon S3 integration with VMware Cloud on AWS

Workloads running on VMware Cloud on AWS SDDCs can access public S3 buckets over the internet. However, this approach is less secure and incurs data egress costs per GB for all data accessed from the S3 bucket. Hence, using an S3 VPC gateway endpoint is recommended for organizations to access data privately from the S3 bucket without exposing it to the public internet. The S3 VPC gateway endpoint is created in the connected VPC. The workload traffic from the SDDC traverses the NSX Edge Tier-0 Logical Router through the X-ENI to the S3 VPC gateway endpoint in the connected VPC and eventually reaches the S3 bucket.

Integrating Amazon EFS

Amazon EFS is a scalable file storage solution that can grow from gigabytes to petabytes of data without pre-provisioning storage or managing storage capacity and performance. EFS supports full filesystem access semantics, including strong consistency and file locking. In addition, Amazon EC2 instances and VMware VMs can access an EFS filesystem simultaneously. *Figure 8.5* illustrates the integration of VMware Cloud on AWS workloads with Amazon EFS using a VPC gateway endpoint.

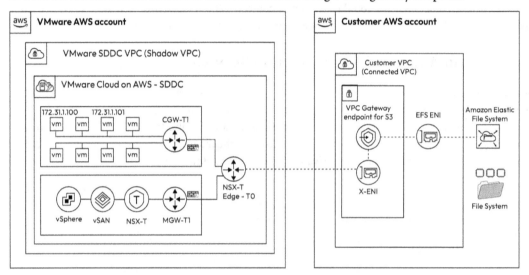

Figure 8.5 – Amazon EFS integration with VMware Cloud on AWS

Workloads running on VMware Cloud on AWS SDDC can utilize an EFS VPC interface endpoint to access EFS filesystems residing in the connected VPC via the NSX Edge Tier-0 Logical Router and X-ENI. Multi-**Availability Zone** (**AZ**) filesystems have ENIs associated with each AWS AZ, enhancing availability and resiliency. Amazon EFS supports a wide range of workloads and applications, including big data and analytics, media processing workflows, and content management. Furthermore, EFS can be utilized as secondary storage to offload VM data from the primary vSAN storage.

Integrating Amazon FSx for Windows File Server

Amazon FSx for Windows File Server is a scalable file storage solution accessible through the **Service Message Block** (**SMB**) protocol built on Windows Server. Amazon FSx provides high throughput and IOPS with consistent sub-millisecond latencies. In addition, an FSx filesystem can be accessed simultaneously by Amazon EC2 instances and VMware VMs. Amazon FSx offers various administrative features, including user quotas, end user file restores, and Microsoft **Active Directory** (**AD**) integration. *Figure 8.6* illustrates the integration of VMware Cloud on AWS workloads with Amazon FSx for Windows File Server and AWS Directory Service, which enables file sharing across multiple VMs.

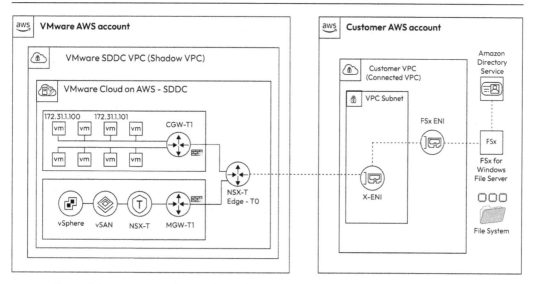

Figure 8.6 – Amazon FSx for Windows File Server integration with VMware Cloud on AWS

Workloads running on VMware Cloud on AWS SDDCs can access an Amazon FSx filesystem in the connected VPC via the NSX Edge Tier-0 Logical Router using the X-ENI. For multi-AZ filesystems, each AWS AZ where the Amazon FSx filesystem is created has a corresponding ENI created within the same AZ to enhance availability and resiliency.

VMs running on VMware Cloud on AWS SDDCs can offload data to Amazon FSx for Windows Server filesystems. The FSx filesystems act as secondary storage to complement primary vSAN storage. A diverse range of use cases that necessitate Windows shared file storage, such as CRM, ERP, custom or .NET applications, and Microsoft SQL Server, can be accommodated by using Amazon EFS for VMware Cloud on AWS SDDC workloads.

To support high availability, security, and scalability, AWS provides a range of fully managed, purpose-built database services, including relational, key-value, in-memory, document, wide-column, graph, time-series, and ledger databases. Among these, Amazon **Relational Database Service** (**RDS**) is a well-known option, enabling organizations to choose from seven popular engines, including Amazon Aurora with MySQL compatibility, Amazon Aurora with PostgreSQL compatibility, MySQL, MariaDB, PostgreSQL, Oracle, and SQL Server. Additionally, Amazon Redshift is a fully managed data warehouse tool that can effectively handle petabyte-scale data analysis.

Amazon QuickSight is a business analytics service that enables users to create visualizations, perform ad hoc analyses, and gain quick insights into their data from any device and at any time. With QuickSight, organizations can expand their business analytics capabilities to a large number of users thanks to its responsive query performance. It provides easy access to data from various sources, such as CSV and Excel files, on-premises databases such as SQL, MySQL, and PostgreSQL, and SaaS applications such as Salesforce, Amazon Redshift, Amazon RDS, Amazon Athena, and Amazon S3.

Athena is an analytics service that allows for interactive querying, utilizing open source frameworks and supporting open table and file formats. With Athena, users can easily build applications or analyze large volumes of data from over 25 different sources, including cloud systems, on-premises data sources, and Amazon S3 data lakes, using either SQL or Python.

AWS Glue is a serverless data integration service that simplifies the process of discovering, preparing, moving, and integrating data from over 70 diverse data sources and managing data in a centralized data catalog. It can be used for analytics, machine learning, and application development. AWS Glue enables organizations to create, run visually, and monitor **extract, transform, and load** (**ETL**) pipelines to load data into their data lakes. *Figure 8.7* illustrates the integration of VMware Cloud on AWS workloads with Amazon RDS (databases) and various AWS analytics services, including Amazon QuickSight, AWS Glue, and Amazon Athena, along with data warehousing using Amazon Redshift.

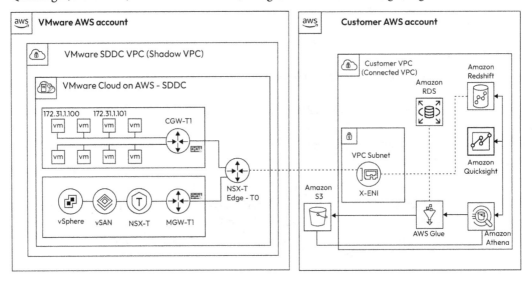

Figure 8.7 – Amazon RDS integration with VMware Cloud on AWS

As seen in *Figure 8.7*, workloads in the VMware Cloud on AWS SDDC have access to Amazon databases such as Amazon RDS and Redshift running in the connected VPC. Organizations can avoid managing complex database servers using Amazon's fully managed databases. The web and application tiers can continue to run on the VMware Cloud on AWS SDDC, while the database tier can be migrated to one of the AWS-managed databases. The traffic between the web tier and app tier in the SDDC is routed through the T1 compute gateway, the T0-NSX-Edge, and over the X-ENI and eventually reaches the database endpoint.

A common use case for organizations is reducing the TCO of storage-heavy or memory-intensive on-premises databases using a purpose-built database such as Amazon RDS. Amazon RDS lets you migrate on-premises relational databases to the cloud and integrate them with VMware Cloud on

AWS SDDC VMs. Amazon RDS also reduces the operational overhead organizations may incur with managing availability, scalability, and **Disaster Recovery (DR)** tasks.

Organizations can benefit from the proximity of data residing in the VMware Cloud on AWS SDDC and gain meaningful insights from their business data by utilizing AWS analytics service integrations. For instance, Amazon Redshift can be used to create a data warehouse that enables running analytics at scale on relational data from transactional systems, operational databases, and line-of-business applications running within the VMware Cloud on AWS SDDC.

Integrating AWS Directory Service

Domain Name System (DNS) is a critical component of any IT infrastructure as it provides hostname-to-IP address resolutions that applications heavily rely on to establish connectivity with other systems and workloads in the organization. Organizations running VMware Cloud on AWS workloads can implement a hybrid DNS solution using fully managed native services such as AWS-managed Microsoft AD and Amazon Route 53 from AWS. *Figure 8.8* illustrates the integration of VMware Cloud on AWS workloads with AWS-managed Microsoft AD.

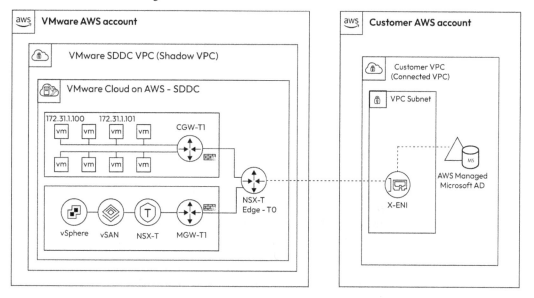

Figure 8.8 – Amazon-managed Microsoft AD integration with VMware Cloud on AWS

AWS Directory Service is a managed service providing directories containing organizational information, including users, groups, and computers. Using AWS Directory Service, organizations can reduce the burden of management tasks, freeing up more time and resources for their business. Organizations can also use AWS Directory Service to provide DNS resolution. The AWS Directory Service IP address can be the DNS forwarder on the VMware Cloud on AWS SDDC environment.

Integrating an Amazon Route 53 inbound Resolver endpoint

Amazon Route 53 is a DNS service that is highly available and scalable. Amazon Route 53 Resolver can respond recursively to DNS queries for public records, Amazon VPC-specific DNS names, and Amazon Route 53 private-hosted zones. The inbound Resolver endpoints can enable DNS queries to an Amazon VPC from another Amazon VPC or VMware Cloud on AWS SDDC segments, or from an on-premises environments. *Figure 8.9* illustrates the integration of VMware Cloud on AWS workloads with an Amazon Route 53 Resolver inbound endpoint.

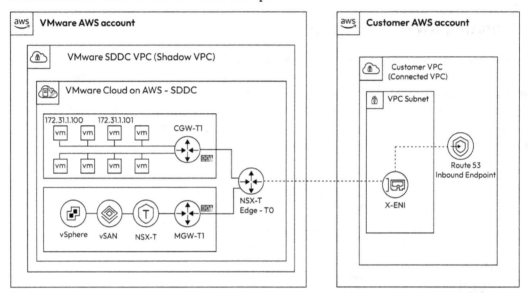

Figure 8.9 – Amazon Route 53 Resolver inbound endpoint integration with VMware Cloud on AWS

The Amazon Route 53 service provides a managed DNS resolver through a Route 53 inbound endpoint, an alternative option for providing DNS resolution to VMware Cloud on AWS environments. The endpoint has the same DNS view as the VPC it resides in, enabling private hosted zone name resolution, internet name resolution, and customizable name resolution through forwarding rules.

Organizations can provision an inbound endpoint directly within the connected VPC, which can have multiple ENIs, each with a unique IP address. To ensure high availability, using at least two ENIs in different AZs is recommended. Each ENI can handle up to 10,000 queries per second, and additional ENIs can be added to scale out.

VMware Cloud on AWS operations and monitoring

A VMware Cloud on AWS SDDC comprises compute, storage, and networking resources and operates within an Amazon VPC. It offers a complete VMware stack, including vCenter Server, NSX software-defined networking, vSAN software-defined storage, and Amazon EC2-powered bare-metal ESXi hosts that provide compute and storage resources to workloads. Daily VMware Cloud operations on AWS require access and management through several consoles. *Figure 8.10* shows the three management consoles most used to manage VMware Cloud SDDC environments and native AWS integrations:

VMware Cloud on AWS Console   vSphere Client (HTML 5)   AWS Management Console

Figure 8.10 – Accessing and managing VMware Cloud on AWS

The VMware Cloud Services Console lets organizations manage the entire VMware Cloud services portfolio across hybrid and native public clouds. Using the VMware Cloud Services Console, organizations can do the following:

- Perform identity and access management functions, including managing users and groups, assigning user roles to resources and services, and viewing the OAuth apps that have access to the VMware Cloud organization

- Manage billing and subscriptions, including information about current costs, such as the last billing statement, manage payment methods or change their default payment method, and add promotional credits and commitments

- Manage organization functions, including creating OAuth apps, switch between organizations, change language and regional formatting, secure the account with MFA, generate API tokens, and edit user profiles.

Figure 8.11 shows the default landing page of the VMware Cloud Services Console, which lists all the VMware services.

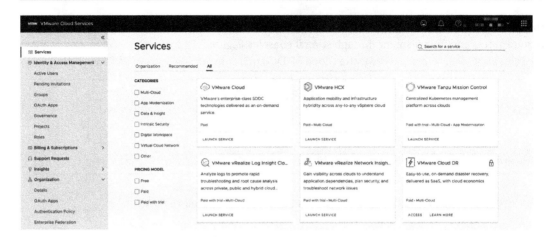

Figure 8.11 – VMware Cloud Services Console

The vSphere Client allows users to connect to vCenter Server systems via a supported web browser and manage vSphere inventory objects. The home screen displays data from the environment in a single, unified view. It allows managing the vSphere environment by performing various functions, such as managing VM operations, managing VM storage policies, performing migrations using vMotion or HCX, configuring **Hybrid Linked Mode** (**HLM**), and using VMware Site Recovery. *Figure 8.12* shows the VMware vCenter console that is used to manage VMware VMs.

Figure 8.12 – VMware vCenter console

The AWS Management Console includes several service consoles for managing AWS resources. The home page is a central location to access all the individual service consoles performing the necessary AWS-related configurations and tasks. The Amazon VPC console is used to access the connected VPC and configure integration with several native AWS services discussed earlier in this chapter. *Figure 8.13* shows the AWS console that is used to integrate native AWS services.

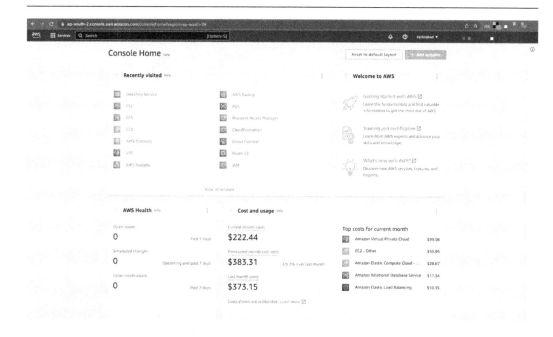

Figure 8.13 – AWS Management Console

VMware Cloud on AWS integrated services

VMware Cloud on AWS has several integrated services, also referred to as add-ons. Organizations can activate or subscribe to these services and integrate them with their VMware Cloud environments from the VMware Cloud Services Console. *Table 8.1* has a list of commonly used integrated services with VMware Cloud on AWS. This is not a comprehensive list; VMware constantly updates the list of services. This chapter will focus on just a few integrated services:

Integrated Service	Category	Active From
VMware Hybrid Extension (HCX)	Migrations & Mobility	Integrated Services tab of the SDDC
NSX Advanced Firewall	Advanced Networking	Integrated Services tab of the SDDC
Site Recovery	Disaster Recovery	Integrated Services tab of the SDDC
VMware Aria Automation	Build & Automation	Integrated Services tab of the SDDC
VMware Aria Operations	Monitoring & Operations	Integrated Services tab of the SDDC

Integrated Service	Category	Active From
VMware Aria Operations for Networks	Monitoring & Operations	Integrated Services tab of the SDDC
VMware Cloud DR	Disaster Recovery	Services section of the Cloud Console
VMware Aria Operations for Logs	Monitoring & Operations	Services section of the Cloud Console
VMware Aria Automation for Secure Clouds	Monitoring & Operations	Services section of the Cloud Console

Table 8.1 – List of VMware Cloud integrated services

VMware Aria Operations (formerly vRealize Operations)

VMware Aria Operations is an AI-driven platform for managing IT operations in private, hybrid, and multi-cloud environments. It can perform continuous performance optimization, efficient cost management, intelligent remediation, and integrated compliance. In addition, the platform includes VMware Aria Operations Manager, which helps organizations configure, investigate, and resolve issues. It is an add-on service providing organizations with multiple deployment options to manage their VMware Cloud on AWS cloud environment. VMware Aria Operations includes all VMware Aria Operations Enterprise edition features and is priced based per VM on demand, for a 1–2-year commitment, or for a 3–5-year commitment.

VMware Aria Operations for Logs (formerly vRealize Log Insight)

VMware Aria Operations for Logs is a powerful log analysis tool that enables scalable log management through interactive and responsive dashboards, advanced analytics, and versatile third-party integrations. In addition, vRealize Aria Operations for Logs provides rich operational visibility and efficient troubleshooting. It offers several key features, such as seamless integration with vRealize Operations for comprehensive end-to-end operations management. It has a built-in understanding of vSphere and other VMware products and can collect and analyze all types of machine-generated log data. It also provides automated alerts to quickly identify and track issues. VMware Aria Operations for Logs is included with VMware Cloud on AWS with an option to upgrade to advanced features.

VMware Aria Operations for Networks (formerly vRealize Network Insight)

VMware Aria Operations for Networks is a comprehensive network monitoring tool that helps you create an efficient, highly available, and secure network infrastructure across various VMware Cloud environments, including NSX, VMware SD-WAN, vSphere, Kubernetes, AWS, and VMware Cloud deployments. Leveraging vRealize Network Insight, VMware Aria Operations for Networks can collect and analyze various metrics, APIs, configurations, metadata, integrations, NetFlow, and sFlow telemetry, and IPFIX flow traffic. Once the traffic is analyzed, vRealize Network Insight provides traffic distribution details and a real-time view of network traffic patterns and collects configuration details and performance metrics for complete visibility. VMware Aria Operations for Networks for VMware Cloud on AWS per-CPU subscriptions are available with a 1–5-year commitment.

The VMware Cloud on AWS subscription includes the VMware Aria Universal Suite (which comprises VMware Aria Automation, VMware Aria Operations, VMware Aria Operations for Logs, and VMware Aria Operations for Networks).

VMware Cloud on AWS troubleshooting

Organizations can deploy monitoring and troubleshooting applications from VMware (including Aria Operations, Operations for Logs, and Operations for Networks) or other third-party vendors. The prerequisite gateway firewall rules should be configured for these tools to perform efficiently.

Additionally, organizations can leverage NSX IPFIX and port mirroring functionality for monitoring and troubleshooting the VMware Cloud on AWS SDDC networking and security. IPFIX, a standard for network flow information export and analysis, can be configured to capture all the flows from VMs connected to a logical segment and then send them to the IPFIX collector. Organizations can specify the collector names as a parameter for each IPFIX switch profile.

Organizations can use port mirroring to redirect all traffic from a particular source to a collector, where the mirrored traffic is sent through a **Generic Routing Encapsulation (GRE)** tunnel to preserve all the original packet information as it traverses the network to a remote destination. Port mirroring has various applications, including troubleshooting, where it can be utilized to detect intrusion, debug, and diagnose network errors. Additionally, it can be used for compliance and monitoring purposes, where all the monitored traffic can be forwarded to a network appliance for analysis and remediation.

Port mirroring requires two groups, a source group for monitoring data and a destination group for copying the collected data. The membership criteria for the source group involve grouping VMs based on the workload, such as a web group or an application group. On the other hand, the membership criteria for the destination group require VMs to be grouped based on their IP addresses. Port mirroring has one enforcement point, where policy rules can be applied to the SDDC environment. Port mirroring can be configured for ingress, egress, or bidirectional traffic.

The VMware Cloud on AWS SDDC console features a **Troubleshooting** tab with a connectivity validator that enables organizations to conduct network connectivity tests to ensure that they have all the necessary network connectivity and firewall rules in place. Currently, the console supports two tests: **HLM** and **Site Recovery**.

With HLM, organizations can manage their on-premises vCenter and VMware Cloud on AWS SDDC vCenter inventories using a unified vSphere Client interface, resulting in a single-pane-of-glass management view. Furthermore, HLM allows organizations to seamlessly migrate workloads between their on-premises data center and cloud SDDC. HLM is based on the **Enhanced Linked Mode**

(**ELM**) feature, a component of vSphere when deployed in the on-premises environment. *Figure 8.14* shows the **Troubleshooting** tab of the VMware Cloud on AWS SDDC console that is used for HLM connectivity use cases:

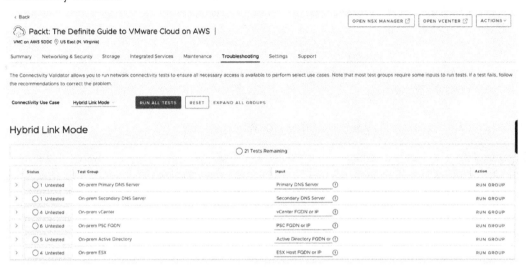

Figure 8.14 – Troubleshooting HLM

The connectivity validator requires certain inputs, including the on-premises DNS server, vCenter Server, and AD services. Depending on the test results, VMware will provide recommendations to correct the problem which could include allowing traffic on on-premises firewalls, AWS Security Groups or NACLs, or VMware Cloud Gateway Firewall.

VMware Site Recovery is a DR as a service add-on to VMware Cloud on AWS SDDCs enabling organizations to protect and recover applications without requiring a dedicated secondary site. The service is provided on demand and is delivered, sold, and supported by VMware. Organizations can use VMware Site Recovery to manage DR, disaster avoidance, and non-disruptive testing capabilities. This solution extends VMware Cloud on AWS and integrates with VMware **Site Recovery Manager** (**SRM**) and VMware **vSphere Replication** (**VSR**) to automate recovering, testing, re-protecting, and failing-back VM workloads. VMware Site Recovery can be implemented between a organization's data center and a VMware Cloud on AWS SDDC or between two VMware Cloud on AWS SDDCs deployed in different AWS Regions. *Figure 8.15* shows the **Troubleshooting** tab of the VMware Cloud on AWS SDDC console that is used for Site Recovery connectivity use cases.

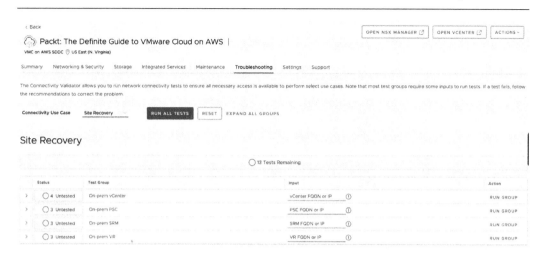

Figure 8.15 – Troubleshooting VMware Site Recovery

To use the connectivity validator for Site Recovery, the FQDN/IP addresses for the on-premises vCenter Server and the Platform Services Controller, as well as the on-premises SRM and VSR server, would be required. *Figure 8.16* shows the **Support** tab of the VMware Cloud on AWS SDDC console.

Figure 8.16 – Support Information

VMware Cloud on AWS organizations who require assistance can contact VMware for support by accessing the VMware Cloud Services Console. To assist organizations, VMware support personnel may request information such as the organization ID and SDDC ID, which can be found on the **Support** tab.

SDDC upgrades and maintenance

VMware is responsible for performing updates on VMware Cloud on AWS SDDCs. These updates, known as SDDC upgrades, ensure that new features and bug fixes are continuously delivered and that software versions remain consistent across the SDDC fleet. *Figure 8.17* shows the **Maintenance** tab of the VMware Cloud on AWS SDDC console.

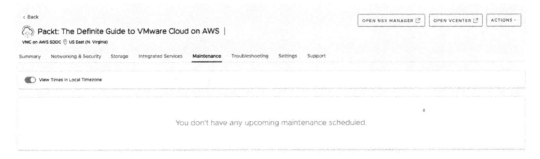

Figure 8.17 – Maintenance information

Odd-numbered releases of the SDDC software (e.g., 1.11, 1.13, 1.15, 1.17, and 1.19) are not mandatory and can only be used for new SDDC deployments. Upgrades and new SDDC deployments will default to the most recent even-numbered release (e.g., 1.12, 1.14, 1.16, 1.18, and 1.20). Upgrades to even-numbered releases are mandatory and will be provided to all SDDCs.

VMware has the discretion to pre-determine SDDC upgrade paths. As a standard practice, VMware does not offer cumulative SDDC upgrades. Therefore, all SDDC upgrades are required to follow a sequential path and cannot be skipped for a subsequent SDDC release (e.g., organizations running version 1.20 cannot skip 1.22 and go to 1.24).

All VMware Cloud on AWS SDDC upgrades are performed across three phases:

- **Phase 1**: Control plane upgrade involves updating vCenter and NSX Edge Tier-0 Logical Router. A backup restore point is created for the management appliances, allowing for a rollback if the upgrade encounters any issues. This phase includes an NSX Edge failover, leading to a brief downtime. Access to NSX Manager and vCenter is unavailable during this period. Despite this, workloads and other resources continue to function normally, subject to outlined constraints. This phase can take approximately 3 to 4 hours.

- **Phase 2**: Host upgrades involve updating the ESXi hosts and host networking software in the SDDC. An extra host (with no additional charges) is temporarily added to the SDDC to ensure sufficient capacity is available for the workloads. vMotion and DRS activities are implemented to facilitate the update. The upgrade process has been optimized to ensure that NSX Edge migrations occur only once during the entire upgrade. Throughout this phase, workloads and other resources continue to operate normally. The completion time for Phase 2 is contingent on the number of hosts in each cluster. Generally, it takes two hours to back up, add, and remove hosts. Additionally, the upgrade process for each host typically requires 45-60 minutes.

- **Phase 3** involves updating the NSX appliances. A backup restore point is created for the NSX Edge appliances, allowing for a rollback if the upgrade encounters any issues. NSX Manager and vCenter access are not available during this phase. Despite this, workloads and other resources continue to function normally, subject to outlined constraints. This phase can take approximately 2 to 4 hours.

Prior to each upcoming SDDC upgrade phase, VMware will inform organizations via email. Organizations can then adjust the maintenance time for SDDC upgrades based on their preferred date and time, aligning with their organization's weekly or monthly maintenance windows. Upon completing each phase, a notification will be sent. There is a waiting period of up to a couple of days between the phases.

Summary

This chapter covered a few AWS service integrations that can be natively integrated with VMware Cloud on AWS workloads, aligning with the migration and modernization strategy embraced by VMware Cloud organizations. Additionally, we provided an overview of day 2 operations, including support, troubleshooting, and maintenance.

In the next chapter, you will learn about, including how to consume, the different APIs available in VMware Cloud on AWS, including CSP, vCenter, and NSX-T. You will also learn how to leverage infrastructure as code with VMware Cloud on AWS.

Infrastructure as Code with VMware Cloud

Infrastructure as Code (**IaC**) is a method used to provision and manage IT infrastructure using code, rather than relying on manual configuration. IaC allows for greater automation, consistency, and the ability to recreate infrastructure management tasks. By leveraging IaC with **VMware Cloud** (**VMC**), users can programmatically provision and manage virtual infrastructure on the **VMC on AWS** platform, leading to enhanced efficiency in automating and handling their cloud environments.

The following are the main topics that will be covered in this chapter:

- Introduction to the VMware Cloud APIs
- Cloud Services Platform APIs
- Consuming Console APIs via the Developer Center
- NSX-T Data Center REST API

Introduction to the VMware Cloud APIs

VMware Cloud, a leading provider of cloud solutions, offers a suite of powerful APIs that empower organizations to harness the full potential of their cloud environments.

In this chapter, we will delve into the VMware Cloud APIs, exploring their significance, capabilities, and the opportunities they present for businesses and developers alike. VMware APIs help simplify manual tasks, facilitate the effective administration of complex environments at a significant scale, and provide code samples and language support for popular programming languages, enabling developers to initiate their projects promptly and with ease.

Whether customers are looking to streamline their cloud operations, optimize resource allocation, or build innovative applications, understanding and leveraging VMware Cloud APIs can be a game-changer. These APIs have the potential to transform your approach to interacting with and overseeing your cloud infrastructure, leading to improved efficiency, agility, and innovation.

VMware Cloud on AWS can be programmatically accessed and controlled through three main APIs. Users need to be familiar with these APIs to automate and develop solutions for their specific use cases:

- Cloud Services Platform APIs

- VMware Cloud on AWS APIs

- SDDC APIs (vSphere API)

Figure 9.1 shows the overview of several VMware APIs, including the SDDC APIs, among others. The diagram also shows the AWS API endpoints.

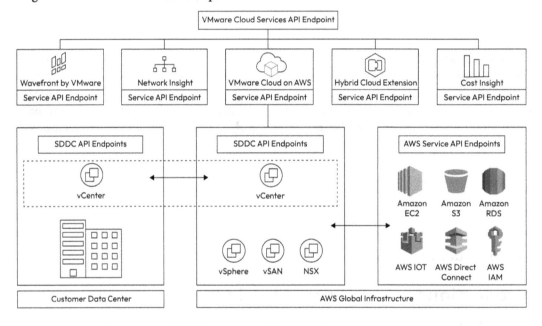

Figure 9.1 – Overview of VMC on AWS APIs

Cloud Services Platform APIs

The **Cloud Services Platform (CSP)** APIs provide customers with a programmatic method to access and manage the capabilities provided by VMware. When working with VMware's cloud services, such as VMC on AWS, the CSP APIs enable customers to automate and manage their cloud environments with greater efficiency. The CSP APIs are the primary mechanism for authentication and user management for VMC on AWS. These APIs provide an authentication endpoint that allows users to access VMC on AWS services. Once authenticated, users are issued an authorization token to be able to access the CSP and VMC on AWS APIs. Furthermore, the CSP APIs offer functionality within the VMware Cloud console for managing users and organizations, including displaying, adding, and removing users. Additionally, CSP APIs include methods for managing permissions, roles, and policies for both organizations and users in VMC on AWS.

VMware Cloud on AWS API

The VMC on AWS API is the primary method for automating and programmatically managing resources in a VMC on AWS **Software-Defined Data Center** (**SDDC**). This API provides a comprehensive set of actions that enables customers and partners to integrate their workflows and tools to manage and automate tasks within the VMC on AWS environment. The API endpoint can execute various functions, such as creating, scaling, and managing SDDCs and adding and removing ESXi hosts. Additionally, the API is used for network operations, including creating and managing virtual networks, firewalls, and security groups. Moreover, the VMC API can retrieve information on tasks and events within the VMC environment.

The VMC API is a RESTful API, which means it can be consumed using any programming language or client that can communicate over HTTP. The API provides flexibility by allowing easy integration into existing tools and workflows. Additionally, the open source vSphere Automation SDKs are available in multiple programming languages including Python, Java, and Ruby, providing a set of libraries and helper functions to make it easier to work with the VMC API. The features of VMC can also be accessed through the command line with PowerCLI or the **Data Center CLI** (**DCLI**).

The VMC API comes with a built-in API Explorer that enables users to test and explore the API's features without any code. This feature simplifies the discovery and testing of the API's functionality and can be accessed through the VMware Cloud Console.

SDDC APIs (vSphere API)

The group of APIs used for managing SDDCs are collectively known as SDDC APIs. The SDDC APIs share the same vSphere APIs that VMware customers are already familiar with and have been using in on-premises vSphere environments. These APIs are provided by VMware's vSphere platform, enabling programmatic access to the capabilities and functionalities of an SDDC, including managing virtual machines, networks, and storage. Using these APIs, customers can automate and integrate their workflows with the SDDC, simplifying the management and expansion of their infrastructure. Since VMware Cloud on AWS is a managed service the permissions for the SDDC APIs are restricted compared to the on-premises vSphere APIs.

The SDDC APIs are RESTful APIs that can be consumed over HTTP using various programming languages and tools, including the vSphere SDKs and PowerCLI. The SDDC APIs is typically used by system administrators, developers, and other IT professionals to automate and manage the VMware Cloud SDDC efficiently and consistently. Some of the tasks used to automate using the API include creating and managing virtual machines, networks, and storage, and monitoring and troubleshooting the SDDC environment.

Generating CSP API tokens

An API token (also known as a **refresh token**) is a key assigned to an individual account used to authenticate to the service via an API. The API token can generate an access token, which can then be used to make API calls to the Organization.

Follow these steps to create an API token:

1.   After logging in to the VMware Cloud Console, from the top-right drop-down menu, navigate to the **My Account** section:

Figure 9.2 – Navigate to My Account on the VMware Cloud Console

2.   From the **API Tokens** tab, click on **GENERATE TOKEN** to create a new API token:

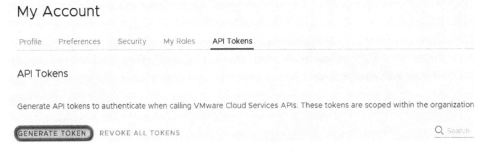

Figure 9.3 – Access API Tokens via the VMware Cloud Console

An Organization can have multiple tokens. Each token has its own set of Organization roles and service roles. Organization roles specify the privileges that an organization member has over organization resources, while service roles determine the privileges when accessing a particular VMware Cloud service.

Figure 9.4 shows the user interface to generate a new API token and assign Organization roles and service roles to the token via the VMware Cloud Console:

Figure 9.4 – Generating API tokens with Organization and service roles

Here are some more details about Organization roles and service roles:

- **Organization roles**: The CSP API should have any of the following Organization roles:

  - Organization member

- Organization administrator

- Organization owner

- **Service roles**: The CSP API should also have a service role. A single token can be granted roles for multiple CSP services. A few examples of service roles are the following:

  - VMC on AWS:

    - NSX Cloud Admin

    - NSX Cloud Auditor

    - Administrator (Delete Restricted)

    - Administrator

  - VMware HCX:

    - Administrator

  - VMware Cloud DR:

    - Global Console Admin

    - Subscription Admin

    - Deployment Admin (Activation)

    - Deployment Admin (Deactivation)

    - Orchestrator Admin

    - Data Protection Auditor

    - Recovery Admin

    - Protection Admin

    - Recovery Tester

    - Recovery SDDC Admin

All the updated CSP roles can be found in the VMware Product Documentation at `https://docs.vmware.com/en/VMware-Cloud-services/services/Using-VMware-Cloud-Services/GUID-C11D3AAC-267C-4F16-A0E3-3EDF286EBE53.html`.

After generating the API token, make sure to securely copy and store it because it cannot be retrieved again. It is crucial to protect the token as it grants access based on the assigned roles. Typically, the API token has a default lifetime of six months, but it can be adjusted to a shorter or longer period to comply with your organization's policies and requirements. Additionally, it is always possible to revoke the API token manually before its expiration.

Consuming Console APIs via the Developer Center

The Developer Center offers various tools to manage the API structure and capture user actions that can be translated into executable code. Developers, automation engineers, and DevOps engineers can access the tools to manage the API structures and capture vSphere Client actions that can be translated into PowerCLI.

Using the API Explorer, you can navigate and execute vSphere REST APIs supported by the system, while also obtaining information and context related to the API requests. The API Explorer simplifies the navigation and execution of vSphere REST API calls. Users first choose an API endpoint from their environment and retrieve a detailed list of vSphere REST APIs. The available APIs depend on the selected endpoint. Further, users can review specific details such as available parameters, expected responses, and response status codes before executing the APIs against a VMware Cloud SDDC environment. *Figure 9.5* shows the available APIs in the VMware Cloud Console Developer Center.

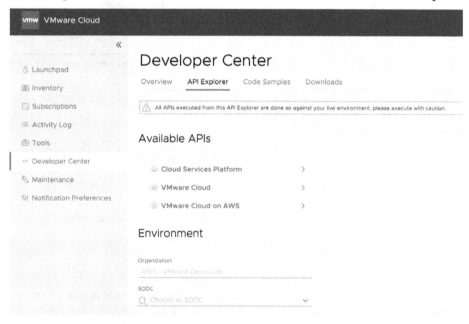

Figure 9.5 – Available APIs in the VMware Cloud Console Developer Center

The API Explorer features an interactive API browser that interacts with the RESTful APIs accessible from the Cloud Services API and the VMC on AWS (VMC) API. The API Explorer is integrated within the Cloud Console and uses the existing refresh token for authentication, eliminating the need for extra authentication steps. Furthermore, it automatically pre-populates specific fields, such as the Organization ID, to improve the user experience when learning about and using these APIs. The API Explorer also allows users to instantly execute the API calls and view the live responses, making it easy to comprehend and understand the given API.

The API reference guides are available at `https://developer.vmware.com/apis`.

NSX-T Data Center REST API

NSX-T is the new default networking stack for VMC on AWS, replacing NSX-V. It offers additional networking and security capabilities and can be controlled using the NSX-T Policy API. To get started with the new API, customers can refer to the official documentation and tutorials provided by VMware.

Unlike NSX-T deployments on premises where the NSX-T API is used, VMC on AWS uses a new NSX-T Policy API that has been introduced to simplify the consumption of NSX-T. Both on-premises and VMware Cloud environments can be consumed using the NSX-T Policy API.

The core of NSX network automation centers around the primary access point into NSX via REST APIs. Like conventional REST APIs, NSX-T APIs facilitate the following API verbs: GET, PATCH, POST, PUT, and DELETE. The table displayed as follows outlines their usage:

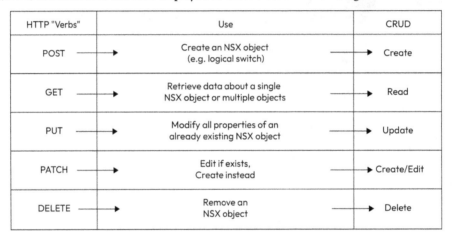

HTTP "Verbs"	Use	CRUD
POST	Create an NSX object (e.g. logical switch)	Create
GET	Retrieve data about a single NSX object or multiple objects	Read
PUT	Modify all properties of an already existing NSX object	Update
PATCH	Edit if exists, Create instead	Create/Edit
DELETE	Remove an NSX object	Delete

Figure 9.6 – NSX-T Policy API verbs

The updated NSX Policy APIs reduce the configuration steps by allowing users to determine an optimal means to achieve the desired outcome. In addition, the NSX-T Policy APIs offer a streamlined data model that can be consumed via an intent-based approach. This data model is based on a hierarchical tree structure, as demonstrated in the following diagram.

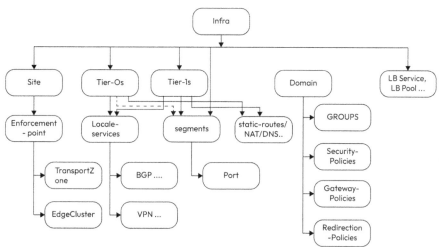

Figure 9.7 – The NSX-T API object model

The hierarchical tree structure is made of strongly typed nodes that have parent/child and peer relationships with each other. Of course, this model maps easily onto the REST APIs. Because the object model is based on a single tree, object names/IDs translate to URIs and are user-friendly Users can configure a given ID, unlike traditional API models where the ID is system generated. This helps to accelerate the development of network automation. Since objects are easily identifiable, they can be referenced without having to make a GET API call to retrieve the system-generated IDs.

Leveraging Terraform for VMware Cloud on AWS

Terraform is an infrastructure provisioning tool from HashiCorp that has become synonymous with *Infrastructure as Code*. This tool allows us to define the desired state of our infrastructure by way of text-based configuration files. From that point, we can manage the entire life cycle of our infrastructure by modifying those files and running a couple of commands.

The Terraform provider for VMC on AWS can be used to configure hybrid cloud infrastructure using the resources supported by VMC on AWS. To use the provider, users need to obtain the authentication token from the Cloud Service Provider by providing the org-scoped API token. The provider client uses the **Cloud Service Provider** (**CSP**) API to exchange this org-scoped API token for a user access token.

The following arguments from the given links are used to configure the Terraform provider for VMC on AWS:

- `https://registry.terraform.io/providers/vmware/vmc/latest/ docs#api_token` (Required) – The API token is used to authenticate when calling VMware Cloud services' APIs. This token is scoped within the organization.

- `https://registry.terraform.io/providers/vmware/vmc/latest/docs#org_id` (Required) – Organization identifier.

- `https://registry.terraform.io/providers/vmware/vmc/latest/docs#vmc_url` (Optional) – The VMC on AWS URL. Default: `https://vmc.vmware.com`.

- `https://registry.terraform.io/providers/vmware/vmc/latest/docs#csp_url` (Optional) – The Cloud Service Provider URL. Default: `https://console.cloud.vmware.com`.

> **Example**
>
> The VMware Cloud community has published code and several blogs on leveraging Terrform for infrastructure automation. Here is a three-part blog in which part 1 demonstrates how to leverage the Terraform AWS Provider along with the VMC Provider to create an Amazon VPC and other constructs including subnets, internet gateways, routing tables, security groups, and S3 endpoint gateways, among other things, as well as deploying a new VMware Cloud on AWS SDDC. In the second part, the VMC provider is used to create VMware Cloud on AWS SDDC Networking and Security constructs that include NSX Segments, Compute Inventory Groups, MGW, and CGW Firewall rules. In the final part, the Terraform VMC Provider is used to add a vCenter Content Library and use the VM templates from the Content Library to deploy virtual machines on the VMware Cloud on AWS SDDC, demonstrating the power of Terraform and how it can be used to automate VMware Cloud on AWS Day1 and Day2 operational tasks.
>
> `https://blogs.vmware.com/cloud/2022/06/30/using-terraform-with-multiple-providers-to-deploy-and-configure-vmware-cloud-on-aws/`
>
> `https://blogs.vmware.com/cloud/2022/07/06/vmware-cloud-on-aws-terraform-deployment-phase-2/`
>
> `https://blogs.vmware.com/cloud/2022/07/15/vmware-cloud-on-aws-terraform-deployment-phase-3/`

Leveraging PowerCLI for VMware Cloud on AWS

VMC on AWS allows customers to use a consistent platform between on-premises VMware environments and the cloud service. This also extends to automation tasks and workflows using PowerCLI, a set of Windows PowerShell modules for managing and automating vSphere. While most existing PowerCLI scripts should work as normal, some may require workarounds to function optimally with VMC on AWS. The workarounds can be found in several blog posts and can help prepare scripts for use with the service. The PowerCLI reference guide is available at `https://developer.vmware.com/powercli`.

vSphere Automation SDKs

vSphere Automation SDKs are essential tools when working with VMware Cloud. These **software development kits (SDKs)** provide a set of resources and libraries that simplify the integration and automation of vSphere-based operations within the VMware Cloud environment. The VMware Cloud on AWS service offers a couple of different RESTful APIs to interact with. The SDKs focus on the VMware Cloud on AWS (VMC) API, as well as providing the authentication method through the CSP API. The vSphere Automation SDKs are open source and can interact with the VMware Cloud on AWS service. These SDKs play a critical role in enhancing the capabilities and extensibility of VMware Cloud, enabling users to harness the full potential of their cloud infrastructure.

VMware provides a rich library of vSphere command-line interface, SDK, and API documentation. Learn about these resources and tools by visiting `https://developer.vmware.com/home`.

Summary

This chapter provided an overview of VMware APIs, which encompassed the Cloud Service Platform API, VMware Cloud API, and vSphere API. It guided you through the process of generating an API token directly from the VMware Cloud Console, and additionally explained how to effectively consume the Console API using the Developer Center. The chapter also provided a brief overview of the NSX-T Data Center REST API. Furthermore, it delved into the strategic use of Terraform for optimizing VMware Cloud on AWS. Finally, it touched upon the significance of vSphere Automation SDKs within the context of VMware Cloud on AWS.

In the next chapter, we will learn about VMware Cloud on AWS Outposts, a fully managed VMware Cloud experience that is tailored to meet the specific requirements of low latency and data residency use cases for customers looking to run VMware Cloud in their on-premises data centers or colocation facilities.

10

VMware Cloud on AWS Outposts

Organizations running on-premises vSphere workloads looking to modernize their workloads and migrate to the cloud use VMware Cloud on AWS to migrate applications into the cloud in a fast and seamless manner, without having to refactor or change any application code or logic.

While most vSphere workloads are a good fit for VMC on AWS, there are still specific workloads that need to stay on-premises or at the edge to ensure low latency, meet local data processing requirements, or maintain compliance with data sovereignty regulations. To address these requirements, VMware and **Amazon Web Services** (**AWS**) introduced VMC on AWS Outposts, which enables organizations to deploy a fully managed VMware Cloud on AWS service on-premises, enabling them to run their vSphere workloads locally while benefiting from the features of the VMC on AWS platform.

The following are the main topics that will be covered in this chapter:

- VMware Cloud on AWS Outposts architecture
- VMware Cloud on AWS Outposts connectivity
- VMware Cloud on AWS Outposts rack components
- Underlying network connectivity for single-rack and multi-rack
- Service connectivity options – public and private
- Scalability and available configurations
- VMware Cloud on AWS Outposts support

What is VMware Cloud on AWS Outposts?

VMC on AWS Outposts is a jointly engineered and fully managed service that runs VMware's enterprise-grade **Software-Defined Data Center** (**SDDC**) software on next-generation dedicated Amazon Nitro-based EC2 bare-metal instances provisioned in an AWS Outposts instance that resides in a organization's on-premises location. VMC on AWS Outposts provides a deeply integrated hybrid cloud environment that can access regional native services in the AWS Region. This enables organizations to seamlessly migrate their workloads to VMC on AWS without re-platforming their virtual machines. The following diagram shows an overview of VMC on AWS Outposts:

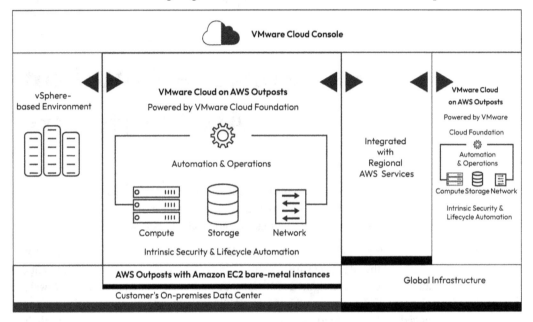

Figure 10.1 – VMC on AWS Outposts overview

Both VMC on AWS and VMC on AWS Outposts share the same infrastructure architecture and operational models, providing a unified hybrid experience. This enables organizations to accelerate their innovation by being able to deploy their workloads in any AWS Region, on-premises facilities, co-location spaces, or organization's data centers.

VMC on AWS Outposts is optimized for VMware workloads with low latency, data residency, or local data processing requirements. AWS delivers and installs the Outposts infrastructure at a organization's on-premises location, along with monitoring, patching, updating, and performing maintenance and replacement of the hardware. VMware provides continuous **Life Cycle Management** (**LCM**) of VMware SDDC software. Organizations always contact VMware for primary support.

Capabilities

VMC on AWS Outposts provides the following capabilities:

- It provides VMware's enterprise-grade SDDC software on next-generation dedicated Amazon Nitro-based EC2 bare-metal instances provisioned in an AWS Outposts that resides in a organization's on-premises location.

- AWS Nitro-system-based bare-metal EC2 infrastructure is designed to provide high performance and enhanced security. This is achieved through the continuous monitoring, protection, and verification of the instance hardware and firmware.

- It offers a fully managed service with continuous LCM, ongoing service monitoring, and automated processes that enhance the infrastructure's health and security. In addition, AWS provides proactive hardware monitoring with break-fix support, while VMware offers first-party services as a single point of contact for hardware and software-related issues.

Use cases

In addition to the conventional use cases, such as data center extension, data center migration, disaster recovery, and application modernization, VMC on AWS Outposts addresses the following use cases:

- **Low-latency compute**: Workloads that are extremely sensitive to latency and exhibit variable latency patterns, including applications used in automated operations on factory floors, medical imaging and diagnostics, high-frequency trading, and school applications or media content accessed concurrently by hundreds of thousands of users.

- **Data residency**: Workloads that must remain in a specific country, state, or municipality due to regulatory, contractual, or information security requirements, including the public sector or highly regulated industries such as healthcare and financial services.

- **Local data processing**: It can be challenging to deal with data-intensive workloads that require hundreds of terabytes of data to be collected and transmitted back to the AWS Region for processing, primarily due to limitations in bandwidth, volume, and costs. However, by leveraging VMC on AWS Outposts, organizations can process data close to where it is generated while maintaining data lakes and ML training in AWS Regions.

Benefits of VMC on AWS Outposts

VMC on AWS Outposts offers a range of benefits, some of which align with the general advantages of VMC on AWS:

- **Consistency across AWS Regions and on-premises: Hybrid Linked Mode** (HLM) allows the integration of both VMC on AWS cloud vCenter and on-premises vCenter, enabling the management of virtual machine workloads using a single pane of glass across both environments.

With this integration, organizations can effortlessly migrate vSphere workloads to VMware Cloud on AWS Outposts using VMware vMotion without any downtime

- **High-performing infrastructure with enhanced security**: The high-performance and secure AWS Nitro system, which powers VMC on AWS, also serves as the foundation for VMC on AWS Outposts. AWS is accountable for all hardware maintenance, updates, and replacement, providing uniform security and operating models for VMware workloads, irrespective of their location.

- **Simplified IT operations**: VMC on AWS Outposts allows organizations to consume a fully managed service in an on-premises environment built on the familiar VMware compute (vSphere), storage (vSAN), and networking (NSX) technologies without the hassle of deploying, monitoring, patching, or updating IT infrastructure. Instead, organizations can effortlessly order, deploy, and scale infrastructure as required, reducing the time and resources required to manage IT infrastructure and increasing IT productivity.

How does VMC on AWS Outposts work?

VMC on AWS Outposts enables AWS to extend the boundaries of an AWS **Availability Zone (AZ)** to bring VMware's SDDC stack from the AWS Region to the on-premises or edge location. Using cloud operating models, organizations can now leverage on-premises hardware to run vSphere workloads.

VMC on AWS Outposts runs VMware's SDDC stack on the AWS Outposts infrastructure. It's important to note that AWS Outposts can only be paired with a single AZ within an AWS Region that offers the VMC on AWS service. AWS Outposts is designed to work as an extension of an AZ and hence cannot work in disconnected mode without connectivity back to the AWS Region it is homed to.

The underlying hardware infrastructure that runs the SDDC is fully managed by AWS, while VMware is responsible for managing all SDDC constructs on the rack.

The logical deployment of an AWS Outposts service is depicted in *Figure 10.2*:

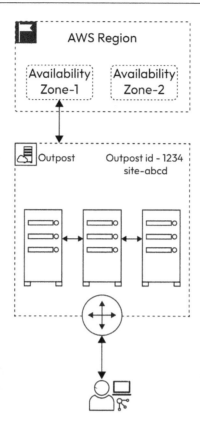

Figure 10.2 – VMC on AWS Outposts connectivity

The architecture illustrates that a logical Outpost contains physical racks that host networking, storage, and computing equipment and is connected to an AWS Region's AZ through the service link.

Two types of traffic are sent back to the parent AWS Region using the service link:

- **Data plane traffic**: All data transmitted between workloads located on AWS Outposts and those residing in AWS is considered data traffic. The organization is responsible for managing network communications between services running on the Outpost and those running in the AWS Regions.

- **Control plane traffic**: The service link is also responsible for transmitting telemetry, state, and health data from various components, including maintenance tasks initiated by AWS (such as software and firmware updates and system commands).

VMware Cloud on AWS Outposts rack

The VMC on AWS Outposts rack is a standard 42U rack provided by AWS Outposts. This rack measures 80 inches (203.20 cm) in height, 24 inches (60.96 cm) in width, and 48 inches (121.92 cm) in depth. It contains bare-metal hosts, network switches, a network patch panel, a power shelf, and blank panels. Outposts racks are designed with high availability in mind, featuring redundant network switches and power connections.

As part of the installation, AWS will deliver the fully assembled rack to your desired location and position it accordingly. Once the installation is complete, the rack will need to be connected to the power and network.

Figure 10.3 – VMC on AWS Outposts rack

Depending on the configuration selected, each Outposts rack will include pre-configured AWS bare-metal Nitro-based EC2 instance(s), with a single rack containing anywhere between 3 and 9 servers that can be used for compute:

Instance Type	i3en.metal
CPU type	Intel Xeon Cascade Lake – 48 cores @ 2.5 GHz (96 HT cores)
RAM	768 GiB
Storage	~45.8 TiB (raw)
Network speed	50 Gbps

Table 10.1 – Hardware specifications of the bare-metal node

Additionally, each Outposts rack is equipped with two physical network devices known as **Outposts Network Devices** (**ONDs**) that connect to the organization's local network. To establish connectivity with the local network, at least two physical links are required between the ONDs and the organization's local network devices. AWS will provide optics that are compatible with the fiber provided at the rack's location.

Figure 10.4 – Outposts Network Device (OND)

The AWS Outposts rack features a centralized and redundant power conversion unit coupled with a DC distribution system integrated into the rack's backplane. The backbone of this power distribution is a central bus bar located at the rear of the rack, ensuring efficient and reliable power delivery to every server housed within. Additionally, the rack accommodates various power supply options, including 5 kVA, 10 kVA, and 15 kVA capacities, all equipped with redundant feeds to enhance reliability. For comprehensive details regarding the rack's specifications, you can refer to the official documentation available at https://aws.amazon.com/outpost/rack/hardware-specs/.

Figure 10.5 – Rack bus bar

AWS is responsible for securing the AWS Outposts infrastructure, similar to how AWS secures the underlying infrastructure in an AWS Region. However, organizations are responsible for securing their applications running on the AWS Outposts rack, just as they are responsible for securing their applications and workloads running in the Region. Organizations are also responsible for maintaining the physical security of their Outposts racks and ensuring reliable network connectivity to the Outposts.

AWS ensures that all organization's data is protected and remains in the their control. The Nitro system in each host encrypts all data at rest, and the encryption key is stored in an removable device called the nitro encryption key (NSK). An NSK is present on each bare metal instance on the Outposts rack; physically destroying the nitro encryption key would mean destroying the data residing on the corresponding bare-metal instance.

Figure 10.6 – Nitro encryption key

Underlying network connectivity

AWS Outposts requires a persistent network connection between the AWS Outposts and an AWS Region to transmit control plane traffic back to the AWS Region. AWS Outposts also needs to establish connectivity to the local on-premises network. The organization is responsible for providing both the local connectivity to the on-premises network and the service link network connectivity back to the AWS Region.

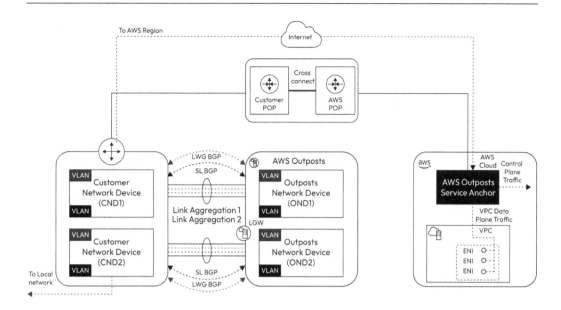

Figure 10.7 – VMC on AWS Outposts underlying connectivity overview

Physical connectivity

Two physical network devices known as ONDs are present on each Outposts rack to enable connectivity to the **Customer Network Devices (CNDs)** that connect to the organization's local network. At a minimum, two physical links must exist between the OND and the CND. The ONDs can accommodate multiple speeds and have symmetrical uplink speeds and the same number of uplinks.

The required uplink speeds and number of uplinks between each OND and CND depend on factors such as the make, model, and configuration and the availability of physical ports on the CND. *Table 10.2* provides various options for the uplink speeds and quantities for each OND:

Uplink speed	Number of uplinks
1 Gbps	1, 2, 4, 6, or 8
10 Gbps	1, 2, 4, 8, 12, or 16
40 Gbps	1, 2, or 4
100 Gbps	1, 2, or 4

Table 10.2 – Physical connectivity uplink speeds and quantity of uplinks

AWS Outposts uses the **Link Aggregation Control Protocol (LACP)** to establish two **Link Aggregation Group (LAG)** connections, one between each OND and CND. The uplinks from each OND are combined into an Ethernet LAG, representing a single network connection. The organization should configure the LAG on the CNDs, while AWS is responsible for the LAG configuration on the ONDs. *Figure 10.7* depicts four uplinks between each OND and CND. Configuring the LAGs using IEEE 802.1q Ethernet trunks is essential to facilitate the transmission of traffic from multiple VLANs between the ONDs and CNDs.

AWS uses **Virtual LANs (VLANs)** to segregate the traffic between the CND and OND. To separate the responsibilities between AWS and organizations, a demarcation line is established at the network ports of the OND. AWS is responsible for managing any infrastructure on its side of the connection, while organizations are responsible for managing any infrastructure on their side. The traffic that flows between the on-premises network and the network of each AWS Outpost includes the following:

- **Service link VLAN**: The service link VLAN facilitates traffic between the VMC on an AWS Outposts rack and the AWS Region, which includes the following:

  - Control plane traffic, including telemetry, state, and health data of the rack and its components

  - Data plane traffic, including traffic that needs to communicate with workloads that reside in the AWS Region

- **Local Gateway (LGW) VLAN**: The LGW VLAN carries workload traffic between VMC on AWS Outposts SDDC network segments and the organization's on-premises network. Additionally, this VLAN facilitates communication between the AWS Outposts rack and the internet via the on-premises network.

The service link VLAN and LGW VLAN are configured on the uplinks connecting the OND and CND and do not have to be extended across the organization's distribution and access switches.

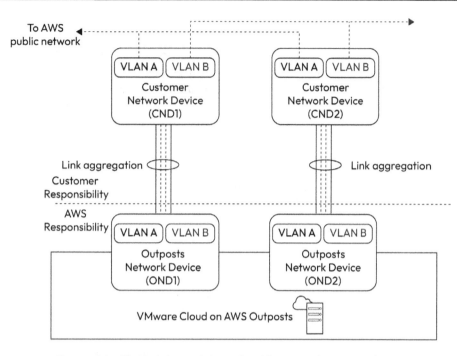

Figure 10.8 – Physical connectivity and LAG between the OND and CND

Once the uplinks are established, the LAGs are configured, and VLANs are created to segregate the traffic, then the Layer 3 connectivity is established using the **Border Gateway Protocol (BGP)** between the OND and CND. *Table 10.3* provides a list of VLANs and their associated traffic (either service link or Local Gateway) that is transmitted on the corresponding uplinks or link aggregations enabled between the CNDs and the ONDs.

VLAN A	Service link BGP 1	OND1 to CND1	LAG 1
VLAN B	Local gateway BGP 1		
VLAN A	Service link BGP 2	OND2 to CND2	LAG 2
VLAN B	Local gateway BGP 2		

Table 10.3 – List of VLANs required for AWS Outposts service links and LGWs

Table 10.3 shows that four BGP sessions, two each on each of the LAGs for service link and LGW traffic, are required.

Service link BGP connectivity

To establish service link connectivity, **external BGP (eBGP)** peering sessions are created between each OND and the CND. A /30 or /31 IP address is used as a BGP peering IP address for each BGP session between the Outposts service link autonomous system and the organization's autonomous system using private **Autonomous System Numbers (ASNs)** to complete the configuration. The following diagram shows the VLANs and subnet information required to establish service link BGP connectivity:

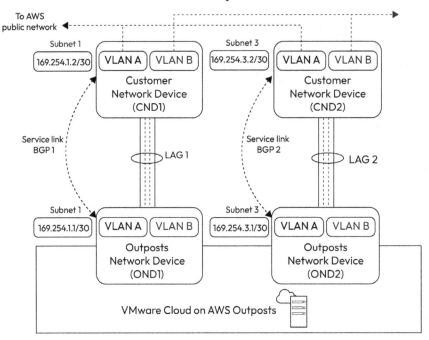

Figure 10.9 – Service link and LGW traffic segregated using VLANs

The following table breaks down the configuration required for the service link BGP connectivity:

VLAN	BGP	Device	LAG	BGP Subnet	OND IP	CND IP	Outposts ASN	Organization ASN
VLAN A	Service link BGP 1	OND1 to CND1	LAG 1	169.254. 1.0/30	169.254. 1.1/30	169.254. 1.2/30	65013	65000
	Service link BGP 2	OND2 to CND2	LAG 2	169.254. 3.0/30	169.254. 3.1/30	169.254. 3.2/30		

Table 10.4 – Sample BGP parameters for service link connectivity

Local gateway BGP connectivity

Similar to service link connectivity, LGW connectivity is also established using eBGP peering sessions between each OND and the CND. A /30 or /31 IP address is used as the BGP peering IP address for each BGP session between the Outposts LGW autonomous system and the organization autonomous system using private ASNs to complete the configuration. The following diagram shows the VLANs and subnet information necessary to establish LGW BGP connectivity:

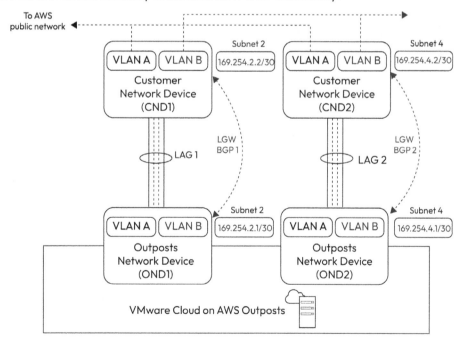

Figure 10.10 – Service link and LGW traffic segregated using VLANs

The following table breaks down the configuration required for the LGW BGP connectivity:

VLAN	BGP	Device	LAG	BGP Subnet	OND IP	CND IP	Outposts ASN	Organization ASN
VLAN B	Local gateway BGP 1	OND1 to CND1	LAG 1	169.254. 2.0/30	169.254. 2.1/30	169.254. 2.2/30	65024	65000
	Local gateway BGP 2	OND2 to CND2	LAG 2	169.254. 4.0/30	169.254. 4.1/30	169.254. 4.2/30		

Table 10.5 – Sample BGP parameters for LGW connectivity

Service link infrastructure subnet

A service link infrastructure subnet that resides on AWS Outposts establishes service link connectivity to the AWS Region. The subnet that connects to the AWS Region uses a /26 CIDR range and can be configured with either public IP addresses that can be reached directly over the internet or private IP addresses that are NAT-ed and can access the internet. The /26 CIDR range is divided into two /27 CIDR blocks to support link and device failures.

Network readiness checklist

Organizations can use the following checklist to gather information that is used to configure Outposts:

Parameter	Description
Number of CNDs	Two recommended
Organization ASN	Existing organization BGP ASN
Number of uplinks	Number of uplinks between each CND and OND (1, 2, 4, 6, or 8 recommended)
Uplink speed	1 Gbps, 10 Gbps, 40 Gbps, or 100 Gbps
Fiber type	SingleMode Fiber (SMF) or Multi-Mode Fiber (MMF)
Optical standard	LX, SX, IR, SR, LR, IR4, LR4, ESR4, SR4, MSA, CWDM4
Service link VLAN	Any VLAN between 1 and 4094
LGW VLAN	Any VLAN between 1 and 4094
LACP LAG 1	Uplinks between Outposts Network Device 1 and Customer Network Device 1

Parameter	Description
LACP LAG 1	Uplinks between Outposts Network Device 2 and Customer Network Device 2
Service link BGP subnet 1	/30 or /31 Subnet 1
Service link BGP subnet 2	/30 or /31 Subnet 3
LGW BGP subnet 1	/30 or /31 Subnet 2
LGW BGP subnet 2	/30 or /31 Subnet 4
Service link ASN	Private ASN for service link
LGW ASN	Private ASN for LGW
Service link infra subnet	A CIDR (/26 required, advertised as two contiguous /27 subnets).
Private connectivity subnet	A subnet created in the AWS Region that acts as an AWS Outposts service link anchor

Table 10.6 – Network readiness checklist

AWS Outposts connectivity to AWS Region

VMC on AWS Outposts requires a persistent connection to a nearby AWS Region designated as the **home region**. A service link connection is set up between the Outposts rack and the home region for management and control plane traffic. The service link can also be used for data plane traffic between AWS Outposts and AWS Region workloads. Continuous service link connectivity with a minimum bandwidth of 500 Mbps (1 Gbps is recommended) is required, which can be established using either of the following options:

- Public connectivity to the AWS Region:
  - Via the internet on-premises
  - Via the internet using an AWS Direct Connect Public Virtual Interface (VIF)
- Private connectivity to the AWS Region:
  - Using an AWS Direct Connect private VIF

Public connectivity

VMC on AWS Outposts public service link connectivity is established using an internet connection at the on-premises organization location. The AWS Outposts rack connects to service link public endpoint IPs using a group of encrypted tunnels using **Transport Layer Security (TLS)**. The following diagram shows VMC on AWS Outposts establishing a service link using the public connectivity model.

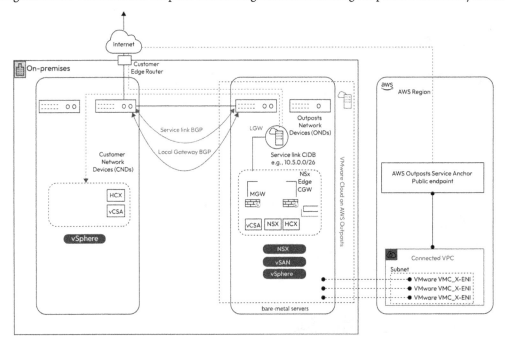

Figure 10.11 – VMware Cloud on AWS Outposts service link public connectivity

Figure 10.11 depicts VMware Cloud on AWS Outposts installed on-premises at the organization, with a service link established over the internet to the AWS Outposts service anchor point public endpoint in the AWS Region. It is critical to have reliable underlying service link connectivity to the AWS Region to ensure that VMC on AWS Outposts remains operational. Therefore, organizations should ensure the availability of resilient and reliable internet connectivity that Outposts can leverage.

For enhanced security, organizations must allow outbound connections from Outposts toward the AWS Region so that the service link tunnel can only initiate connections from Outposts to the Region, as indicated in the following table:

Protocol	Source Port	Source Address	Destination Port	Destination Address
UDP	443	Outposts service link /26	443	AWS Region's (homed to Outposts) public routes
TCP	1025-65535	Outposts service link /26	443	AWS Region's (homed to Outposts) public routes

Table 10.7 – Prerequisite firewall rules for public connectivity

Private connectivity

VMC on AWS Outposts can leverage AWS Direct Connect private VIFs for the service link private connectivity. A set of **Elastic Network Interfaces (ENIs)** within an Amazon VPC is created to establish the service link connectivity to the AWS service anchor private endpoint. This Amazon VPC is created in the VMware-owned and managed AWS account in the AWS Region, and connectivity is established over an AWS Direct Connect private VIF. Organizations may also use an AWS **Direct Connect Gateway (DXGW)** for cross-Region Direct Connect access if necessary. However, it's important to note that AWS Outposts private connectivity does not support using AWS Transit Gateway or site-to-site IPsec VPNs.

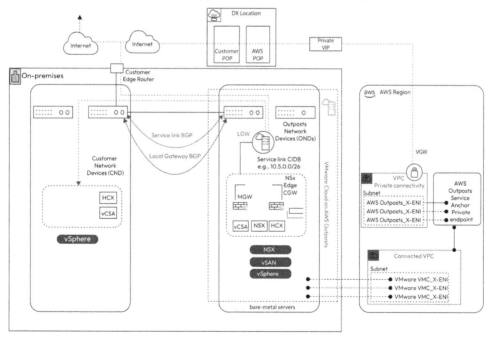

Figure 10.12 – VMware Cloud on AWS Outposts service link private connectivity

Figure 10.12 depicts VMC on AWS Outposts (on the left) connected to the AWS Outposts service anchor in the AWS Region via the service link private connectivity. The AWS Region (on the far right) contains a **Virtual Private Gateway** (**VGW**) attached to the Amazon VPC hosting the ENIs that connect to the AWS Outposts service anchor private endpoint.

Using the private connectivity option eliminates the need for the service link traffic to traverse the public internet. It also prevents organizations from having to use large public allow lists on their on-premises firewalls. This is because the AWS Outposts service anchor private endpoint now uses the ENIs in the VMware-owned Amazon VPC. It will also enable organizations to use AWS Direct Connect features to monitor the connectivity using Amazon CloudWatch metrics.

To ensure robust and resilient private connectivity, organizations should consider using redundant DX locations and DX partners. It is highly recommended to review AWS DX resiliency recommendations to choose a DX architecture that meets the organizations' specific availability requirements.

Service link disconnection

Irrespective of whether you're using private connectivity or public connectivity, VMC on Outposts is not designed for operating in disconnected mode for long durations. In the case of a network outage that results in the service link connectivity being disconnected, the following will occur:

- Virtual machines and VMware vSAN storage will continue to run and be accessible via the LGW
- API calls to the AWS Region will fail (downloading from the content library, creating new logical networks, and so on)
- Metrics will be spooled locally for a limited period
- If there is a host reboot as a result of a power outage, during a service link disconnection, VMware vSAN will be inaccessible for that host

VMC on AWS Outposts configuration

VMC on AWS Outposts streamlines IT operations by providing a fully managed solution. AWS takes care of delivering, installing, monitoring, patching, updating, and maintaining the Outposts hardware at the organization's on-premises location. In addition, VMware ensures continuous LCM of VMware SDDC and provides direct first-party support. The following components are included with VMC on AWS Outposts:

- Standard 42U rack hosting AWS Outposts components
- Amazon Nitro-based EC2 bare-metal servers with local SSD storage
- VMware SDDC software including vSphere, vSAN, NSX-T, and vCenter Server

- VMware **Hybrid Extension (HCX)** Enterprise license
- VMware global support

While VMware Cloud on AWS supports a variety of EC2 bare-metal instance types including *i3.metal*, *i3en.metal*, and *I4i.metal*, VMware Cloud on AWS Outposts supports only the *i3en.metal* instances.

Specifications	Amazon EC2 i3en.metal
Compute	
CPU type	Intel Xeon Cascade Lake (dual socket)
CPU cores	48 cores @ 2.5 GHz (96 HT cores)
Custom core count	8, 16, 24, 30, 36, or 48
Memory	768 GiB
Storage	
Type	vSAN with local NVMe All Flash
Capacity and optimization	~45.8 TiB (raw) – compression enabled (40.35 TiB usable per host)
Network	
Physical speed	100 Gbps (currently 50 Gbps supported) In-transit encryption on the NIC for east-west traffic

Table 10.8 – Hardware specifications for Amazon EC2 i3en.metal instance type

Scalability

VMC on AWS Outposts offers several node configurations starting with a minimum of three-node configuration (with one additional dark capacity node) to a maximum of nine nodes (with one additional dark capacity node). The dark capacity is used as an auto-remediation task in case of host failures. However, the replacement of the physical hardware can take up to 48 hours from the time a confirmation has been provided, subject to logistical constraints.

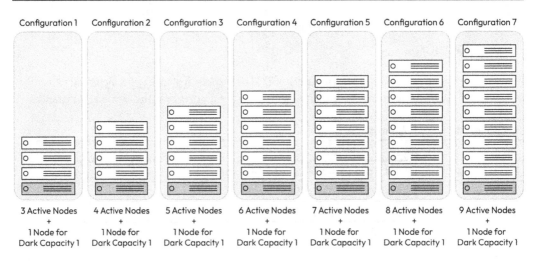

Configuration 1	Configuration 2	Configuration 3	Configuration 4	Configuration 5	Configuration 6	Configuration 7
3 Active Nodes + 1 Node for Dark Capacity 1	4 Active Nodes + 1 Node for Dark Capacity 1	5 Active Nodes + 1 Node for Dark Capacity 1	6 Active Nodes + 1 Node for Dark Capacity 1	7 Active Nodes + 1 Node for Dark Capacity 1	8 Active Nodes + 1 Node for Dark Capacity 1	9 Active Nodes + 1 Node for Dark Capacity 1

Figure 10.13 – VMC on Outposts single-rack configurations

Depending on the organization footprint, a VMC sizing exercise determines the number of nodes required. Each rack, as denoted in the figure, has one additional node reserved for dark capacity that triggers autoscaling in case of a hardware failure or physical health deterioration of any of the active nodes.

Similar to other hyper-converged infrastructure offerings, a VMC on Outposts rack can only scale out. Additional bare-metal hosts can be added to scale the compute and/or storage capacity. There are some functional restrictions in terms of scaling out. Organizations can pick any of the seven configurations available; however, the rack can be scaled out in increments of three nodes at a time.

Each rack, in addition to the Amazon EC2 i3en.metal server(s), has additional nodes used for LCM functions and a pair of ONDs. For organizations who are looking to scale their VMC infrastructure beyond the maximum capacity of nine nodes in a single rack, there is a multi-rack option that can scale up to a maximum of four racks.

Let us look at the scalability of VMC on AWS Outposts single-rack and multi-rack configurations:

	Single rack	Multi-rack
Rack capacity	Min: Three nodes Max: Nine nodes in a single rack	Min: Three nodes Max: Nine nodes in a single rack
Outposts logical unit capacity	Single rack: Maximum of nine active nodes	16 racks: Maximum of 36 active nodes across 4 racks
Number of SDDCs	1 SDDC, 10 clusters (subject to availability of nodes)	1 SDDC, 10 clusters (subject to availability of nodes)

	Single rack	Multi-rack
Connectivity to organization network	A pair of ONDs connect to a pair of CNDs	A pair of ONDs connect to a pair of CNDs for configurations up to four racks For multi-rack configurations, the ONDs in each rack connect to ONDs in all the other racks
Service link connectivity to AWS Region	A logical Outposts unit establishes a single service link connection back to the AWS Region, independent of the number of racks in the Outposts logical unit (each rack does *not* establish its own service link)	

Table 10.9 – Comparing single-rack and multi-rack configurations

Multi-rack network connectivity

A VMC on AWS Outposts multi-rack configuration can accommodate multiple racks, with a maximum capacity of four racks within a single Outposts logical unit. The classification of a logical Outposts unit may vary based on its size and scale, with different categorizations to suit various deployment scenarios.

In a VMC on AWS Outposts multi-rack environment, note the following:

- The ONDs in each rack are redundantly interconnected with the ONDs in the other racks to provide highly available network connectivity between them. AWS is responsible for ensuring network availability within the Outposts infrastructure.

- Both ONDs in each rack are also connected with a pair of CNDs.

- A single service link is established for connectivity back to the AWS Region.

The following diagram shows the VMC on Outposts multi-rack architecture that spans four racks, offering greater capacity and scalability.

VMC on AWS Outposts support

VMC on AWS Outposts provides organizations with first-party support through VMware. Organizations can take advantage of the 24/5 in-service chat support available in English across all global Regions.

Moreover, organizations can contact VMware's enterprise support personnel. Regular updates, upgrades, and patching of the VMware SDDC software are performed by VMware, while AWS carries out software upgrades and patches on the hardware. AWS handles the monitoring of the AWS infrastructure, publishing Outposts health metrics, and notifying VMware proactively about units that require maintenance. VMware will inform organizations of scheduled maintenance. The modular design of AWS Outposts allows for hardware replacement, as necessary. In the case of physical maintenance, VMware will coordinate with organizations to schedule a visit to their site. The following process diagram illustrates the sequential stages of the support process, commencing with a organization's initial contact with VMware for assistance and concluding with the resolution of the support case.

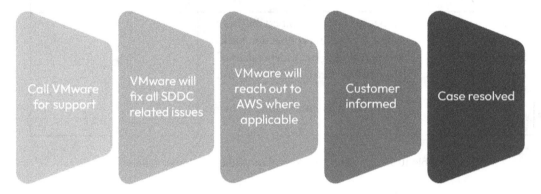

Figure 10.15 – VMware Cloud on AWS Outposts support process

This chapter has provided a deep dive into the VMware Cloud on AWS Outposts service, including the use cases, benefits, underlying network connectivity, SDDC scalability, and multi-rack capabilities. As the service continues to evolve, it can run the same SDDC capabilities as VMware Cloud on AWS in a Region. VMware and AWS have been jointly validating additional services, including the likes of VMware HCX and **VMware Site Recovery** (**VSR**). Additional add-on services and other native AWS service integrations are being developed and validated. For further information, reach out to a VMware or AWS representative.

Summary

This chapter covered VMC on AWS Outposts's architecture, connectivity, and rack components, along with details of the underlying network connectivity for single-rack and multi-rack environments. It also covered both service link options: public and private. The chapter also covered scalability aspects and reviewed the available configuration options, as well as how VMware provides first-party support for VMC on AWS Outposts.

In the next chapter, we will learn how to right-size the infrastructure for VMC on AWS using VMware's sizing tools and how to estimate and manage costs to run workloads on VMC on AWS.

Part 3: Leveraging Design Considerations and Best Practices

Part 3 focuses on ensuring a seamless adoption of VMware Cloud on AWS. It covers key topics, including best practices to optimize the adoption process, strategies for avoiding common pitfalls, and answers to **frequently asked questions (FAQs)**. It also provides essential insights into crucial configuration elements required to deploy the SDDC and set up a hybrid cloud environment. It serves as a prelude to the purchase and onboarding process. The goal is to provide valuable insights and guidance to enhance the overall experience of integrating VMware Cloud on AWS, offering practical advice to streamline the adoption journey and address potential challenges.

This part consists of the following chapters:

- *Chapter 11, Knowing Best Practices, FAQs, and Common Pitfalls*
- *Chapter 12, Appendix – Preflight Checklist Before Onboarding*

11

Knowing the Best Practices, FAQs, and Common Pitfalls

Incorporating a new service into the enterprise infrastructure landscape is not easy. A lot of factors must be considered to make the project a success. In this chapter, you will learn how to make the adoption of VMware Cloud on AWS as smooth as possible.

The following are the topics to be covered in this chapter:

- Best practices
- Avoiding common pitfalls
- FAQs

Best practices

When you are designing, implementing, and operating a service, it's vital to follow common best practices to prevent performance, availability, and security issues. In this section, we will summarize the most common best practices for VMware Cloud on AWS.

Design and architecture

A solid design is the basis for successful implementation and a positive user experience. Never start deploying the service before completing the design phase. Once production workloads are running on the SDDC, it will be very hard to redesign the implementation without affecting the user experience. Most production outages occur in infrastructures that are deployed without a proper architecture design.

The standard industry flow for the design and architecture phase is as follows:

- Discovery workshops with key business and technical stakeholders
- Key design decisions

- Logical and physical design
- Implementation

Let's see more details about each of these activities in the following section.

Discovery workshops with key business and technical stakeholders

This is one of the most important steps of the design phase. Failing to properly collect and document key requirements, along with risks, constraints, and assumptions, may affect the implementation of the whole service. For example, if an organization has a strict deadline to migrate workloads from a data center but you fail to check whether a direct connect is available for the project, it may not be possible to accomplish the migration in the required amount of time. Or if a organization has workloads with hardware accelerators or an extremely high number of **input-output operations per second** (**IOPS**) and you did not properly identify them, you might not be able to migrate and/or meet performance SLAs later on, leading to project suspension.

As a result of discovery workshops, your team should have a clear understanding of the business and technical requirements. These will be the foundation for your design, and you should ensure the new cloud infrastructure can meet all of them. Here are some typical examples of the requirements for the hybrid cloud platform:

- An example of a business requirement – a new platform must guarantee four nines of availability (99.99%)
- An example of a technical requirement – a new platform must be able to host VMs with up to 256 GB of RAM

In addition to requirements, you should capture constraints and document assumptions. Assumptions may pose risks to the project by affecting timelines or making some of the requirements not achievable. Your design should provide a clearly documented risk mitigation procedure.

The following examples illustrate possible constraints, assumptions, and risks:

- Constraints:
  - Some VMs use **Raw Device Mapping** (**RDM**) to support Windows Server Failover Clustering
  - Direct Connect is available but does not support the MaCsec feature
- Assumptions:
  - Technical personnel will receive adequate training to ensure proper Day 2 operations of the service
  - The networking team will be able to implement the required networking changes in a timely manner

- Risks:

  - If network configuration cannot be completed by the defined timeline, migration of the workload will not be possible

  - If the training budget is already exhausted, necessary technical training must be provided as a part of the project, possibly increasing costs

All requirements, constraints, assumptions, and associated risks must be clearly documented and acknowledged by the project's stakeholders. You may find some of the identified requirements might be overwritten by senior management or even completely removed. It's not uncommon to see every application team requiring the highest possible availability for their application service even if only 15% of the application's workload is considered mission-critical.

Key design decisions

Upon completion of the discovery workshop, you will move on to creating the design and architecture for VMware Cloud on AWS. The main goal of your design is to map business and technical requirements into product capabilities, taking constraints and assumptions into account, and mitigating risks whenever possible. All design decisions must be clearly documented, presented, and acknowledged by the project's stakeholders before moving to the more detailed logical and physical architecture. A solid design is the foundation of the successful operation of the environment. Let's illustrate the design decision making process using some examples:

- Requirements:

  - 5% of the workload must have 99.999%, 15% of the workload must have 99.99%, and the other 80% must have a 99.9% availability guarantee

  - The most critical workloads are SQL Server databases

- Constraints:

  - Applications using critical SQL Server databases do not support SQL Server Availability Groups

  - The design must provide the most cost-effective solution possible

- Assumptions:

  - The DBA team has experience of running SQL Server in a virtual environment

- Risks:

  - The organization is in the process of negotiating a new ELA with Microsoft. This final negotiating will take place after the deployment phase of VMware Cloud on AWS

Considering the requirements, constraints, assumptions, and risks, outlined here, the following design decisions were made:

- The design will require two separate SDDCs:

  - A standard SDDC with a 99.9% availability guarantee

  - A stretched cluster SDDC with a 99.99% availability guarantee

  Justification: VMware Cloud on AWS does not support a mix of standard and stretched clusters within a single SDDC at this time. Only the stretched cluster will satisfy the requirement for a 99.99% SLA. Using only stretched clusters will violate the budget constraint.

- SQL Server databases must be deployed on the stretched cluster SDDC and leverage a **Windows Server Failover Cluster** (**WSFC**) cluster with shared disks. The default managed storage policy must be used to ensure shared **Virtual Machine Disk Files** (**VMDK**) are replicated between AZs.

  Justification: Critical SQL Server databases require a 99.999% availability guarantee. This availability requirement cannot be achieved by the infrastructure and requires application-level redundancy to ensure the service is available during upgrades/application maintenance. Using SQL Server Availability Groups is not possible with the current version of applications. VMware Cloud on AWS provides support for shared disk clusters (`https://blogs.vmware.com/apps/2021/01/wsfc-validation-vmware-vmc.html`) natively with vSAN (limitations apply; for example, there's no support for the online disk extension), including stretched cluster support.

  Risk: Stretched clusters have a performance impact on SQL Server workloads due to vSAN synchronous replication between AZs, which adds latency to all write I/O. To mitigate this risk, reconfiguration of the VM and SQL Server may be required.

- Both SDDCs will require activation of Windows Server licenses. SQL Server licenses should follow the BYOL approach.

  Justification: The process of the new ELA negotiation with Microsoft is ongoing. The new ELA will have updated terms and conditions reflecting the licensing restrictions introduced on October 1, 2019. These restrictions require Windows Server licenses to be acquired from VMware. SQL Server licenses are still eligible for BYOL with Software Assurance. ELA includes Software Assurance by default.

  Risk: The negotiation process is not finalized yet. The total number of available SQL Server licenses cannot be provided on time. An additional budget should be considered if new SQL Server licenses are required.

This example indicates the level of detail needed in your design document. However, by no means is this a full list of possible requirements. It's not uncommon to see hundreds of different requirements, constraints, assumptions, and risks that need to be considered for design decisions.

Upon completion of the design, key design decisions must be presented to the key stakeholders, along with a high-level architecture proposal and cost estimates. Expect to have corrections from the stakeholders. All corrections must be properly captured; requirements, constraints, assumptions, and risks must be updated accordingly; and design decisions should be reviewed to accommodate the new requirements of the organization.

Logical and physical design

Once design decisions are approved, you will move on to creating a logical design for the infrastructure, including compute, storage, networking, operations, and other additional components of your design. Your logical design must follow the design decisions.

For example, let's map the following design decisions to the logical design.

The design will require two separate SDDCs:

- Standard SDDC with 99.9% availability
- Stretched cluster SDDC with 99.99% availability

To properly accommodate this requirement, your logical design should include the following:

- The number of hosts and host types per SDDC
- The number of vSphere clusters
- Desired AWS Region and AZs for the deployment
- AWS account and connected VPC
- Network connection between SDDCs
- SDDC group
- vTGW and DXGW
- Recommendation for workload placement
- eDRS policies configuration
- Storage policies configuration
- VMware Aria Operations for Logs alerts and dashboards
- VMware Aria Operations custom dashboards

When creating a logical design, you will map the design decisions on the current product's capabilities. In some cases, it would not be possible to satisfy a design decision, because of product interoperability or known bugs. All changes must be properly documented, and design decisions should be updated and communicated to the project stakeholders. Do not move on without getting all the required approvals; it may affect the product implementation later!

Upon completion, the logical design must be presented to the relevant technical teams, with the feedback captured and incorporated into the design.

Logical design is a foundation for a physical design. The physical design depicts the necessary configuration information, including the following:

- Management subnet CIDR for both SDDCs

- Workload segments CIDRs

- eDRS policy thresholds

- Custom storage policy thresholds

- BGP configuration, including ASN, peer-to-peer network CIDR, VLAN, and so on

- HCX Service Mesh and Uplinks configuration

The main goal of the physical design is to ensure necessary configuration information is available for the implementation and configuration workbooks. Even at this stage, you may encounter additional risks that were not captured before. It's very common to see a lack of available VLANs, BGP limitations, and so on. Some of them may affect your design decision and may require revisiting the logical design.

Implementation

The level of detail of your physical design must be sufficient to create configuration workbooks, including the following:

- The detailed set of network parameters for VPN connections

- BGP details per connection, neighbor configuration, and so on

- Mapping of resource thresholds to custom eDRS policies

- vTGW configuration details

Now you are finally ready to start the deployment. The deployment team must review the configuration workbooks, highlight any deviations or missing information, and start the infrastructure deployment.

The infrastructure deployment task, despite all the common opinions, is very straightforward if all the design and architecture work has been done correctly. VMware Cloud on AWS features fully automated provisioning of the SDDC. Other configuration tasks are easy to follow using the Cloud Services Console and/or the familiar VMware Web Client. You can automate the deployment using PowerCLI or VMware Cloud on the AWS Terraform provider (`https://blogs.vmware.com/cloud/2020/02/12/getting-started-terraform-provider-vmware-cloud-aws/`).

Make sure you follow the configuration runbooks, note any deviations, and enjoy VMware Cloud on AWS SDDC being deployed quickly and reliably.

Migration

Upon completion of the deployment, you can hand over the newly built VMware Cloud on AWS infrastructure to the operation team. Planning and executing workload migration is a separate project, requiring you to follow the same approach as outlined for the infrastructure deployment. In this chapter, we will cover the key best practices to consider.

Identify the migration scope

In many cases, the scope will be defined as a list of applications and underlying VMs. The list must be prioritized and segregated into migration waves based on the criticality of the application: start with the `test&dev` workload and finish with the most critical one after gaining enough experience.

Identify dependencies

This step is crucial for the success of the project. Failing to correctly identify all connected services will affect user experience after migration and may lead to escalations. Migrating only part of the application landscape will cause intra-application traffic to start traversing the WAN link between your on-premises (or other cloud) and VMware Cloud on AWS SDDC, causing high network latency, and affecting application performance.

VMware Aria Operations for Networks is your primary tool for visualizing the traffic flow and correctly mapping dependencies. Additional NSX monitoring tools described in *Chapter 6* can also be used for troubleshooting.

Identify migration tools

VMware Cloud on AWS supports different migration tools to help move your workload. You can find out more in *Chapter 7*. For most migration projects, consider using VMware HCX to facilitate migrations.

VMware HCX deployment

While HCX design and deployment could easily be a topic for a separate book, let's point out the most important design decisions to make:

- Consider using AWS DX for migration traffic. You must configure the HCX Service Mesh on the cloud side to use DX. By default, HCX uplinks are mapped to public IPs.

- Consider using Layer 2 extensions to prevent the IP addresses of your application from changing. Consider and discuss the pros and cons of Layer 2 extensions with your networking and security teams (there are a number of security concerns when transmitting Layer 2 broadcast traffic over WAN links).

- Make sure you understand the traffic flow for a VM residing on the Layer 2 extended network. For example, all traffic to an Amazon VPC goes first to your default gateway located on-premises, and after that will be routed back to AWS. The **Mobility Optimized Network** (**MON**) feature discussed earlier, in *Chapter 3*, helps to overcome this issue for traffic between segments within the same SDDC.

- Consider using the RAV migration type, combining the benefits of bulk migration with the ability to live-migrate workloads using vMotion.

- Make yourself familiar with the HCX configuration limitations (for example, no support for migrating a VM with SCSI bus sharing enabled).

- Plan for the future: if you plan to use a Layer 2 extension for a long time, consider enabling high availability for your Layer 2 extension appliance.

- Consider possible VM Virtual Hardware compatibility mismatches between your on-premises and VMware Cloud on AWS, especially when using the i3.metal host type. The per-VM EVC feature may help to overcome this difficulty.

Workload optimization

Moving workloads to VMware Cloud on AWS SDDC does not necessarily mean that the underlying VM configuration is optimized for the service. Depending on your on-premises vSphere configuration and selected options (especially the host type), you may need to perform VM configuration optimization to run efficiently and effectively on VMware Cloud on AWS. We will discuss the most important recommendations based on the main virtual resources: CPU, memory, storage, and networking. We will also touch upon VM management.

CPU

Processors are categorized into families. Typically, processors within the same family have similar sets of features, and processors within the same family and generation support the exact same set of CPU features or capabilities. The CPU capabilities or features available to virtual machines depends on the processor family and generation of the underlying physical hosts.

When virtual machines are migrated from a cluster with one host type to another cluster with a different host type, it is important to understand the vMotion compatibility between both the clusters, and if required reconfigure the virtual machines by enabling **Enhanced vMotion Compatibility** (**EVC**). If is also important to understand how vCPUs are presented to your VM:

- **Total number of vCPUs**

    You cannot configure more vCPUs on a single VM than the total number of logical CPUs (including hyperthreaded cores) available on the host. The following table depicts the maximum number of vCPUs on a single VM per instance type:

Instance Type	Physical/Logical CPU Cores	Max vCPUs per VM
i3.metal	36/36 *	36
i3en.metal	48/96	96
I4i.metal	64/128	128

*Hyperthreading is disabled on i3 hosts

Table 11.1 – Host instance type CPU capabilities

> **Note**
>
> The maximum number of vCPUs per VM is the configuration for a single VM. You can assign more vCPUs than a host has for different VMs (CPU overcommitment). This configuration might have performance issues.

When migrating from on-premises, make sure that you are within the specified limit. You must adjust the number of vCPUs to match the maximum number available on the host to be able to start a VM.

- **Cores per socket setting**

  From vSphere 5.0 onward, you can control how vCPUs are presented to a VM as virtual sockets or virtual cores. This configuration might affect some applications (such as SQL Server and Oracle) that have their own CPU schedulers. As a best practice, always match the number of virtual sockets to the number of physical sockets in your system. On VMware Cloud on AWS, all host types currently have a two-socket configuration. Configure your VM to have no more than two virtual sockets. If the total number of vCPUs fits within a single physical socket, expose just a single virtual socket.

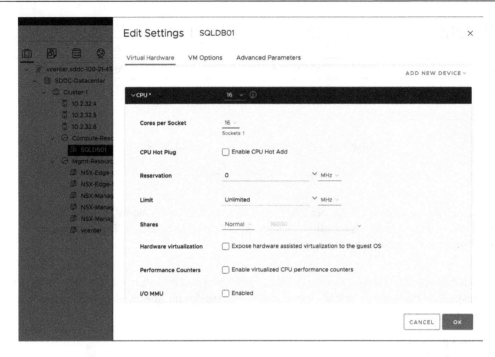

Figure 11.1 – Virtual Hardware settings – validate Cores per Socket

> **Note**
> This best practice is still applicable to the new vNUMA calculation algorithm.

Let's review the following examples:

- A VM with 16 vCPUs running on any host type should be configured with 1 vSocket/16 cores, as shown in *Figure 11.1*

- A VM with 24 vCPUs running on an i3 host should be configured with 2 vSockets/12 cores; when running on i3en or i4i, there is 1 vSocket/24 cores

- A VM with 72 vCPUs running on any supported host type should be configured with 2 vSockets/36 cores (you cannot configure 72 vCPUs on i3)

- **vNUMA**

  It's a best practice to recheck the vNUMA configuration after you migrate VMs to a new hardware platform because the underlying physical NUMA configuration of the host types might be different.

The following table outlines the physical NUMA configuration of VMware Cloud on AWS host types. As a best practice, a VM with a number of vCPUs lower or equal to the number of cores in a single physical NUMA node should be configured as a single NUMA VM.

Instance Type	NUMA Configuration	Max vCPUs per VM to Fit into a Single Physical NUMA Node
i3.metal	2 nodes, 18 cores, 256 GB RAM	18
i3en.metal	2 nodes, 48 cores, 384 GB RAM	48
I4i.metal	2 nodes, 64 cores, 512 GB RAM	64

Table 11.2 – VMware Cloud on AWS host physical NUMA CPU configuration

Let's review the following examples:

- A VM with 16 vCPUs running on an i3 host should have only a single virtual NUMA node

- A VM with 64 vCPUs running on an i3en host should have two virtual NUMA nodes

- A VM with 64 vCPUs running on an i4i host should have only a single virtual NUMA node

For a complex configuration, where a VM requires more memory than a single physical NUMA node has, but the number of vCPUs fits into a single NUMA node, refer to the detailed NUMA configuration discussed in the VMware documentation (`https://www.vmware.com/content/dam/digitalmarketing/vmware/en/pdf/solutions/sql-server-on-vmware-best-practices-guide.pdf`).

To validate the current virtual NUMA configuration, you can use in-guest tools or use a PowerShell script (`https://github.com/vbondzio/sowasvonunsupported/blob/master/Get-vNUMA-config.ps1`). VMware support might be able to assist in retrieving the vNUMA configurations for VMs running on VMware Cloud on AWS.

If you need to change the vNUMA, simply add or remove vCPUs and reboot the virtual machine – the underlying physical NUMA configuration of the host will be used to recreate the vNUMA configuration for the VM.

- **CPU Hot Plug (Hot Add)**

  The CPU Hot Add feature allows us to quickly adjust the number of vCPUs without needing to reboot a VM.

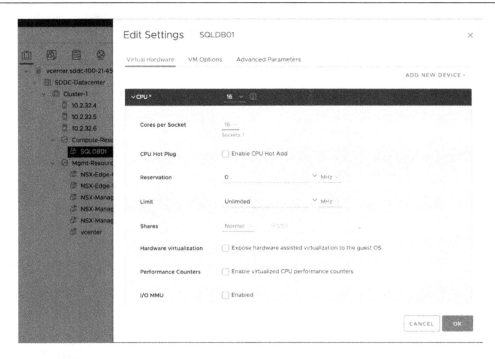

Figure 11.2 – CPU Hot Plug configuration

While this feature might be useful from an automation or test and dev perspective, it also has a known performance impact. A VM with CPU Hot Add enabled does not have vNUMA configuration, which might lead to unbalanced memory access across NUMA nodes. If you are looking for the best performance for your applications, we recommend disabling CPU hot-add for all VMs.

Memory

Memory compute resources are required for all VMs to be able to execute the application workload. Memory management with VMware Cloud on an AWS SDDC is not very different from on-premises, with just a couple of best practices to follow:

- Do not overcommit host memory for your production application workload.

  While it's possible to assign more memory to VMs than a physical host has, it might seriously affect the performance of your application. Most modern applications are designed to use memory as a disk/application cache even if the real application payload is not consuming all the assigned memory. If swapping or ballooning occurs on the physical host, an application might experience up to a tenfold increase in latency compared to a non-overcommitted environment. This is not different on VMware Cloud on AWS, especially with vSAN and NSX consuming additional memory on the host. It's recommended to leave at least 10% of the physical memory available for additional SDDC services.

- Consider sizing memory to fit into a single NUMA node.

  Single NUMA VMs tend to perform better and utilize fewer resources than wide NUMA VMs. As the configuration of your host on-premises might be different, make sure to recheck the memory allocation after migration. You can use the following table for references:

*If your application workload requires significantly more memory, make sure to create a symmetrical CPU/memory configuration and expose vNUMA correctly.

Instance Type	NUMA Configuration	Recommended Max Memory Setting per VM in GB*
i3.metal	2 Nodes, 18 cores, 256 GB RAM	256
i3en.metal	2 Nodes, 48 cores, 384 GB RAM	384
I4i.metal	2 Nodes, 64 cores, 512 GB RAM	512

Table 11.3 – VMware Cloud on AWS host physical NUMA memory configuration

The correct configuration of vNUMA settings for your workload may improve the performance of your applications and can help you to use the compute infrastructure more efficiently.

Storage

As discussed in *Chapter 5*, vSAN is the default storage type for your SDDC. vSAN storage provides a lot of benefits but also has a number of trade-offs:

- Dependency on network

- Host compute resource consumption

- Different queue limitations and maximum thresholds

These challenges and overall vSAN architecture define some of the best practices that might be different from the existing storage configuration in your on-premises estate. You should treat migration to vSAN as comparable to a migration to a new storage array (for example, a move from NetApp NFS storage to Pure storage with FC connectivity). Each storage vendor, vSAN included, has its own set of recommendations and best practices for your workload. Do not expect the same approach that worked well for an NFS datastore to work the same on vSAN.

We will review the most important configuration settings:

- I/O queues

  When migrating to vSAN, your primary goal is to spread the I/O flow in as many streams as possible. To achieve this, we recommend implementing the following configuration changes:

  - Split large (>1 TB), high-I/O VMDKs into smaller disks and use as many VMDKs as possible.

- Distribute VMDKs between the maximum number of virtual SCSI controllers (up to four per VM).

- Choose the best-performing storage policy aligning with SLAs. For workloads with a heavy write pattern (SQL Server transaction log, `tempdb`), use RAID1 whenever possible.

- Use the VMware **Paravirtual SCSI** (**PVSCSI**) controller type. This controller type has higher throughput with lower latency and CPU utilization and supports up to 254 queues per controller.

> **Note**
>
> We do not recommend using the vNVMe controller due to known performance issues. In general, you achieve better throughput with lower CPU utilization using the PVSCI controller type.

- **Object space reservation**

  It's often recommended to set the advanced setting for **Object Space Reservation** (**OSR**) (`https://core.vmware.com/blog/demystifying-capacity-reporting-vsan`) to 100%. However, this setting does not influence the performance of your workload; it's just a reservation. A VMDK with 100% OSR or 0% OSR is able to sustain the same amount of IOPS.

Figure 11.3 – Object space reservation setting

The difference between setting the OSR to 0% and 100% is with OSR set to 100%, your workloads are protected if a vSAN datastore becomes full, which might lead to critical conditions for your workload. On VMware Cloud on AWS, due to Elastic DRS and the elastic compute capacity, an SDDC can never reach over 80% vSAN datastore utilization. Using the default 0% setting of OSR (thin provisioning) will help you to lower the cost and still maintain the same performance level as with OSR set to 100%.

> **Note**
>
> For clusters with shared disks on VMware Cloud on AWS, you can use VMDKs with OSR set to 0%.

- **I/O alignment**

  vSAN implementation on VMware Cloud on AWS uses physical NVMe drives with 4Kn physical drive formatting – 4,096 bytes per physical sector size. Due to the specifics of the VMDK implementation, a logical disk presented to a VM always has a physical sector size of 512 bytes. This discrepancy might cause severe (up to 300%) performance degradation caused by unaligned I/Os. This especially affects small I/O, between 512 and 4,096 bytes.

  While an application can choose to use an I/O size as increments of 512, vSAN on the backend always operates with 4,096 bytes. For an I/O smaller than 4,096 bytes, a so-called **read-modify-write (RMW)** condition might arise, causing three I/Os in the backend for a single guest I/O. You can learn more at `https://blogs.vmware.com/apps/2021/12/enhancing-performance-vmc-on-aws-sql-server-trace-flag-1800.html`.

In most cases, proper alignment can be achieved by selecting an NTF block size to be 4,096 bytes or an increment of 4,096 bytes when formatting the logical disk within the Guest OS. However, some applications (SQL Server, Oracle) featuring their own I/O subsystem may be affected and require additional in-application tuning to mitigate possible performance issues.

Networking

Networking inside SDDC is powered by NSX. For your workload, it does not mean a lot of changes in terms of performance; however, it might have a much broader influence on the traffic flow, security principles, and so on.

One of the key changes our organizations notice from the network perspective is the change to the **maximum transmission unit (MTU)**. On VMware Cloud on AWS SDDC (`https://docs.vmware.com/en/VMware-Cloud-on-AWS/services/com.vmware.vmc-aws-networking-security/GUID-1B51A82F-1AB5-4D35-A170-1044A3A85913.html`), all east-west traffic supports an MTU of up to 8,950 bytes, while north-south traffic depends on the communication channel chosen. When using DX, you can set MTU up to 8,900 bytes, and when using a VPN connection, the only option is 1,500 bytes.

We recommend retesting the MTU after migration to make sure packet fragmentation is not happening. Don't set different MTU sizes within a network!

> **Note**
>
> Due to the specifics of the overlay network, the "classic" jumbo frame size of 9,100 bytes is not supported.

VM management

VM management involves a detailed understanding of VM lifecycle management and the VM configuration:

- **VM configuration**

    A VM first created in an on-premises environment might have a number of virtual devices or advanced configuration settings, and no or limited support on VMware Cloud on AWS. VMs with serial or parallel ports are not supported, and you cannot configure or move an encrypted VM. A full list of settings can be found in the VMware documentation (`https://docs.vmware.com/en/VMware-Cloud-on-AWS/services/com.vmware.vsphere.vmc-aws-manage-data-center-vms.doc/GUID-B8E9A999-9ACB-46ED-A80A-6AF288B513F9.html`).

- **VM lifecycle management**

    VM lifecycle management includes two of the most common operations:

    - VMware tools update

    - Hardware compatibility (aka virtual hardware)

- **VMware Tools**

    VMware Tools provides a packaged set of drivers that improve the guest OS experience and enable VMware-specific devices (such as a PVSCSI adapter or a VMXNET3 network adapter). VMware constantly releases new VMware Tools versions to enhance existing, or provide new, functionality. In general, we recommend you always update VMware Tools to the latest supported version. Some caution is required – VMware Tools updates are comparable with driver updates on a physical server. Performing a test rollout using a test environment is highly recommended.

- Hardware compatibility

    This is probably one of the most underrated features of VMware vSphere. It's not uncommon to see VMs still using **virtual Hardware (vHW)** 6 or 8 and running on the latest generation of Intel CPUs. Such configurations drastically reduce VM performance and the adoption of new hardware features.

    Hardware compatibility not only defines the applicable set of hardware capabilities available for the VM configuration – for example, virtual hardware 11 introduced support for 4 TB RAM and 128 vCPUs per VM – but also added support for hardware accelerators, new CPU instructions, and so on. For example, if you are running a VM with vHW 11 on a host with an Intel Skylake CPU, your VM would not be able to take advantage of any Skylake native instruction. Support for Skylake was introduced in vHW 17.

We strongly recommend using the latest available virtual hardware that's compatible with the host and CPU types.

Updating vHW is very simple – you can schedule the update to happen on the next VM reboot. However, caution is required – upgrading vHW is comparable to a change of a motherboard in your physical server. You might see new devices appearing in the guest OS or even an application requiring relicensing due to changes in the underlying hardware components.

Figure 11.4 – Upgrading VM compatibility using the web client

> **Note**
>
> vHW upgrades cannot be rolled back. vHW requires a certain ESXi version to run. For example, a VM with vHW 18 cannot be started on an ESXi 7.0. If you are planning to potentially reverse migrate your VM back to on-premises, choose the maximum supported vHW between two environments.
>
> Currently, VMware Cloud on AWS supports vHW 19 and below.

Day 2 operations

The Day 2 operations of the infrastructure is one of the key elements of a successful implementation. Often, underestimating Day 2 operations leads to a suboptimal solution design, which is hard to maintain, leading to dissatisfaction. Day 2 operations is the phase when your team will spend most of the time working with the environment.

As a best practice, your architecture should be built with the primary focus on the Day 2 operations:

- Ensure you engage the IT operations team when presenting key design decisions.
- Plan to train the IT operations team on the new technologies.
- Include runbook updates as a part of your design implementation.
- Explain the key lifecycle management changes when moving to VMware Cloud on AWS.
- Validate current monitoring/backup/automation tools for compatibility. Recommend updating or switching to other tools if necessary.

VMware Cloud on AWS can streamline the Day 2 operations of the environment:

- Infrastructure lifecycle management (https://vmc.techzone.vmware.com/resource/infrastructure-lifecycle-management-done-you-vmware-cloud-aws) is covered by the vendor – VMware
- Log management/operations/automation tools in the VMware Aria product portfolio are available as integrated services that ease deployment and integrations
- Many complex Day 2 operations procedures are offered as additional, non-billable services – cluster conversion, capacity management, and advanced network troubleshooting

However, VMware Cloud on AWS also differs from an on-premises vSphere environment in a few key ways:

- Most of the infrastructure-level settings (ESXi host, vSphere cluster, vCenter) are predefined by VMware and cannot be changed. The settings' values may be different from what you are using in your environment.
- The permission model does not allow full access to the environment, including vCenter, ESXi, and NSX manager. This may limit some operations and/or optimization you are performing in your on-premises environment.
- Backup compatibility: VMware requires each vendor of a backup solution to undergo a certification process to validate the compatibility with VMware Cloud on AWS. Make sure your current backup solution is certified or you will need to plan a transition to a different product/vendor. You can check the following kb article outlining certification for various backup solutions (https://kb.vmware.com/s/article/76753).

Make sure to address key Day 2 operations challenges in the design phase. It's not helpful if you find out your backup vendor is incompatible after workload migration!

Contract documentation

VMware offers VMware Cloud on AWS as a managed service. As a consumer of cloud services, you should double-check all the relevant contract documentation before making a purchase decision. VMware has simplified and consolidated access to contract documentation on a separate web page (`https://www.vmware.com/agreements.html`). Use this page to look for terms and agreements for VMware products and services. For VMware Cloud on AWS, we recommend you review the following set of documents:

- VMware Cloud Service Guide (`https://www.vmware.com/content/dam/digitalmarketing/vmware/en/pdf/agreements/vmware-cloud-services-guide.pdf`): This guide defines the terms applicable to all cloud services provided by VMware. The guide has a separate section dedicated to VMware Cloud on AWS, covering the requirements for an AWS account, details of Microsoft product licensing, PCI compliance, capacity requirements, and much more. This guide is your first port of call to understand some of the configurations and options available with VMware Cloud on AWS.

- **Service Level Agreement** (**SLA**): The SLA document serves as a basis for understanding availability with VMware Cloud on AWS. This document outlines the availability commitments, SLA events, requirements, and the definition of SLA Credits (`https://www.vmware.com/content/dam/digitalmarketing/vmware/en/pdf/support/vmw-cloud-aws-service-level-agreement.pdf`).

Avoiding common pitfalls

In the previous section, we were focused on how to do things right. However, it's also important to highlight the most common scenarios, configurations, and design decisions where a resulting configuration proved to be ineffective and error-prone.

Compute

Compute resources provide the necessary CPU and memory resources for virtual machines. Let's review the most common misconfigurations and/or suboptimal design choices:

- **Sizing**

  It's often the case that VMware Cloud on AWS SDDCs are either undersized or oversized. Undersized environments lead to low performance and a bad user experience, while oversized environments are expensive in terms of cost per VM. Opting for a right-sizing exercise and expanding on-premises vSphere environments as an afterthought may result in running into extended procurement cycles. However VMware Cloud on AWS benefits from the flexible and elastic capacity of public clouds. Paired with the right Elastic DRS policy, organizations can achieve cost savings by leveraging the scale-in option of the Elastic DRS policy, and performance burst, if required, by scaling out their cluster when demand grows. We recommend using custom

Elastic DRS policies, which give you much better control not only over the storage resources, but also CPU and memory.

- **Host type**

    Another common misconfiguration we observe a lot is selecting the wrong host type. We observe most issues with configurations involving the i3.metal host type. i3.metal might be suitable for running general-purpose workloads, but its outdated CPU (Broadwell) and lack of hyperthreading (and as a result, its low amount of CPU resources) makes resource contention very possible, especially with entry-level clusters (`https://vmc.techzone.vmware.com/resource/entry-level-clusters-vmware-cloud-aws`). A two-host i3.metal cluster is limited to 35 simultaneously running VMs, as most of the CPU resources are allocated to management VMs. Such a cluster might be suitable as a management cluster but should not be considered for production implementation. i3.metal **End of Sale (EoS)** naturally eliminates this problem; however, you still might be tempted to take i3.metal using an on-demand subscription for your ongoing project to profit from the cost. We strongly recommend not doing so at this point and consider i4i.metal, which has a much more powerful and modern CPU.

- **SDDC upgrade and lifecycle management**

    Most of the observed issues are tied with the wrong expectations: VMware releases a new SDDC software bundle every 6 months. This bundle is based on the latest vSphere + NSX version at the release time. With all the excitement, there are a couple of issues to underline:

    - Do not expect your SDDC to be upgraded overnight. For a brownfield (existing) SDDC, the estimated upgrade time is 6+ months. Depending on the complexity of your SDDC, it may be more.

    - Version inconsistency: VMware Cloud on AWS SDDCs always use the latest available build for deployment. You cannot specify a build version when deploying your SDDC. Current bundles use vSphere 8, while your on-premises environment might be still on vSphere 7. It may have a negative effect on reverse migration, potential incompatibility with management/automation/monitoring tools, and prevent you from raising the virtual hardware level of the VMs you migrate to the cloud.

- **Configuration management**

    VMware Cloud on AWS is offered as a managed service. Most ESXi/vSphere cluster/vCenter configurations are predefined and cannot be changed. If your applications or automation tools depend on a particular advanced setting, make sure to clarify the configuration before deployment. You would not be able to change the value after deployment.

Storage

Storage resources are crucial for storing an application's data. You should encompass both capacity and performance requirements while designing, implementing, and operating the infrastructure. We will review the most common misconfigurations and/or suboptimal design choices:

- **Sizing**

  Storage resources define two different dimensions of resources – storage capacity and storage performance. While sizing an environment, very often only one of these dimensions, in most cases capacity, will be considered. This approach is a direct path to failure. Even if your SDDC will have enough storage to host your workload, the resulting performance in many cases is inadequate and will lead to lengthy and costly escalations.

  When sizing storage, make sure to follow the recommendation of VMware Cloud Sizer (`https://vmc.vmware.com/sizer`) both in terms of capacity and performance. Double-check your sizing assumptions and tweak them using the advanced sizer if needed.

Figure 11.5 – VMware Cloud Sizer – Sizing Assumptions

- **Storage policies**

  vSAN is very easy and intuitive to manage with storage policies directly in vCenter. There's no need to work with the storage team, and it's easy to make changes. However, it could work against you. You could be tempted to use RAID5 for all your workloads and free up more space than you'd get with RAID1. RAID5 has a known performance implication, especially for workloads with predominantly small writes, causing a lot of overhead with RAID5. If the initial sizing has been done with RAID5 configuration, you may not have enough hosts to switch to RAID1 if needed. If you find yourself in this situation, decide whether you can split some of the VMDKs and dedicate small VMDKs to some particular data type – the database transaction log and tempdb are good candidates for such optimizations.

Networking

The network communication with workloads deployed on your SDDC is a key part of the overall user experience and, probably, one of the most complex design sections. Network configuration is under the organization's control; VMware only provides underlying network connectivity with the hardware AWS infrastructure.

Let's highlight the most common network misconfigurations:

- **Insufficient connection between on-premises and the VMware Cloud on AWS SDDC**

  It's a common practice to initially configure an IPSec VPN over the internet to achieve basic connectivity between on-premises and the SDDC and to secure the traffic flow. However, a VPN tunnel over the internet is not suitable for a mass migration of the workload. Live vMotion over the internet is not supported. Unpredictable bandwidth and latency affect the migration timeline making it unpredictable. For a large-scale migration and/or a hybrid cloud use case, you need to plan for a dedicated private connection to your SDDC.

- **Underestimating Level 2 network extension complexity**

  HCX and/or NSX Standalone Edge provide a unique feature – the ability to stretch a Layer 2 broadcast domain for a selected VLAN and allow the workload to retain the original IP addresses. This feature enormously helps to seamlessly migrate applications without an impact on the client configuration. On the other hand, this feature has several trade-offs, impacting workload availability and/or performance:

  - For workloads deployed on a Layer 2 extended segment (even with the MON feature enabled), all traffic sent to destinations residing outside of the SDDC network will first reach the default gateway, located on-premises. It may cause unexpected high latency when accessing workloads residing in native AWS VPC, including the connected VPC.

  - Workloads have a clear dependency on the on-premises default gateway. If the link between on-premises and the SDDC stops functioning, the workload on the extended leg of the segment would not be able to reach the default gateway and communicate with the external destination.

  - Undersized HCX Layer 2 extension appliances: All broadcast traffic within the VLAN must traverse the extension appliances on both sides of the tunnel. If the appliance is overloaded and/or does not have enough resources, the workload residing in the SDDC drops all external connections. This scenario is often observed with entry-level clusters based on the i3.metal host type. You can scale out and deploy multiple extension appliance pairs and distribute extended segments between appliances.

- Extension appliance availability: As mentioned earlier, the Layer 2 extension has a direct dependency on the HCX appliance. If the appliance stops working, becomes corrupted, or restarts, the network communication is affected. If you plan to maintain the extension after the migration is complete, use the HA feature of HCX extension appliances. Bear in mind that for a complex environment with a lot of extended VLANs, configuring HA will reduce compute and storage resources on both sides of the environment, including the SDDC. You may need to scale out the vSphere cluster hosting appliance on the SDDC side, incurring additional costs.

- Security concerns: Many security teams tend not to allow a Layer 2 extension over the public internet as it poses security risks and exposes sensitive broadcast traffic to the internet. When not properly addressed in the design phase, it might drastically affect your migration plans if you were planning to live migrate and retain the IP addresses. The best solution is to use a dedicated DX line and pass the extension traffic over the DX, which must address most of the concerns of the security team.

- **Identify network dependencies after migration**

   Many organizations claim that performance suffers after migrating workloads to the cloud. Some of these concerns are due to not following the best practices while migrating; however, in many cases, it has nothing to do with the SDDC. For a complex distributed application when not all components were properly identified and migrated to the cloud, the traffic may have additional hops traversing the WAN link(s), adding not foreseen latency to the application. An example of this is a migration of a SQL Server database warehouse, where the centralized integration service (SSIS) was left on premises, causing all the data to be first moved back to on-premises and then retransmitted to the SDDC. The impact of this configuration on the application was measured at a 300% increase in the OLAP cube generation time. The troubleshooting and search for affected traffic flows may be a complex and time-consuming task. VMware Aria Operations for Networks can help you visualize the traffic flow for a selected application.

FAQ

In this section, we will cover the most common questions we get from organizations that are interested in VMware Cloud on AWS. You can also find the comprehensive FAQs list published on the VMware Tech Zone website (`https://vmc.techzone.vmware.com/vmware-cloud-aws-frequently-asked-questions`).

How is VMware Cloud on AWS different from "just" a vSphere deployment?

VMware Cloud on AWS includes not only vSphere, but also vSAN and NSX, providing an all-in-one solution for organizations' needs. VMware Cloud on AWS is offered as a service, in contrast to an on-premises vSphere deployment, removing the burden of lifecycle management from IT teams.

How does VMware Cloud on AWS fit into the "public cloud first" strategy?

VMware Cloud on AWS provides enterprises with a quick, secure, and scalable option to mass migrate thousands of applications to the public cloud. VMware Cloud on AWS offers a lot of native public cloud benefits, including elastic capacity, without the need to refactor or rearchitect applications.

What are the key technical differentiators of VMware Cloud on AWS?

VMware Cloud on AWS helps you quickly deploy a vSphere-based SDDC on the public cloud, simplifying hardware and infrastructure management. The ability to flexibly manage capacity with eDRS and provide native AZ resiliency with stretched clusters are key technical differentiators of VMware Cloud on AWS SDDCs.

How does VMware Cloud on AWS enforce security for my workloads?

Migrating enterprise line-of-business applications to a public cloud infrastructure might raise a lot of security questions. VMware Cloud on AWS provides a secure way to deploy, operate, and decommission applications in the public cloud with the help of VMware NSX. VMware Cloud on AWS ensures security on the hardware (encryption in transit, self-encrypted NVMe drives, etc.) and infrastructure level (vSAN datastore encryption is always on, NSX firewalls are activated by default and configured to drop all incoming traffic, etc). VMware Cloud on AWS uses the shared responsibility model (`https://www.vmware.com/content/dam/digitalmarketing/vmware/en/pdf/products/vmc-aws/vmware-shared-responsibility-model-overview-vmware-cloud-on-aws.pdf`) to provide transparency in achieving security and compliance for your workload.

How can I get started?

VMware Cloud on AWS is easy to deploy (`https://vmc.techzone.vmware.com/vmc-aws-quick-start`) – you can create a new SDDC with just a couple of clicks and, in two hours, enjoy full-featured VMware Cloud on AWS SDDC functionality. You can use the free trial program (`https://www.vmware.com/products/vmc-on-aws/free-trial.html`) to get to know VMware Cloud on AWS right now!

Summary

In this chapter, we focused on defining best practices when planning, designing, and operating a cloud environment based on VMware Cloud on AWS. As well as best practices, it's also important to learn about and understand examples of suboptimal design choices and their potential influence on the infrastructure. Reviewing the most common questions and answers will help you summarize the most important points about VMware Cloud on AWS.

In the next chapter, we will review some configuration examples.

12
Appendix: Preflight before Onboarding

In this chapter, we will cover the most important configuration items you need when you deploy the SDDC and configure a hybrid cloud environment.

You will find a detailed description of the configuration steps and items from previous chapters of this book.

Purchasing and onboarding

When purchasing the service and preparing for the first SDDC deployment, you need to choose a couple of options. These options may have a large impact on the further operations of the service, so make sure your choices are well thought out, as you will not be able to change some of them moving forward.

Purchasing and funding

When purchasing the service, you can select one of the following options:

- A direct VMware purchase
- AWS resell
- Purchasing through a **Managed Service Provider** (MSP)

VMware Cloud on AWS supports all three routes to the market. Depending on your purchase strategy, you may find one or other better suited to your needs.

> **Note**
> Some services available for VMware Cloud on AWS can only be purchased directly from VMware, for example, Microsoft host-based licenses for workloads on VMware Cloud on AWS.

When purchasing from VMware, you can choose how you want to pay for the service:

- VMware Purchasing Programs: You can select from a different range of programs, most of them offering so-called **Credits**. You can use credits toward payment for VMware Cloud on AWS. Consult a VMware sales representative to get more details about available programs. (More details on VMware Purchasing Programs can be found here: `https://customerconnect.vmware.com/web/vmware/spp-landing`.)

- Pay by invoice: You can activate pay by invoice using the VMware Cloud Console.

- Pay with a credit card: Applicable for small purchases up to $25,000.

Consumption options

When deploying VMware Cloud on AWS SDDC, you have a choice between the following:

- Subscription: Your commitment to buy a certain amount of host capacity for a defined period. When purchasing a subscription, you select the AWS Region, host type, and the number of hosts. You can pay upfront or monthly. If purchasing from VMware or AWS, you can select the following:

  - Flexible subscription: The terms of the subscription (number of hosts, region, host types) can be changed over time (limitations apply)

  - Standard subscription: The terms of the subscription are fixed and cannot be changed

- On-demand: You can run VMware Cloud on AWS SDDC using on-demand prices. You are free to select the region, host type, and the number of hosts.

Typically, a standard 3-year term subscription is the most cost-effective option, while on-demand prices are the highest. Depending on your use case, one or another option might work better. In our experience, a flexible subscription is the right balance between flexibility and cost savings.

Accessing and configuring the VMware Cloud Console

There are a couple of steps required before you can start consuming VMware Cloud on AWS. You use the VMware Cloud Console to provision VMware Cloud on AWS SDDC. If you are already using any of the VMware Cloud services, you can just log in to the VMware Cloud Console and look for VMware Cloud on AWS in the **Services** inventory:

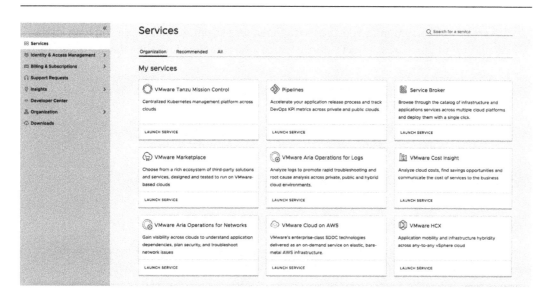

Figure 12.1 – VMware Cloud Console Services inventory

However, if it's the first time you're using VMware Cloud services, you should get access to the VMware Cloud Console.

The following steps outline the procedure to get started with the VMware Cloud Console:

1. Receive a welcome email: Upon processing your purchase, VMware will send an email with an activation link. Use this link to log in to the VMware Cloud Console.

> **Note**
> VMware will use the email address designated as the "Fund owner's" to send the activation link.

2. Setup an Organization. An Organization provides authentication boundaries for your VMware Cloud services. Each Organization can be entitled to different services. A user can access multiple Organizations and switch between them in the VMware Cloud Console.

3. Setup VMware Cloud service accounts: After gaining initial access to the VMware Cloud Console and creating an Organization, you can entitle user accounts to access to VMware Cloud on AWS. You can use manual assignment, or you can federate VMware Cloud Console with your identity provider. If your design includes federation for the VMware Cloud Console, it's important to configure the federation feature before you deploy VMware Cloud on AWS SDDC.

4. Create a term subscription. If you purchased a term subscription, it's important to create a subscription object in the VMware Cloud Console before you deploy an SDDC. Creating a subscription matching your purchase is a organization's responsibility – VMware does not

pre-create a subscription in your VMware Cloud Organization. Make sure you have all the details of your purchase contract before creating a subscription, including the following:

- AWS Region
- Host count and host type
- Subscription type – flexible or standard
- Subscription duration – 1 year or 3 years

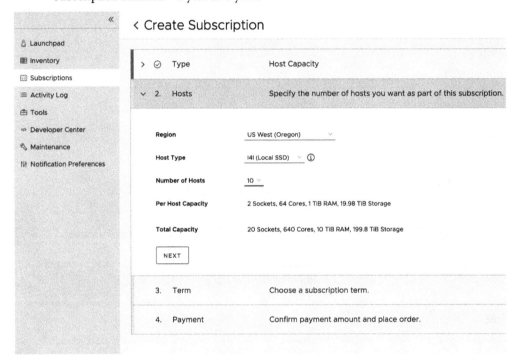

Figure 12.2 – Creating a subscription for VMware Cloud on AWS

> **Note**
>
> You can deploy a VMware Cloud on AWS SDDC without creating a subscription. In this case, VMware will use on-demand prices for billing. If you purchased a subscription but did not create a subscription object in the VMware Cloud Console, on-demand prices will be applied. If you deploy your SDDC using a different AWS Region or host type, or use more hosts, on-demand prices will be applied as well.

SDDC deployment

When preparing for the deployment of your first SDDC, you need to collect the configuration data in advance. The settings ideally should be captured at the design stage, as discussed in the previous chapter.

The following table depicts the configuration items you need to provide to successfully deploy your first SDDC:

Configuration section	Configuration item	Description
SDDC (see *Figure 12.3* for details)	Name	Free text field. You can change the name after the deployment as well. It is recommended to use the company naming convention.
	AWS Region	AWS Region where your SDDC resides. The Region should fit your subscription, AWS VPC configuration, and AWS DX configuration (if in use).
	Deployment	Single host – for POC only, for 60 days only. Multi-host – production deployment. Stretched cluster – a deployment across two AWS AZs.
	Host type	Select one of the available host types. The host type should fit into your subscription, design, and workload requirements. You have a choice between: • i3.metal • i3en.metal • I4i.metal See *Figure 12.4* for the deployment wizard where the host type is specified. VMware constantly adds new instances. Check the VMware documentation for the available instances.
	Number of hosts	Count of ESXi hosts in your **first** cluster. If your design requires a multi-cluster setup, you will add additional clusters after the SDDC is provisioned with the first cluster.

Configuration section	Configuration item	Description
AWS Connection (see *Figure 12.2* for details)	AWS account	This is an AWS account you own. Choose the account according to the design and security requirements.
	Choose a VPC	Select an AWS VPC (the VPC should be precreated) in your AWS account. This VPC will become a connected VPC after the deployment.
	Choose subnet(s)	Select a subnet in your VPC (the subnet must be precreated). The subnet must have enough free IPs for the SDDC deployment (to accommodate ESXi hosts' ENI interfaces). The subnet also defines the destination AZ. You cannot change the subnet after the deployment. If you deploy a stretched cluster SDDC, you must select two subnets in two different AZs.
SDDC networking	Provide the management subnet CIDR	You should provide a private network subnet with enough IP addresses for the SDDC management (vCenter, ESXi hosts, vSAN network, etc.). It is recommended to use a /23 subnet if you plan to deploy more than 10 hosts. You cannot change the subnet after the deployment. Make sure the subnet does not overlap with the on-premises or other connected networks (including AWS).

Table 12.1 – SDDC Configuration Details

You can review the deployment wizard in *Figure 12.3*:

∨ 1.	SDDC Properties	Give your SDDC a name, choose a size, and specify the AWS region where it will be created.

SDDC Name	Prod
Cloud	○ ZEROCLOUD ● AWS
AWS Region	US West (Oregon) ∨
Deployment	○ Single Host ● Multi-Host ☑ Stretched Cluster ⓘ
Host Type	I3en (Local SSD) ∨ ⓘ
Number of Hosts	4 ∨
Host Capacity	2 Sockets, 48 Cores, 768 GiB RAM, 45.84 TiB Storage
Total Capacity	8 Sockets, 192 Cores, 3 TiB RAM, 183.36 TiB Storage

SHOW ADVANCED CONFIGURATION

NEXT

Figure 12.3 – SDDC deployment wizard SDDC Properties

You can review the VPC and subnet details of the SDDC wizard in *Figure 12.4*:

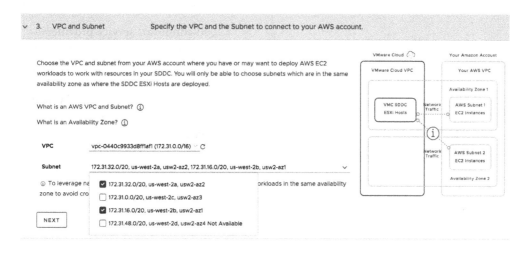

Figure 12.4 – SDDC deployment wizard. AWS VPC and subnet

After you have provisioned the SDDC, you must configure access to the vSphere Web Client to manage your SDDC through VMware vCenter Server. You will use the NSX manager UI to create a Management Gateway Firewall Rule. By default, access to vCenter is not allowed. You will specify an IP or a subnet and entitle it to access vCenter. An "allow all" rule is not possible.

Hybrid cloud configuration

If your design requires establishing a connection on-premises, several configuration changes have to be made to enforce the connection. If you also need to configure HCX for migration, it adds some complexity to the deployment. The following table lists the relevant configuration items to be considered for the hybrid cloud deployment:

Configuration section	Configuration item	Description
Network configuration	VPN	Policy-based or route-based. See the networking section in *Chapter2* for more details on VPNs
	AWS DX (see *Figure 12.5*)	You can choose to use the AWS DX service to gain predictable latency and possibly higher throughout for your workload. You can leverage the following: • AWS DX provisioned as a private VIF to your SDDC. • AWS DX VIF connected to an AWS DX Gateway (DXGW). You will use an SDDC group and a vTGW to connect your SDDC(s) to a DXGW. • Cloud connector service providers – cloud connector service providers can offer an alternative by sharing cloud connectivity lines. From the SDDC perspective, the connection still would be in the form of a private VIF or a connection to a DXGW.

Configuration section	Configuration item	Description
	Dynamic routing support	VMware Cloud on AWS supports only the BGP dynamic routing protocol. You can filter incoming/outcoming routes and/or announce 0.0.0.0./0 to route all SDDC traffic through the selected connection. If you have multiple connections from on-premises to the cloud, it is important to synchronize the routing information (e.g., avoid announcing 0.0.0.0/0 through DX and specific subnets through a route-based VPN)
SDDC management	vCenter Server	Reconfigure to use a private IP
(see *Figure 12.6*)	NSX manager	Reconfigure to use a private IP
	HCX manager	Reconfigure to use a private IP
Firewall	Management Gateway Firewall	Ensure your on-premises CIDRs required access to vCenter/NSX Manager/HCX Manager is included in the management firewall rules.
	Compute Gateway Firewall	Ensure you add on-premises CIDRs and map them to the DX/VPN interface.
Migration Service	Activate HCX	HCX Enterprise is included with VMware Cloud on AWS SDDC.
	Pair HCX managers	Configure a pairing between on-premises and the cloud. You can have multiple site pairs if needed.

Configuration section	Configuration item	Description
	Configure a network profile. (See *Figure 12.7*.)	Configure HCX on VMware Cloud on AWS to use the "directConnectNetwork1" network profile. Add a non-overlapping private CIDR (different from the SDDC management network). HCX will use this network to establish connectivity between the appliances. The SDDC workflow will automatically add the subnet to the BGP route distribution and create the required firewall rules.
	Create a service mesh	Override the network uplink configuration to use the directConnectNetwork1 network profile while configuring the service mesh.
	Configure network extension	The HCX network extension service can extend vSphere vDS VLAN-based port groups to the cloud. You can enable high availability for your NE appliances (you need to configure an HA group before extending a VLAN).
Migrate workloads	Identify VMs to be migrated	Identify VMs building an application and migrate them as a part of the same migration group.
	Select migration type	Select between the following: • vMotion • bulk migration • **replication-assisted vMotion (RAV)** See *Chapter 3, which* covers HCX migrations in great depth for more details.
	Configure schedule	Use this option to define the switchover/start of vMotion. If using bulk or RAV, you need to make sure HCX has enough time to replicate virtual machine data.

Table 12.2 – Hybrid Cloud configuration details

You can review the Direct Connect configuration in *Figure 12.5.*

Figure 12.5 – AWS DX VIF attached to an SDDC

You can review the FQDN configuration in *Figure 12.6*:

Figure 12.6 – Configure vCenter Server, HCX, and NSX FQDN resolution

You can review the configuration of HCX to leverage AWS **Direct Connect** (**DX**) connection in *Figure 12.7*:

Figure 12.7 – VMware Cloud on AWS HCX network profile: uplink over AWS DX

Next steps

Now that you have completed the basic SDDC setup and connected the SDDC to on-premises, you can use the following list to get further information about the services and next steps:

- Review the roadmap: `https://www.vmware.com/products/vmc-on-aws/features-and-roadmaps.html`

- Review the FAQ: `https://vmc.techzone.vmware.com/vmware-cloud-aws-frequently-asked-questions`

- Review configuration maximums: `https://configmax.esp.vmware.com/guest?vmwareproduct=VMware%20Cloud%20on%20AWS&release=VMware%20Cloud%20on%20AWS&categories=68-0,52-0,3-0,53-0,54-0,55-0,56-0,57-0,58-0,75-0,76-0`

- Review the VMware Cloud on AWS release notes: `https://docs.vmware.com/en/VMware-Cloud-on-AWS/services/rn/vmware-cloud-on-aws-release-notes/index.html`

Index

www.packtpub.com

Subscribe to our online digital library for full access to over 7,000 books and videos, as well as industry leading tools to help you plan your personal development and advance your career. For more information, please visit our website.

Why subscribe?

- Spend less time learning and more time coding with practical eBooks and Videos from over 4,000 industry professionals

- Improve your learning with Skill Plans built especially for you

- Get a free eBook or video every month

- Fully searchable for easy access to vital information

- Copy and paste, print, and bookmark content

Did you know that Packt offers eBook versions of every book published, with PDF and ePub files available? You can upgrade to the eBook version at www.packtpub.com and as a print book customer, you are entitled to a discount on the eBook copy. Get in touch with us at customercare@packtpub.com for more details.

At www.packtpub.com, you can also read a collection of free technical articles, sign up for a range of free newsletters, and receive exclusive discounts and offers on Packt books and eBooks.

Other Books You May Enjoy

If you enjoyed this book, you may be interested in these other books by Packt:

AWS Observability Handbook

Parth Pandit, Robert Hardt

ISBN: 978-1-80461-671-0

- Capture metrics from an EC2 instance and visualize them on a dashboard
- Conduct distributed tracing using AWS X-Ray
- Derive operational metrics and set up alerting using CloudWatch
- Achieve observability of containerized applications in ECS and EKS
- Explore the practical implementation of observability for AWS Lambda
- Observe your applications using Amazon managed Prometheus, Grafana, and OpenSearch services
- Gain insights into operational data using ML services on AWS
- Understand the role of observability in the cloud adoption framework

DevSecOps in Practice with VMware Tanzu

Parth Pandit, Robert Hardt

ISBN: 978-1-80324-134-0

- Build apps to run as containers using predefined templates
- Generate secure container images from application source code
- Build secure open source backend services container images
- Deploy and manage a Kubernetes-based private container registry
- Manage a multi-cloud deployable Kubernetes platform
- Define a secure path to production for Kubernetes-based applications
- Streamline multi-cloud Kubernetes operations and observability
- Connect containerized apps securely using service mesh

Packt is searching for authors like you

If you're interested in becoming an author for Packt, please visit `authors.packtpub.com` and apply today. We have worked with thousands of developers and tech professionals, just like you, to help them share their insight with the global tech community. You can make a general application, apply for a specific hot topic that we are recruiting an author for, or submit your own idea.

Share Your Thoughts

Now you've finished *VMware Cloud on AWS Blueprint,* we'd love to hear your thoughts! Scan the QR code below to go straight to the Amazon review page for this book and share your feedback or leave a review on the site that you purchased it from.

`https://packt.link/r/1803238194`

Your review is important to us and the tech community and will help us make sure we're delivering excellent quality content.

Download a free PDF copy of this book

Thanks for purchasing this book!

Do you like to read on the go but are unable to carry your print books everywhere?

Is your eBook purchase not compatible with the device of your choice?

Don't worry, now with every Packt book you get a DRM-free PDF version of that book at no cost.

Read anywhere, any place, on any device. Search, copy, and paste code from your favorite technical books directly into your application.

The perks don't stop there, you can get exclusive access to discounts, newsletters, and great free content in your inbox daily

Follow these simple steps to get the benefits:

1. Scan the QR code or visit the link below

https://packt.link/free-ebook/978-1-80323-819-7

2. Submit your proof of purchase

3. That's it! We'll send your free PDF and other benefits to your email directly

www.ingramcontent.com/pod-product-compliance
Lightning Source LLC
Chambersburg PA
CBHW080610060326

40690CB00021B/4642